The Indiana Constitutional Convention Of 1850-1851

Donald F. Carmony

Master's Thesis,
Indiana University, 1931

A publication of the Indiana Supreme Court's "Courts in the Classroom" project

Indianapolis, Indiana

Prepared for publication by
Bethany L. Natali & Elizabeth R. Osborn

Published & distributed by:
Indiana Supreme Court
Indiana State House
200 W. Washington Street
Indianapolis, IN 46204
courts.in.gov

in association with:
IBJ Book Publishing
41 E. Washington Street, Suite 200
Indianapolis, IN 46204
www.ibjbp.com

ISBN 978-1-934922-03-3
First Edition

Printed in the United States of America

TABLE OF CONTENTS

INTRODUCTION

This volume contains a complete reprint of the 1931 master's thesis of Dr. Donald F. Carmony, one of Indiana's best known and most respected state historians. Carmony's thesis explores and explains Indiana's second constitutional convention, held in 1850-1851, with references to a significant number of primary source materials.

When Indiana ratified its second constitution in 1851 we had plenty of company, including neighboring Ohio and Kentucky, who were re-writing the constitutions crafted by the first generation of settlers. Hoosiers and other mid-nineteenth century Americans saw a need to change their constitutions to better reflect the growing democratization in American society and politics.

Indiana's new constitution addressed issues such as the creation of more elected offices, revisions to the judiciary, reform of the criminal justice process, dispensing with private bills in the legislature, and changing the operating procedures for parts of state government.

While the passage of time has resolved certain high profile issues debated at the convention (like the state banking system, the rights of freemen, and the property rights of women), readers might be surprised at how many of the questions debated in 1851 are still a part of our political discussion. The passion with which delegates debated issues such as taxation, public education, and the role of state and local government will likely hold the interest of many Hoosiers.

Carmony's important work has never been easily accessible to the average researcher, teacher, or student. The Court wishes to express its appreciation to Duane Carmony and Lowell Carmony, Carmony's two sons, for making their father's work available to the Court in connection with this publication. I had the good fortune to know Dr. Carmony, so making his work available is a matter of special satisfaction.

This edition is part of a series of publications sponsored by the Indiana Supreme Court through its "Courts in the Classroom" project. We hope this project will help educate Hoosiers about Indiana's legal past by making more materials about the history of the courts and the law readily available to them. You can find information about this and other publications, as well as educational programs and special events, from the Court's website (*www.in.gov/judiciary/citc*).

Randall T. Shepard
Chief Justice of Indiana

Editors' Note

Donald F. Carmony completed this master's thesis in 1931. Written between two world wars, just fifteen years after Indiana's centennial, his work is as valuable for its own historical context as for the information he provides, interprets, and distills. With these historical considerations in mind, the editors have attempted to use a light touch in compiling this edition, making it as accurate to the original document as possible, while also making it comprehensible to the modern reader.

Carmony's thesis is presented here in nearly the same manner as it appeared upon its completion in 1931. A few changes have been made to better the aid the reader. Endnote and bibliographic citations have been modernized using the Turabian style. Typographic and grammatical errors and inconsistencies—which would have been difficult to correct in 1931 using a typewriter—have also been corrected for this edition. Underlined titles of books and phrases have been italicized.

In very few instances language in the original document was illegible. In the case where the original language was illegible, but the likely content could be determined, the editors have used brackets to indicate the probable word.

In addition to his historical interpretation and explanation of

Indiana's 1850-1851 constitutional convention, Dr. Carmony rendered an invaluable service to the historical community by collecting and reproducing large portions of primary source material relating to the convention. Where possible, this material has been proofread against the original sources. The unique characteristics of the quoted sources, including style and formatting, have been retained as much as possible.

Readers looking for more information on this subject may find the author's bibliography to be a valuable resource. In addition, the editors have also included a "For Further Reading" section containing other works by the author and works pertaining to the subjects discussed within this edition.

The editors would like to thank Becky Sutton for transcribing this piece from the original typewritten manuscript found in the graduate library at Indiana University and to Sarah Hachey for creating the Index. Thanks are also due to Ashley Reller, a student at Indiana University, and to Grant Gerard, Melissa A. Fanning and Erin J. Gobel, public history students from Indiana University at Indianapolis, for their work in preparing this edition for publication.

BLN & ERO
Indianapolis, 2009

AUTHOR'S BIOGRAPHY

I was born on a farm in Shelby County, Indiana, in 1910, near where my great, great, paternal grandfather and family had settled in the 1820s. They arrived soon after various Indian tribes had ceded much of central Indiana to the United States. For a year or so after my paternal grandmother died, my parents lived with grandfather in the double log cabin where my father was born. A frame lean-to along its back provided two additional rooms, making four rooms for three adults and three small children. The dug well was between the cabins and the log barn, with its frame addition, and the outhouse was nearby on the other side of the cabins.

My elementary education was completed in seven years in four one-room, red brick schoolhouses, which offered grades one through eight, taught by my father. I was one of nineteen who graduated from Manilla High School, across the line in Rush County, in 1925. Because I had never missed a day since entering the first grade, the county superintendent gave me a medallion.

During the teens and twenties I did a variety of chores and labor on the family farm before mechanization and electricity revolutionized farming and farm life. Despite long hours and much hard work, I enjoyed these years, which in some respects resembled the pioneer life, about which I write in this book, more than life of the 1990s.*

In the fall of 1925 I entered Indiana Central College, now the University of Indianapolis, expecting to major in mathematics and probably combine farming and teaching at the high school level as my career. Soon my interest in history exceeded that in mathematics, and I completed majors in both subjects, graduating *cum laude* in June, 1929. During the summer I was invited to teach history at Indiana Central College on a part-time basis, while pursuing the doctorate in history from Indiana University. I soon became full-time, and continued on its faculty for a decade.

As a graduate student at Indiana University during the thirties, I became much interested in Indiana history under the capable and charming teaching of Logan Esarey. From 1939 until "retirement" in 1980, I was a member of the faculty in history at Indiana University, teaching at the Fort Wayne, South Bend, and Indianapolis Extension Centers, but principally on the Bloomington campus. I began teaching Indiana history while on the faculty of Indiana Central College, but the transfer to Indiana University gave me much more time for its study and teaching. I received the Ph.D. in history from Indiana University in 1941. The pioneer era has long been my area of principal interest. From 1954 until 1975 I edited the *Indiana Magazine of History*.

From service on several state commissions and committees, including that as chair of the Indiana Sesquicentennial Commission, 1959-1967, I gained valuable insights about politics, politicians, and government. This experience increased my understanding of and appreciation for the role that politicians exercise in local, state, and national government.

- DONALD F. CARMONY, 1998

*Reprinted with permission from the Indiana Historical Bureau & Indiana Historical Society. Donald F. Carmony, "Preface," in *Indiana 1816-1850: The Pioneer Era*, vol. II, *The History of Indiana* (Indianapolis: Indiana Historical Society, 1998), ix-x.

Preface

This thesis is submitted as a partial fulfillment of the requirements for the degree Master of Arts from Indiana University.

In a survey of the primary sources, the records of the convention and the contemporary newspapers, sources were found to be comprehensive and well preserved. The Indiana State Library has the most source material. However, both the Indianapolis Public Library and the Indiana University Library have sources not found in the State Library. Kettleborough's was a most valuable guide.

I wish to express my appreciation to Dr. Logan Esarey for his suggestions and help. He was kind enough to give me the utmost freedom and privileges in my work. Any errors or questionable opinions are solely my own. Acknowledgement is due to Miss Esther McNitt, and her assistant at the Indiana Section of the State Library, for the very courteous and helpful attention given my needs there. Miss Edith Hagelskamp,* a student at Indiana Central College, prepared the maps and organized much of the data used.

The reader is urged to give careful attention to the sources contained in the appendix. These are lengthy, but being primary sources they contain very valuable facts, some of which are very interesting in reflecting the Indiana of the period under study. The maps used were verified by original tables taken from the State Archives.

The written Indiana Constitution of 1851 is not a great document. However, it was representative and worthy of the men and age in which it was framed. Judged by present day standards it does not attract one; viewed as a product of pioneer Indiana it is about what one would expect. It has had but few formal amendments added; usage and interpretation have very much altered its original meaning. My personal opinion is that its purposes have been largely achieved and that it should be revised; but perhaps not until the political atmosphere is more favorable to sound politico-economic thought.

Donald F. Carmony, Instructor
Indiana Central College
Indianapolis, Indiana

* *Editors' Note:* Edith Hagelskamp later became the author's wife.

Photo Courtesy Allen County/Fort Wayne Historical Society

This aqueduct is a part of the Wabash and Erie Canal project near Fort Wayne, Allen County.

Aqueducts and canals were a common sight in Indiana in the 1830s and 1840s. Attempting to imitate the financial success of New York's state-funded Erie Canal project, states around the country entered into a flurry of canal construction. Most of these projects were poorly planned, rarely completed, and led states to the brink of bankruptcy. Indiana's ill-fated canal building project, resulting in extreme financial duress, was one of the best-publicized and most often cited reasons for convening a new constitutional convention.

CHAPTER I

CONSTITUTIONAL ORIGINS

Every government, past and present, has been or is based upon a constitution. A constitution consists of all the rules, forms, usages, principles, conventions, and traditions which determine the structure of a government and define its powers. The difference between written and unwritten constitutions is merely one of degree. In a written constitutional system most of these rules, usages, forms, and traditions have been set to writing; in the unwritten constitutions these rules and customs are to be found in precedents which have become established. In the United States both the national and state governments are built upon the written constitutional system. They have become so deeply imbedded in the American system of government that one who criticizes them adversely may be charged with political heresy. It is difficult for the average American to see that the unwritten British system has many advantages. However, either system may be adaptable to some conditions which the other is not.

Lord Bryce lists rigid or so-called written constitutions as one of "the three chief contributions which the United States has made to political science regarded as an Applied Science or Practical Art."[1]

This is merely another way of saying that "a written constitution is an American institution."[2] The written constitution is a product of the modern age of history. However, in both the ancient and medieval periods of history there was a distinction between laws which were regarded as fundamental and permanent and those which were regarded as temporary and changeable.[3] This distinction is the fundamental step in constitutional evolution. Written constitutions were not used in the United States first but their adoption here "represented the first successful attempt of a people to create, consciously and deliberately, a system of government, and to enact the principles of a political philosophy into law."[4] They were the product of a long evolutionary process, with roots in the ancient and medieval periods, which found a favorable environment in the new world. Here they burst forth into full bloom as a result of the conditions created by the revolt of the thirteen colonies from the British Empire.

Written constitutions, in this country, were a development of colonial experience and an outgrowth of the embryo system of popular government which developed in the democratic environment of the frontier.[5] The first mainspring for their development came from the charters originally granted to various trading companies.[6] Since these companies began as business agreements, the executive was given extensive powers. Each colony had at least one charter and was familiar with such a system of government. These charters were often very liberal and the fact that they were written in black and white made them bulwarks of popular and individual liberty when the public opinion of the people called for their observance. In debates and struggles with the agents of the Crown the colonial assemblies had often found that a threat to reread the charter and study it was sufficient to gain what they desired.[7] This feeling that a written constitution would serve as bulwarks of popular liberty was perhaps the greatest single factor leading to the adoption of written constitutions by every colony when the revolution began. These colonial charters furnished the idea or model upon which these first constitutions were built.[8] Furthermore, these written constitutions were helpful in fostering the growth of popular government as they made it possible for the people to exert a greater influence in forming policies of government. They made it possible to establish a representative democracy. A written constitutional system was also favored because it tended to become more rigid and conservative. This was in accord with the negative philosophy of government, which was ushered in as a part of the colonial revolt from Great Britain.[9] The colonial experience and environment greatly enriched and modified colonial and state institutions but, as Dr. Channing has so aptly stated, "The political institutions of all of the colonies were bottomed on those of England."[10] The French and continental influences played a minor part.

The early American written constitutions did not become a craze of governments for a brief period and then pass into oblivion, as had other previous attempts. The English Civil War had produced three written constitutions. One of these, the "Instrument of Government" drawn up by Cromwell's officers in 1653, was in actual operation for about three years;[11] this was the "earliest written organic law to be put into actual everyday use."[12] The adoption of written constitutions, based upon the colonial charters, by all of the thirteen colonies gave these instruments a favorable opportunity for growth. The liberals of Europe soon came to regard a written constitution as necessary in a liberal political system. During the French Revolution several written constitutions were used for various periods of time. The reactionaries after the Congress of Vienna, under the leadership of Prince Metternich, made sporadic attempts to suppress these written documents, which had become attached to the general movement for more representative democracy. The restored French Bourbon Louis XVIII was forced to grant a constitution to his subjects (Charter of 1814). Later written constitutions were adopted in Belgium (1831), Switzerland (1843), the North German Confederation (1867), and many other countries. Since the World War, the number of written constitutions has further increased. In the early part of the last century Latin American countries began to adopt written constitutions, which show the influence and imprint of the American example. A written constitution lies at the basis of almost all of the Occidental systems of government and has made inroads into the other systems. The British unwritten constitution is the outstanding exception. It is example enough to show that a written constitution is not absolutely essential to a liberal system.

The purpose of a constitution is to determine the structure and machinery of government, to distribute the powers and functions of government, and to provide the necessary organs and officials to give effective motivating power. A written constitution usually contains four or five general provisions. First is an outline of the framework of government. This, in American practice, calls for the establishment of three separate departments: an executive, a bicameral assembly, a court system, and the other common boards and commissions. In the second place a constitution makes provision for both territorial and functional distribution of powers. In the forty-eight American commonwealths this territorial distribution recognizes the existence of national, state, and local units. Functional distribution apportions power among the so-called executive, legislative, and judicial departments. A third field includes articles dealing with such topics as finance, education, corporations, banking, public utilities, monopolies, taxation, and industrial legislation. In the early constitutions such articles were either in embryo or altogether missing. In the last century these articles have increased in length and number because of the growing complexity of economic and social life plus the distrust of the people toward the work of legislatures. A fourth field usually makes provision in regard to the extent of the franchise, the time and manner of holding elections, and to regulate evils in elective machinery and methods. Another part of the constitution usually makes provision for revision or amendment; revision for basic changes and amendment processes for minor alterations. Lastly, and often included among the very first articles of the constitution, is a bill of rights, regarded as necessary to protect individual rights and liberties. These six general provisions are usually found in the constitutions of every state in the United States.[13] Today many students of political science have come to place less emphasis upon written constitutions and to attach a greater importance to evolving better methods of securing efficient and more effective machinery and officials. It is very possible that written constitutions may someday be discarded as hindering progress in political evolution. The trend is apparently in this direction but its realization, if it comes into being, would take a long period of political readjustment. At present written constitutions have about as much influence in democracies as the Bible has among some religionists who have a feeling that one should stay close to the "written word."

The development of written constitutions is only the foundation of constitutional origins in the United States. The constitutional convention has been the agency which has made these written documents adaptable to applied political science. A constitutional convention is a body whose primary, if not sole function, is to frame a new organic law for the state or to formulate amendments to the existing constitution. However, its work usually consists of thorough revision of the already existing constitution; minor changes are often made by amendment. Such an assembly, which is an unicameral body, is usually given more than ordinary attention by the electorate. It is often said that its members are better qualified and more concerned in the public welfare than the members of state legislature. Perhaps partisan influences are less active in these than in regular law-making bodies. Among those elected as delegates are lawyers, farmers, professional politicians, journalists, businessmen, and since the nineteenth amendment women have served in this capacity.

Every state constitution, now in operation, was framed by constitutional convention. The constitutional convention is the generally accepted method of revision. In this convention (and contrary to the general trend) it is interesting to note that the first constitution of Indiana provided for change only through the medium of a constitutional convention; the present constitution does not even mention the calling of a convention although it is generally recognized that such a right exists.[14]

The modern practice in constitution making is the result of three fundamental steps.[15] The basic step came with the development of the distinction between constitutional and statutory law as has already been discussed. This distinction was recognized in colonial government and many laws were set aside on the basis. The second step came in the development of the constitutional convention as a body distinct and separate from the legislature. This development came during and immediately after the American Revolution. It was later fostered by both the Jeffersonian Republicans and Jacksonian Democrats. The third and final step came in the adoption of the practice of submitting the work of the convention to the people for approval or rejection. This was a much nearer approach to true representative democracy. With the adoption of this third step, which is generally used, democracy was made more real in affairs of government.

Since 1776 there have been more than two hundred of these conventions or an average of one convention for each state for every generation; that is as far as averages are concerned but some states have had but one and others have had several.[16] According to this schedule Indiana is already long past due a revision in the organic law.[17] There is evidence to warrant a belief that the next two decades will usher in a period of considerable constitutional changes in order to meet the new problems of government, caused to a great extent by the complexities of industrial life. It is important, especially in this age when the state is supreme over other institutions, that the people understand the background of constitution making. It is the state that exerts the strongest power over the people.

This chapter has been included only to serve as a background of constitutional history and has no direct bearing on the immediate circumstances involved in connection with the constitutional convention of 1850-1851.

[1] James Bryce, *Modern Democracies* (New York: McMillan Company, 1921), 2:27.

[2] William W. Cook, *American Institutions and Their Preservation* (Norwood: Norwood Press, 1927), 21.

[3] Charles Grove Haines and Bertha Moser Haines, *Principles and Problems of Government* (New York: Harper & Brothers Publishers, 1921), 189; William F. Willoughby, *The Government of Modern States* (New York: Century Company, 1919), 95.

[4] Raymond Garfield Gettell, *History of American Political Thought* (New York: Century Company, 1928), 299.

[5] Claude Halstead Van Tyne, *The Causes of the War of Independence* (Boston: Houghton Mifflin Company, 1922), ch. 2; Frederick Jackson Turner, *The Frontier in American History* (New York: H. Holt and Company, 1920), chs. 1, 9, and 13.

[6] Edward Channing, *The American Revolution*, vol. 3, *History of the United States, 1761-1789*, (New York: McMilliam Company, 1912), 434; Max Farrand, *Fathers of the Constitution* (New Haven: Yale University Press, 1921), 40-41; Van Tyne, *The American Revolution 1776-1783* (New York: Harper & Brothers Publishers, 1905), 137.

[7] Van Tyne, *War of Independence*, 33-36. Gives typical examples of this struggle.

[8] The constitution of Rhode Island was exactly like the colonial charter except for a few details and lasted until after the Dorr Rebellion; likewise, the first constitution of Connecticut was based upon the charter and lasted until 1818.

[9] Frederic Austin Ogg and P. Orman Ray, *Introduction to American Government* (New York: Century Co., 1922), 86; Van Tyne, *The American Revolution*, 145; Gettell, *History of American Political Thought*, 329.

[10] Channing, *The American Revolution*, 431.

[11] Ogg and Ray, *Introduction*, 25.

[12] Channing, *The American Revolution*, 434-435.

[13] Any standard college textbook in political science discusses these provisions more in detail.

[14] Section one, article one, of the constitution says: ". . .the people have, at all times, an inalienable right to alter and reform their government."

[15] Walter Farleigh Dodd, *Revision and Amendment of State Constitutions* (Baltimore: Johns Hopkins Press, 1910), 30.

[16] Arthur N. Holcombe, *State Governments in the United States* (New York: The MacMillan Company, 1926), 471.

[17] The first constitution of Indiana went into effect in 1816; the second in 1851.

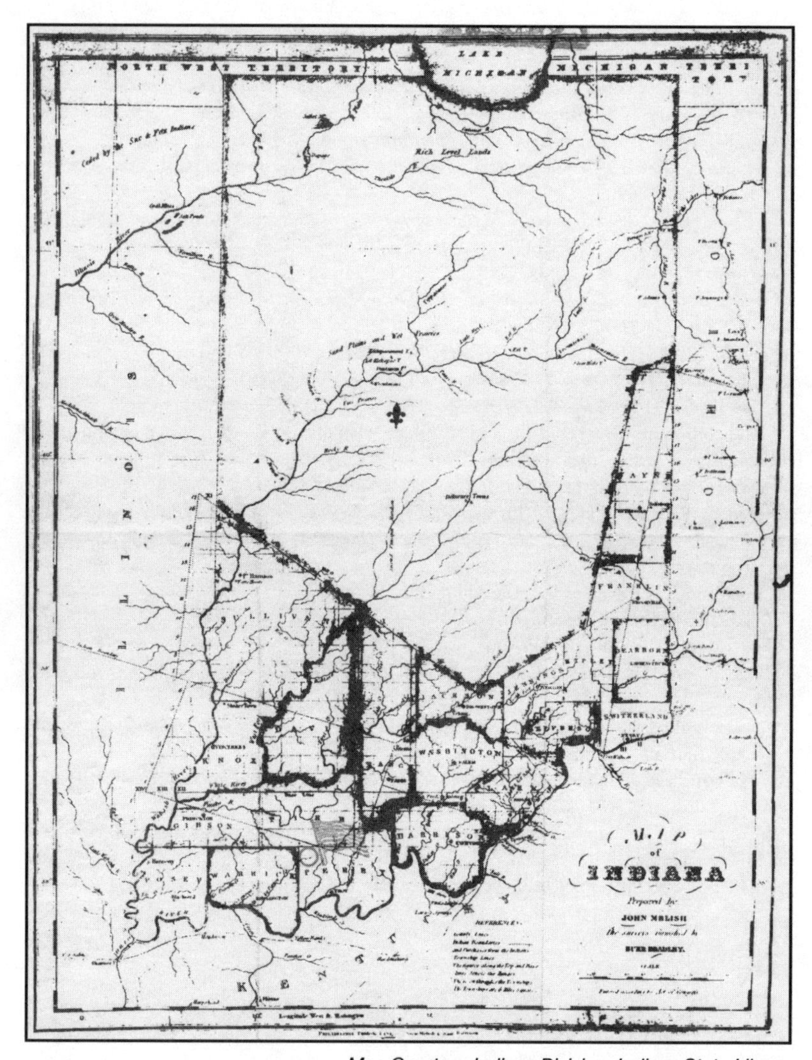

Map Courtesy Indiana Division, Indiana State Library

This 1817 map of Indiana reflects initial settlement patterns from the south. In 1824, the state's capital was moved northward from Corydon, the site of the first constitutional convention, to the more central location of Indianapolis. By 1850, when delegates gathered for the second constitutional convention, the population of Indiana had grown to roughly one million inhabitants and the pattern of settlement had begun to move north.

CHAPTER II

Influences Leading To The Convention

It is not difficult to explain why Indiana held a constitutional convention in 1816, because framing a constitution was a necessary step for statehood which the people were eager to achieve. It was a political revolution of the most peaceful sort. The first constitution of Indiana was much like the constitutions of Ohio and Kentucky, much of it being copied from them.[1] It was in accord with the political philosophy of the time and compared favorably with its contemporaries. It lasted less than two generations; however, many of its phrases and clauses are copied almost verbatim in the present constitution. The new constitution changed few principles of the old one. Not many citizens of the state can enumerate the differences between the first and second constitution of Indiana.

The framers of the first constitution were imbedded with a liberal Jeffersonian conception of government. A cardinal premise of this philosophy was that the people have at all times an inalienable and unalterable right to change the political system under which they live. The old constitution provided that every twelve years the question of calling a constitutional convention should be submitted to the people.[2] This "twelve-year clause," as the ascending process came to be called, was debated by politicians, editors, and politically-minded people generally. Varied interpretations of its meaning were advanced by those who discussed it. Those who opposed changes in the organic law tended to take a strict-construction view of this article and regard it as limiting referendums to the regular twelve-year period. This doctrine was expressed in the act which made provision for the referendum in 1840, at the end of the second twelve-year period.[3] Those who favored constitutional changes contended that the twelve-year clause was merely directory and that the General Assembly could submit the question to a popular vote at any election. This group quoted the Bill of Rights as declaring all power to be inherent in the people and giving the people and giving the electorate "at all times an unalienable and indefeasible right to alter or reform their government in such a manner as they may think proper."[4] All accepted this doctrine of popular sovereignty but the strict constructionists contended that the twelve-year clause was merely a method of giving it motivating power.[5] They argued that there must be some regulation for constant agitation, which would cause political instability. The loose construction view finally prevailed because it was found to be the most adaptable to the trend of the period. Governor James Whitcomb, the first Democratic governor of Indiana, gave a very concise interpretation of this view in his message to the General Assembly on December 6, 1848.[6]

The General Assembly submitted referendum proposals to the people in the general elections in 1823, 1828, 1840, 1846, and 1849.[7] Only two (1828 and 1840) came at the close of regular twelve-year periods.[8] The members of the General Assembly made many other unsuccessful attempts to submit referendums to the people.[9] For something like a decade after 1816, political parties were not very well organized in the state. It was the era of personal politics. During the later twenties, the Whig and Democratic factions began to appear. It is impossible to divide opponents and proponents of constitutional revision solely on the basis of party loyalty. The issue crossed party lines in peculiar ways, some of which indicate that in general the Democrats were more friendly to constitutional revision than the Whigs.[10]

There were many factors which led to the calling of a constitutional convention. Many states had called conventions in the generation before 1850. The advent of Jacksonian Democracy was everywhere sweeping away the old order and inaugurating a new era of more democratic rule. Indiana, in calling a convention, was doing what her neighboring states were likewise doing.[11] The chief criticisms of the old constitution were launched against the working of the General Assembly, the election machinery and system of office holding, the lack of real democracy in the judicial department, the abuse of power by the governor, and the administration of county government. In addition some economic and social changes were advocated.

Perhaps the chief criticism was launched against the working of the General Assembly. Under the old constitution this body was given very broad powers; the exercise of these powers had been abused. The internal improvements system had plunged the State into a debt that was never fully paid. The system was a failure and the people wanted the credit and honor of the State restored to its former status. Some change must be made which would make it impossible for such a catastrophe to occur again.[12] There was general demand that the power of the General Assembly be restricted in financial matters. Another criticism was directed against local and special legislation. The legislative sessions had come to be cluttered up with private and local bills that could be regulated by a general law or through an administrative agency. Acts were continually being passed to incorporate railroads, academies, private schools, libraries, and the like. The General Assembly vacated alleys, provided for street improvements, changed names for individuals, and assumed the authority to grant divorces.[13] Some of these practices became ridiculous at times.[14]

The worst evil of these practices was the impetus it gave to log-rolling, lobbying, and trading of votes. Closely allied to local and special legislation was the attack against annual sessions of the General Assembly. However, the demand for biennial or triennial sessions did not meet with the unanimous support of the people or press. On the other hand, it was contended that the State did not have sufficient business to require annual sessions and less frequent sessions would save thousands of dollars to the people as well as rid the state of constant political turmoil.[15] It would also break up the meeting of a clique of politicians at the State Capitol every year. It was urged that the duration of legislative sessions should be limited and provision should be made for special sessions to be called for by the governor. The appointive power of the General Assembly was looked upon with disfavor since it was commonly regarded as a method of awarding partisan friends with offices; this power could better be invested in the electorate.[16]

Other changes advocated in the working of the General Assembly were: *viva voce* voting in the General Assembly, elections in the assembly to be decided by a plurality vote, all members to be chosen from single districts, and rigid restriction on the number of senators and representatives.[17] It is evident that much of the criticism directed against the working of the General Assembly was not of such a nature as to demand constitutional changes to meet the demands of its critics. But sometimes it takes a political revolution to make real changes in political affairs. It may be kept in mind that Indianans have never become famous for praising the work of their General Assembly and that none ever meets without receiving severe criticism.

The method of electing officials and the system of office holding received a large amount of criticism. In this field the people were being led by the spirit of Jacksonian Democracy and the end in view was to bring the government as close as possible to the people; popular election of all officials was regarded as the only method of doing this.[18] If the electorate chose the officials the politicians would then be made directly responsible to the people.

Tenure of office should be restricted so that ruling dynasties could not develop.[19] It was argued that constant rotation in office would ensure honesty and faithful public service. Pluralism should be abolished in all of its forms. The farmers, which meant that it was statewide in its demand, favored postponing the regular election until later in the year as August was a busy month for them.[20] There was a demand for liberalizing of the suffrage requirements; most of this agitation was to get the foreign vote.[21] Both parties took part in this movement. Some advocated *viva voce* voting and the abolition of the poll tax was urged by others. All in all it was a movement to bring the government closer to the people by instituting complete representative democracy with brief tenure of office holding.

Several alterations were proposed in the judicial department of the government. The people had no sacrosanct respect for law and desired very meager and single judicial machinery. Popular election of all judicial officials was advocated as a primary need.[22] These should serve for fixed terms and if successful could be reelected. Associate judges and probate courts were considered a useless growth and a source of waste for public taxes. It was argued that the circuit courts be given authority to try divorce cases and to impeach local officials. There were some who believed that the grand jury system was archaic and advocated its abolition. There was a popular demand that court procedure and proceedings be codified and simplified.[23] All technicalities and special forms should be abolished, it was urged. The judicial department had been too far from the understanding and the reach of the people.

Under the old constitution the governor had very little power. Hence there was no great amount of criticism against this official. However, it was contended that his power of appointment should be given to the people and that restrictions should be placed about his pardoning power.[24] Popular election of officials would bring the administrative department closer to the people and free them of dependence upon the General Assembly. There was a desire to make county and local government more democratic.

Almost every proposed reform had an economic coloring but some reforms were primarily economic. There was a statewide demand for lower taxes and less expense in operating the government. It was urged that all needless expense and machinery should be abolished.[25] As already indicated, it was desired that the General Assembly be so restricted as to prevent future financial disasters or a new state debt. The banking question was a favorite topic of discussion. The State

Bank was attacked because the people regarded it as a monopoly that was too closely attached to the leading Whig merchants and politicians.[26] The exclusive state banking system was not in accord with the spirit of the age; there were very few attacks against the management of the State Bank and its soundness was apparently accepted by the people. Some argued that the state system was not competent to meet the growing needs of the state. It was suggested that private or free banking be established.[27] Hard money and good security were regarded as necessary elements of any system. It was urged that there should be a general law for the chartering of corporations and proper regulation of monopolies.[28] There was no experience to guide the people in these matters; hence no united support of any one plan. A further demand was made for the aid of the state in promoting agricultural and mineral development.

There were those who took occasion to remind the more privileged that there were the less fortunate who should be protected and guarded by the state. The growth of popular government plus the changes taking place as a result of the Industrial Revolution turned the attention of the folks to education. It was the era of agitation for a statewide system of common schools.[29] The higher institutions of learning were looked upon with disfavor by the rank and file of the people. The old constitution had made provision for an excellent state school system but the General Assembly had done little about it. Many speakers then offered education as the panacea for almost all of the ills of human society.[30] There were those who desired changes in the status of women in society; for the most part this was a demand for more equal property rights with men. To give force to this agitation many stories were circulated of degraded men who married women, secured their property, and then left them to become dependents upon society.

Imprisonment for debt was regarded with disfavor, except in cases of fraud. A homestead exemption was desired to protect and preserve home life. It was urged that provision should be made to care for the unfortunates of the state in a creditable manner.

It might be expected that the freemen of Indiana were active

Duplicate

ıslation to relieve the Negro of the restrictive d been placed about him. Distinctly the opposite ing. There are those who contend that the early ıstitutional revision in Indiana was largely due troduce slavery in the state.[31] The working of Railroad and the long debates over the slavery ress had agitated the people and there was a that free blacks be barred from the state.[32] It ...ch the people failed to solve. The average white ..n in 1850 regarded the problem as being one of exclusion (of blacks from the state) or amalgamation; the latter was unthinkable to them. The commonwealth of Indiana did not propose to be the "promised land" for those "lost sons of Africa."

[1] Ruth E. Brayton, "The Constitution of 1816" (master's thesis, Indiana University, 1929), ch.3. This lists and discusses various parts copied from these two constitutions.

[2] Indiana Constitution (1816), art. 8, sec. 1. "Every twelfth year, after this constitution shall have taken effect, at the general election held for Governor there shall be a poll opened, in which the qualified Electors of the State shall express, by vote, whether they are in favour of calling a convention, or not, and if there should be a majority of all the votes given at such election, in favour of a convention, the Governor shall inform the next General Assembly thereof, whose duty it shall be to provide, by law, for the election of the members to the convention, the number thereof, and the time and place of their meeting; which law shall not be passed unless agreed to by a majority of all the members elected to both branches of the General Assembly, and which convention, when met, shall have it in their power to revise, amend, or change the constitution." The remainder of the section forbids the introduction of slavery or involuntary servitude except for the punishment of crimes; this is forbidden even through a process of constitutional revision.

[3] *Laws of a General Nature Passed at the Twenty-fourth Session of the General Assembly of the State of Indiana* (Indianapolis: J. Livingston, 1840), 21-22. "And for the purpose of more expressly calling the attention of the people of the State, is the propriety of voting for or against said proposed convention, it is hereby made the duty of the several sheriffs of the State, to give six weeks public notice, in a newspaper, if one is published in his county; if not, by written notices in all townships in said county, in writing, calling upon the people to vote for against a convention; and that, in the language of the present constitution, there will not be a convention called unless a majority of all the votes given at such election, shall be in favor of a convention, and urging the people to vote for or against said convention, and setting forth in said notice, that said voting for or against said convention, is in obedience of the constitution of this State, and that the vote for or against another convention for the space of twelve years."

[4] Indiana Constitution (1816), art. 1, sec. 2.

[5] *Indiana State Journal,* 30 December 1816, calls a referendum at any other time "a forced interference not warranted by a fair construction of that instrument." (That instrument—the constitution.)

[6] "Governor's Address to the Senate and House of Representatives," *Journal of the State of Indiana during the Thirty-third Session of the General Assembly* (Indianapolis: John D. Defrees, 1849), 25: "In framing the constitution it was doubtless borne in mind that this future condition of the State might require corresponding modifications of that instrument. But by securing the people the privilege of voting upon the question every twelfth year, their power to exercise that right in any other year for which their representatives should ask suitable provisions, was not taken away. If it was taken away, it was competent, by lengthening the interval for the vote to any imaginable extent [and] virtually bind posterity in some future time and prevent any amendment whatever." "The Democratic Majority," *Indiana State Sentinel*, 13 August 1846, p.2, takes a very similar view.

[7] *Laws of the State of Indiana Passed and Published at the Seventh Session of the General Assembly of the State of Indiana* (Corydon: Carpenter and Douglas, 1823), 121; *Laws of the State of Indiana Passed and Published at the Twelfth Session of the General Assembly of the State of Indiana* (Indianapolis: Smith and Bolton, 1828), 22; *Laws of a General Nature Passed at the Twenty-fourth Session of the General Assembly of the State of Indiana* (Indianapolis: J. Livingston, 1840), 21; *Local Laws of the State of Indiana Passed at the Thirtieth Session of the General Assembly* (Indianapolis: J.P. Chapman, 1846), 97; *General Laws of the State of Indiana Passed at the Thirty-third Session of the General Assembly* (Indianapolis: John D. Defrees, 1849), 36.

[8] It is worthy of note that the referendum of 1849, which led to the convention, was not held at the end of a regular twelve-year period.

[9] Charles Kettleborough, *Constitution Making in Indiana: A Source Book of Constitutional Documents with Historical Introduction and Critical Notes* (Indianapolis: Indiana Historical Commission, 1916), 1:xxxv: "Forever unsuccessful attempts were made to provide for the calling of the convention in 1820, 1821, 1826, 1827, 1829, 1830, 1831, 1833, 1835, 1836, 1841, 1843, 1844, 1846 and 1847."

[10] A reading of the contemporary literature is not convincing.

[11] W. W. Thornton, "The Laws of Indiana as Affected by the Present Constitution," *Indiana Magazine of History* 1, no. 2 (1905): 30-31. Iowa and New York had adopted constitutions in 1846, Illinois and Wisconsin in 1849, Kentucky and Michigan in 1850, and Ohio and Maryland did in 1851.

[12] Ibid., 30.

[13] A browsing into the law of the General Assembly as the public had for each session will reveal the nature and extent of this local and special legislation.

[14] Jacob Piatt Dunn, *Indiana and Indianans* (Chicago: American Historical Society, 1919), 437. Dunn quotes from the *Chamberlain's Gazetteer*: "A few years later a Senator submitted a petition for a divorce, on the grounds that the wife had borne a colored child, and as he states there was no doubt of the fact, a bill granting the divorce passed without objection to its third reading. Before its final passage, however, the Senator rose and said that there was another fact not yet stated, which possibly ought to have some influence, and this was that both man and wife were colored persons." This put an end to the bill.

[15] *Indiana Statesman*, 5 October 1850; *Indiana State Journal*, 2 January 1850; *Indiana State Sentinel*, 25 July 1846.

[16] *Indiana State Sentinel*, 27 June 1850, suggests that it is a fortunate thing for democracy that most of the offices are not held by Democrats.

[17] *Report of the Debates and Proceedings of the Convention for the Revision of the Constitution of the State of Indiana, 1850* (Indianapolis: A. H. Brown, 1850), 40, 44-45, and 52; Kettleborough, *Constitution Making in Indiana*, 60-62. These references list the changes advocated.

[18] *Indiana State Sentinel*, 27 June 1850, states that it is generally conceded by Democrats, Whigs, and Free Soilers that popular election of all officials will be provided for in the new constitution.

[19] Ibid., 15 August 1850. A writer, signing the name "Ricklery" writes: "One office and one term in the true principle of Democracy."

[20] October or November was suggested as a more favorable time.

[21] Indiana Constitution (1816), art. 6. This constitution gave suffrage to "every white male and citizen of the United States, of the age of twenty-one years and upward . . ." *New Albany Ledger*, 4 December 1850, says, "Dr. Franklin once put the question to some gentlemen who advocated the property qualification for voting, 'If a man who owns a Jackass is entitled to vote, and one who does not is not as entitled, who votes, the man or the ass?' The question was well put and no one attempted a reply." This indicates the feeling against property qualifications; which had been abolished in the first constitution.

[22] *Indiana State Journal*, 21 January 1830; *Indiana State Sentinel*, 4 July 1850.

[23] *Indiana State Journal*, 15 June 1850, says that little improvement had been made in law reform for centuries, common law had absurd technicalities, submission of evidence and pleadings was not satisfactory, the spirit of criminal law should be Christianized and humanized. [Law] should all be codified.

[24] *Indiana State Journal*, 4 May 1850, a letter from "Justitis" says that in sober moments most people regard the pardoning power as an evil because it destroys confidence in the judiciary and encourages crime.

[25] *Debates*, 263: "The great reason why the people voted for a call of this convention, was embraced in the hope of being able to economize expenditure expenses; and are the people to be deceived in regard to this matter?"

[26] Thorton, "Laws of Indiana," 30.

[27] *Indiana Statesman*, 9 October 1850 and 13 November 1850; *Indiana State Journal*, [Day and Month Unknown] 1830; Dunn, *Indianans*, 446.

[28] *Indiana State Journal*, 21 January 1850.

[29] *The Common School Advocate* was established in 1846 and the oft-debated school referendum was held in 1849.

[30] *Madison Weekly Courier*, 27 July 1850: "There is no fear of a people's liberties where education becomes popular."

[31] Dunn, *Indianans*, 436: "The earlier efforts were probably connected with a desire for the introduction of slavery, and were defeated on that ground, as has been mentioned, by the party in power."

[32] *Indiana State Sentinel*, 25 July 1850: "The candidates for the convention in Marion county, Whigs as well as Democrats, advocate strong measures to prevent the further emigration of people of color to the State." *Indiana Statesman*, 11 September 1850, quoted from the *[New Albany] Ledger* that many delegates had taken a strong stand against the further emigration of free blacks to the state and believed that "the free Negroes would consult their own interest and that of posterity by emigrating to the colored mans El Dorado, Liberia."

Photo Courtesy Indiana State Library

George Whitfield Carr, delegate from Lawrence, served as president of the convention.

Carr was born in 1807 and spent his childhood on his family's farm in Charlestown, Indiana. Carr moved to Lawrence in 1831 to operate a tannery. Prior to the convention, Carr served as a five-time representative and three-time senator in the Indiana Legislature. Following the convention, Carr continued in public service as receiver of the land office in Jeffersonville from 1852 to 1854. J. P. Dunn, *Indiana and Indianans*, (Chicago: American Historical Society, 1919), 442.

CHAPTER III

The Referendum And Election Of Delegates

In his message to the General Assembly December 6, 1848, Governor James Whitcomb, the first Democratic governor of Indiana, recommended that the General Assembly submit a referendum to the people opening a poll for and against a proposed constitutional convention. The governor favored voting on the referendum at the regular August election. He discussed the growing evil of local and special legislation and stated that a remedy of this one condition would abundantly justify the calling of a convention. Furthermore, he continued, it would lessen the expenses of legislation nearly one-half and within two years after the adoption of the new constitution save enough to pay the expenses incidental to calling a convention. Governor Whitcomb expressed the opinion that a large majority of the people favored changes in the organic law.[1]

December 15 Senator Alonzo A. Morrison (Democrat) introduced a bill to provide for the proposed referendum.[2] Three days later the bill was read a second time and referred to a select committee of one from each congressional district.[3] The committee was instructed to report a bill providing for *viva voce* voting and to indicate the probable expenses of such a convention. December

30 the select committee reported the bill making provision for *viva voce* voting and a few minor amendments. The committee stated that it lacked sufficient data to make a report concerning the cost of a convention. The bill was engrossed to third reading and January 2, 1849, passed the Senate by a vote of thirty-four to twelve; twenty-six Democrats and eight Whigs voting for it, one Democrat and eleven Whigs voting against it. January 10 the bill was introduced in the House, read twice, then laid upon the table. Three days later the bill was taken from the table and passed by a vote of eighty to two; forty-seven Democrats and thirty-three Whigs voting for it, no Democrats and two Whigs voting against it.[4] January 15, 1849, the bill was approved by Governor Paris C. Dunning, who had succeeded Governor Whitcomb after the election of the latter to the United States Senate December 17, 1848.[5]

The act, which was very brief, made provision for using the regular elective machinery and procedure. Section one directed that a poll be opened to enter "all the votes given for or against a convention to alter, revise, or amend the Constitution of this State." Section two gave every qualified voter in the state the right to vote on the referendum. Section three provided for *viva voce* voting. Sections four, five, and six provided for the elective machinery and procedure. It was made the duty of the secretary of state to make an official report of the poll to the next General Assembly. In the early part of January 1849, while the bill to provide for a convention was under discussion in the General Assembly, the Democratic State Convention adopted a resolution favoring a convention and enumerating certain reforms that it considered necessary.[6] Previous to this, the Free Soil State Convention had adopted a resolution recommending that the constitution be so amended as to provide for the popular election of all officials.[7] The referendum was not an important issue in the campaign and little attention seems to have been given to the subject of constitutional revision at the time. State politics were then dominated by national issues, the chief of which was the whole question of slavery. After the August poll had been reported the editor of the *Indiana State Journal*, the leading

Whig organ of the state, announced that he had been among those who voted for the convention and did so because he favored several important alterations of the constitution.[8]

Governor Whitcomb's opinion that the people would approve a referendum calling for a convention was verified at the polls on August 6, 1849. The official returns, as recorded by the secretary of state in the *Documentary Journal*, gave a total of 81,500 votes for the convention to 57,418 against. A total of 138,918 votes were cast on the referendum; the total poll of the election, without the report of Fayette County from which no return on the total vote was given, was 147,851. There were seventy-three of the ninety-one counties that voted for calling a convention.[9] All of the counties that voted against the referendum were from central and southern Indiana, except Jasper. It is interesting to note that Ohio County, the only county that later voted against adopting the new constitution, gave 516 votes for to 329 votes against calling a convention. No satisfactory explanation of this geographical distribution of the vote can be given. Perhaps the northern counties, being newer districts, had more to gain and less to lose by constitutional changes than the older counties farther south. It should be kept in mind that, at this time, the southern counties were the ones that exercised the dominant power. However, a study of the map shows that every section of the state voted in favor of a convention.[10] The *Indianapolis State Sentinel* charged the Whigs with responsibility for the defeat of the proposition in Marion County. The *Indiana State Journal*, answering for the Whigs, made no direct reply to this attack but pointed out that there had been very little interest in the proposal and asked, "How will the *Sentinel* account for the fact that many Whig counties voted for it, and many Democratic counties against it?"[11] If the Whigs endeavored to defeat the referendum it must have been a subtle campaign on their part; contemporary newspapers do not indicate such an attack. The Democrats were in power and favored the measure, which had apparently become popular with the people, and they may have desired to discredit the Whigs before the campaign for the election of delegates began to bubble.

The vote on the referendum left no doubt as to the wishes of the electorate. In pursuance of this poll Governor Dunning, in his message to the General Assembly December 4, 1849, gave the official returns of the voting and recommended that the General Assembly call a convention. The governor urged that partisan influences and considerations be forgotten in arranging for the organization and personnel of the convention.[12] On the same day, in fact before the governor had delivered his message, Senator Frank P. Randall (Democrat) introduced a bill to provide for the holding of a convention.[13] The bill passed first and second readings and was referred to a select committee of the one from each congressional district.[14] December 14 the select committee reported the bill with amendments and recommended its passage. The bill and proposed amendments were laid on the table to be considered at a later date. A study of the *Senate Journal* indicates that the chief debate came in regard to the apportionment of delegates. January 3, 1850, the bill was taken from the table and passed. The vote on final passage is not recorded in the *Senate Journal.* January 4 the bill was introduced in the House and read a first and second time. One week later it was approved, with amendments, by vote of fifty-five to thirty-eight.[15] It was necessary to appoint two conference committees to iron out the differences between the two houses. January 18, 1850, the bill was approved by Governor Dunning; three days more than one year after he had signed the bill providing for the referendum in 1849.[16]

The bill contained seventeen sections, being rather lengthy. It probably called into being the only constituent assembly ever provided for by the General Assembly. It contained several items worthy of attention: all who were eligible to vote for members of the General Assembly were given the right to vote for delegates to the convention; all who were entitled to vote were eligible to be elected delegates; the delegates were to be chosen at the regular August election; the delegates, when properly assembled, were to have full power to make "such amendments to, alteration of, and changes in the same, as they may deem proper;" the work of the convention was to be submitted to the people for approval or rejection; the delegates, except in two instances, were to be chosen in *exactly* the same districts as members of the General Assembly were then chosen; members of the convention were to be paid four dollars *per diem* while in actual attendance at the convention; the convention was authorized to submit one or more amendments as distinct propositions if they so desired; the convention was to meet at the Capitol on the first Monday in October (October 7, 1850) and be organized by the secretary of state.

The bill was based upon the principle that the people were sovereign, hence all the qualified voters were given the right to vote and the people were likewise to have the final word before the new constitution could be adopted. The section providing for the election of delegates from the regular senatorial and representative districts was confusing to the voters and local politicians.[17] There was no difference between the two classes except the fiat of the General Assembly, which designated that the senatorial and representative districts be used. While the bill was under discussion in the General Assembly it was criticized by the *Indiana State Journal* as making provision for too many delegates, for providing that the election of delegates be in August, and for postponing the assembling of the convention so long after the election of delegates. The *Journal* contended that one hundred delegates would have been sufficient and, to remove the subject from politics, that the delegates should have been chosen at a special election.[18] They were not averse to a convention but merely to certain provisions of the bill which were not very satisfactory to them.

On submitting the referendum in 1849, and in all subsequent acts leading to the calling of the convention, both the Whigs and Democrats had supported convention measures. The difference had been one of degree, for a larger percent of Democrats than Whigs had voted for legislation friendly to the convention. The campaign for the election of delegates soon injected the partisan issue and the party newspapers took occasion to issue political invective against their opponents. Feeble attempts were made to secure a non-partisan election of delegates but the Democrats, with victory appearing certain for them, did not wish to compromise with the Whigs who, so the *Indiana Sentinel* asserted, had never given the Democrats anything when the latter were in power.[19] The Whig offer to divide the ticket in Marion County was refused. The *Indiana State Sentinel*, as the organ of orthodox democracy in the state, called for a full election of *regular* Democrats.[20] The Democrats circulated a letter asking for a complete victory and warning against all compromises with the Whigs.[21] There was an undercurrent of Free Soilism in the campaign. Perhaps the average citizen would say that the Whigs deserve praise for having endeavored to secure the election of non-partisan delegates. Perhaps it would be more accurate to say that it was altogether a matter of political opportunism and that the situation would have been entirely reversed had the Whigs been the majority with the Democrats seeking concessions from them. The Democrats had the advantage and, as all political parties usually do, they made use of their superior numbers by electing a convention dominated by their party.

The election returns showed a sweeping victory for the Democrats who won about two-thirds of the seats in both the convention and the General Assembly. They were elated by their success over the "Whig wire-workers" and rejoiced that they met the "enemy in open fight" and won.[22] The *Indiana State Sentinel* assured its readers that Indiana was a Democratic state and that the Whigs won only when democracy was asleep.[23] The *Indiana State Journal* explained the election by saying, "Very little excitement existed among the people and they seemed to be controlled by other party considerations, for many strong Democratic counties elected Whigs and many Whig counties elected Democrat."[24] The *Indiana Statesman*, established in 1850 as a revolt from the Dunkerism of the *Sentinel*, was pleased with the Democratic victory but noted that several good Democrats had been defeated.[25] The *Indiana State Sentinel* reported ninety-six Democrats and fifty-four Whigs elected to the convention; this corresponds very closely with the reports of the *Indiana Statesman* and the *Indiana State Journal*.[26]

The election in Union County was contested between Benjamin F. Brookbank (Whig) and James Osborn (Democrat). The election had been very close and there were irregularities in its conduct. Brookbank came to the convention and took a seat on the first day of its session. But the election committee refused to accept his credentials and recommended that the election go back to the people. A large majority of members of the convention concurred in this recommendation. In this "second election," as the *Indiana State Journal* termed it, Brookbank was successful by more than twenty votes. The Democrats had replaced Osborn by Judge Vinsant as their candidate. November 15 Brookbank was admitted to the convention after more than a month of the session had passed.[27] During the labors of the convention one delegate died and two resigned. James Vanbenthusen (Democrat) of Shelby County died on November 1; he had attended the convention the day before his death. He was the oldest delegate in the convention. James Elliot (Democrat) of Shelby County was elected to fill the vacancy and took his seat December 6. Elliot was a director of the State Bank. December 21 Richard A. Clements of Daviess was sworn in as a delegate to fill the vacancy caused by the resignation of Elias S. Terry (Whig). Terry had resigned to accept an appointment as recorder of the land office at Washington. Early in January, William Holliday (Democrat) of Orange resigned his seat in the convention in consequences of bad health. He was succeeded by William R. Johnson (Democrat) of Orange January 18. During the election to fill the vacancy caused by the resignation of Holliday, the *Indiana Statesman* sent out the report that the new delegate need not hurry as "he'll get here in time to have his picture taken!"[28] If he did arrive in time to have said picture taken it must have been lost along with other pictures of the delegates. Counting the three delegates elected to fill vacancies, there were 153 delegates who served in the convention. A list of the regularly elected delegates may be found in the appendix.

The work of the convention is better understood when one is acquainted with the delegates. Contemporary newspapers of both parties expressed their faith and confidence in the ability and fair mindedness of the delegates chosen.[29] The delegates were a representative body of Indiana citizens. A table prepared by Baker and McFarland, which has very interesting data about all of the 150 delegates elected to the convention, shows that only thirteen of the delegates were born in Indiana; twenty-two were born in Kentucky, nineteen in Virginia, nineteen in Pennsylvania, seventeen in Ohio, sixteen in New York, each of these five states furnishing more delegates than did Indiana. North Carolina furnished ten delegates, Tennessee seven, Maryland seven, South Carolina four, Massachusetts four, Connecticut two, with one each from Delaware, Vermont, New Jersey, and New Hampshire. Scotland was the birthplace of Robert Dale Owen, James Dick, and G. H. Ballingall. Ireland was the birthplace Beattie McClelland, D. Milligan, and Allen Hamilton. This is a very clear picture of the westward movement of population in that period of the history of the state; not a single delegate came from a state west of Indiana, although 137 delegates came from states east and south of Indiana and the British Isles. The same table shows that twelve of the delegates had lived in Indiana less than ten years, that there were six delegates twenty-seven years of age and under, that there were five delegates sixty-six years of age and above (four of these being sixty-six, the fifth seventy-two), and there were ten delegates in the convention who were not married.[30]

Twenty-one delegates had been members of the General Assembly of 1848-1849 which submitted the referendum to the people. Fourteen delegates were members of the General Assembly of 1849-1850, which issued the call for the convention.[31] Seventy-five of the members had seen service in the General Assembly and twenty-five more made this the stepping-stone to later legislative service.[32] Twelve members sat in the General Assembly of 1851-1852, which codified the laws under the new constitution.[33] Many had political careers, other than in the General Assembly, after the convention was over: Schuyler Colfax and Thomas A. Hendricks became vice presidents; John Pettit and Thomas A. Hendricks served as United States senators; Thomas A. Hendricks and Alvin P. Hovey became governors of Indiana; Samuel Hall became lieutenant-governor; Horace Biddle, Alvin P. Hovey, and John Pettit served on the Indiana Supreme Court bench; James W. Borden, Alvin P. Hovey, and Robert Dale Owen became ministers to foreign countries; William McKee Dunn became a judge advocate general of the United States; John P. Dunn and Joseph Ristine became auditors of state; Schuyler Colfax, Robert Dale Owen, David Kilgore, James Lockhart, Smith Miller, Thomas Smith, William S. Holman, Thomas A. Hendricks, William McKee Dunn, James B. Foley, and Alvin P. Hovey later served as congressmen.[34] Robert H. Milroy and Alvin Hovey served as generals in the Civil War.[35] Among the leading delegates of the convention were: E. K. Bascom, James W. Borden, M. G. Bright, J. P. Chapman, Schuyler Colfax, G. F. Cookerly, D. M. Dobson, W. M. Dunn, B. R. Edmonston, W. C. Foster, T. W. Gibson, Milton Gregg, Thomas A. Hendricks, W. S. Holman, A. P. Hovey, Daniel Kelso, P. M. Kent, David Kilgore, James Lockhart, R. H. Milroy, A. F. Morrison (Marion), Robert Dale Owen, A. C. Pepper, James Rariden, Daniel Read, John Pettit, David Wallace, and T. D. Walpole; Colfax, Dunn, Gregg, Kilgore, Rariden, Wallace, and Walpole were Whigs, the others Democrats. An analysis of the table, referred to above and found in the appendix, reveals that almost half of the delegates were farmers, about one-fourth of them were lawyers, about one-eighth were physicians; the remainder were merchants, editors, printers, bankers, teachers, and so on. The spirit of the convention was dominated by the agrarian interests and Whig business was almost undreamed of by the delegates; it may be justly called the "farmers convention" but there need be no apology attached to that title for none other could have better represented the Indiana of that period.

[1] *Journal of the State of Indiana during the Thirty-third Session of the General Assembly* (Indianapolis: John D. Defrees, 1849), 23. Governor Whitcomb also called attention to the fact that the time was appropriate; he thought the work of a convention could be completed before the presidential campaign of 1852 would be inaugurated.

[2] Ibid., 95.

[3] Ibid., 124. The members of this committee were: Godlove S. Orth, William A. Porter, Elisha G. English, William H. McCarty, David P. Holloway, James M. Sleeth, Lovel H. Rousseau, William P. Dole, Cyrus Taber, Franklin P. Randall. Orth was chairman.

[4] Ibid., 532.

[5] Ibid., 36. Also in Charles Kettleborough, *Constitution Making in Indiana: A Source Book of Constitutional Documents with Historical Introduction and Critical Notes* (Indianapolis: Indiana Historical Commission, 1916), 1:192-193 .

[6] *Indiana State Sentinel*, 11 January 1849. The convention favored biennial sessions, *viva voce* voting in the legislature, and a very stringent regulation against a public debt.

[7] Ibid., 14 February 1849. The convention was held August 30, 1848.

[8] *Indiana State (Daily) Journal*, 3 December 1849. He favored biennial sessions of legislature, popular election of all state officials, a general banking law with ample provision to protect bill holders, a reasonable homestead exemption, and distribution of fines and penalties for law violations to the benefit of the common schools.

[9] *Documents of the General Assembly of Indiana at the Thirty-fourth Session Commencing December 3, 1849* (Indianapolis: John D. Defrees, 1849), 81. Miscellaneous Records of Secretary of State (State Archives), 1845-1860 , 333-334. Also see accounts of Indianapolis newspapers.

[10] This map was copied from the Records of the Secretary of State, referred to in note nine.

[11] *Indiana State (Tri-Weekly) Journal*, 24 August 1849.

[12] *Journal of the Indiana State Senate during the Thirty-fourth Session of the General Assembly Commencing December 3, 1849* (Indianapolis: John D. Defrees,1849), 20.

[13] Ibid., 11. The session had begun the day before.

[14] Ibid., 12. The members were: Franklin P. Randall, Smith Miller, Elisha G. English, George Berry, David T. Holloway, Wm. G. Montgomery, Ambrose D. Hamrick, Michael A. Malott, Franklin Hardin, and Henry Day. Kettlebrough, *Constitution Making in Indiana*, 1:196, notes the committee consisted of six Democrats and four Whigs.

[15] *Journal of the House of Representatives of the State of Indiana during the Thirty-fourth Session*, 649.

[16] *General Laws of the State of Indiana Passed at the Thirty-fourth Session*, 29.

[17] *New Albany Weekly Ledger*, 1 August 1850; *Indiana State Sentinel*, 20 June 1850; *Report of the Debates and Proceedings of the Convention for the Revision of the Constitution of the State of Indiana, 1850* (Indianapolis: A. H. Brown, 1850), 127.

[18] *Indiana State (Daily) Journal*, 3 January 1850; *Indiana State (Weekly) Journal*, 7 January 1850. The *Journal* expressed the hope that the House would alter the bill to meet these objections; but such was not the result.

[19] *Indiana State Journal*, 27 April 1850. The editor asserted that there would be no assurance that both parties would carry the program out in good faith, that the Whig members of the last General Assembly had recommended a full ticket for their party, that there would be a need for parties in the convention, and that Indiana should ever rest on a "safe and Democratic foundation."

[20] *Indiana State Sentinel*, 27 June 1850; Ibid., 11 July 1850; Ibid., 25 July 1850. *Sentinel* desired the enemy (Whigs) to be treated as spies and all must "beware of the pretended Democrat."

[21] Kettleborough, *Constitution Making in Indiana*, 1:212, has copied as much of the circular as pertains to the convention from the *Daily Lafayette Courier*, 1 March 1850.

[22] *Indiana State Sentinel*, 16 August 1850. The *Sentinel* said that "they were alarmed for fear of the result—knowing the tactics used."

[23] Ibid.

[24] *Indiana State Journal*, 17 August 1850.

[25] *Indiana Statesman*, 4 September 1850. They name Hon. E. H. C. Chamberlain of Elkhart defeated by "a corrupt coalition of disorganizers and Whigs," Hon. Charles W. Gatheart "who unfortunately resides in a Whig district," Hon. D. B. Herriman "noted like Shakespeare's alderman for his good round belly," and Hon. Jere. Smith of Randolph district known for his legal ability and integrity. "These were some of the best men whose absence will be more regretted by others than by themselves."

[26] *Indiana State Sentinel*, 20 August 1850. Thirty-three Democrats and seventeen Whigs are listed as senatorial delegates, sixty-three Democrats and thirty-seven Whigs are listed as representative delegates. The *Indiana State Journal*, 31 August 1850, lists sixty-five Democrats to thirty-five Whigs as representative delegates. The *Indiana Statesman*, 4 September 1850, lists sixty-two Democrats and thirty-two Whigs as representative delegates. The *Journal* and the *Statesman* agree with the *Sentinel* in regard to senatorial Delegates.

[27] *Debates*, 125-131, contains a discussion of the disputed election.

[28] *Indiana Statesman*, 15 December 1850. The *Statesman* no doubt referred to the picture of the delegates that was being prepared; the Indianapolis newspapers have several items in regard to such a picture but no record of the picture could be found.

[29] *Indiana State Sentinel*, 15 August 1850, notes, "As an [Indianan] we are proud of the man selected to alter and amend our constitution showing that the people have not been unmindful of the high duty that is to be preformed. So have talent, age, and experience, and both parties represented by their best men." The result will be a "good Democratic Constitution" worthy of the age and the state.

Indiana State Journal, 12 October 1850, states, "From the character of the delegates elected, and the spirit which seems to animate them, we feel justified in predicting that they will assume these duties with a determination to act in such a manner as will secure to the people of the State a constitution under which all their rights will be amply protected and their prosperity and happiness insured in so far as it is possible to do so."

Indiana Statesman, 2 October 1850, states, "The convention is admitted by all to embody more talent, more eloquence, than any other deliberative body that has ever assembled here since the organization of the State. Both parties have presented their ablest men for the suffrages of the people, and both have sent up delegates who will do them no discredit."

[30] A Photostat copy of this table is enclosed in the appendix. The only copy the writer was able to find is the one being preserved in a vault in the Indiana Section of the State Library.

Editors' Note: The Photostat copy is not included in this edition.

[31] Legislative Reference Bureau; from typed records kept there.

[32] Logan Esarey, *From Its Exploration to 1850*, vol.1, *The History of Indiana*, (Fort Wayne: Hoosier Press, 1924), 516; Esarey notes that few delegates had university or college training and that the great Whig lawyers of the state were absent.

[33] Legislative Reference Bureau, typed sheets. Franklin Hardin, Christopher Graham, and George Berry were "hold over" Senators and were members of the General Assembly and the convention, both of which were in session at the same time.

[34] W. W. Thornton, "Constitutional Convention of 1850," Indianapolis: Debate sponsored by the Indiana State Bar Association (Address delivered 1902). A pamphlet in the State Library, this was an address delivered before the Indiana State Bar Association in 1902.

[35] Ibid.

Photo Courtesy Indiana Historical Society

During the first part of the convention, delegates met in the hall used by the House of Representatives in the old Capitol Building. This was the first capitol building built in Indianapolis. It was eventually torn down and replaced by the current building, which was completed in 1888.

CHAPTER IV

Organization and Structure

The act calling for the election of delegates provided that the delegates should assemble October 7, 1850 and be organized by the secretary of state.[1] A subsequent act appropriated $40,000 to defray the expenses of the convention and a joint resolution of the General Assembly authorized the governor, auditor, and secretary of state to select a suitable hall to be used by the convention; the rent of the hall not to exceed one hundred dollars per month.[2] The large and attractive Masonic Hall had just been completed but the attempt of this committee to secure it was unsuccessful because the commissioner of the hall refused to rent it for the price offered.[3] The committee consisting of Joseph A. Wright (governor), J. P. Drake (treasurer), and E. W. H. Ellis (auditor) then had the hall of the House of Representatives prepared for the use of the convention. Later when the General Assembly convened, the convention made arrangements to use the Masonic Hall for the remainder of the session.[4] An attempt was made to have the convention moved to Madison but this seems to have been more talked about than actually considered.[5]

The press of the state gave more than usual attention to the meeting of the convention.[6] Many newspapers promised their readers to give full reports of the work of the convention; subscribers were urged to take advantage of this opportunity to acquaint themselves with the labor of the delegates. Some of the newspapers offered special club rates to enlarge their circulation. Advertisements in the Indianapolis papers, especially in regard to rooming and boarding houses, made appeals for the patronage of the delegates.[7]

"The Convention assembled in the Hall of the House of Representatives, at 10:00 o'clock A.M. and was called to order by the Hon. Charles H. Test, Secretary of State. . . ."[8] The secretary of state called the roll and the delegates were all present but Messrs. Jones of Bartholomew, Conduit of Morgan, Colfax of St. Joseph, Ritchey of Johnson, Taylor of LaPorte, Hovey of Posey, and Blythe of Vanderburgh.[9] The delegates were administered the oath of office by Isaac Blackford, the senior judge of the Supreme Court.[10] The secretary announced the presence of a quorum and the convention proceeded to the election of a permanent chairman. Borden of Allen, Adams, and Wells, nominated George W. Carr of Lawrence for chairman, stating that the dignity and impartiality with which that gentleman had presided over the last two sessions of the House was a sufficient guarantee of his fitness for the position.[11] No other nominee was suggested and Carr was elected by a vote of 136 to six. The election was *viva voce*. As soon as the presiding officer had been chosen, Mr. Pettit said, "That in consequence of the amount of business which it was desirable should be done out of doors, he would move that the convention do now adjourn until tomorrow morning at 9 o'clock." Kilgore of Delaware moved to amend Pettit's motion so that the convention would meet at two o'clock in the afternoon. Kilgore wanted to know something about the informal business to be done out of doors and said that the "within door members" should be informed as to how the delegates were to be chosen. His amendment carried and the convention took a recess until two o'clock in the afternoon. There is evidence to indicate that the Democrats nominated the officers at caucus meetings; apparently the Whigs made no effort to select officials.[12]

When the afternoon session opened, three more delegates

appeared and were sworn in by Biddle of Cass, Howard, and Pulaski counties.[13] There was prolonged debate as to the number of secretaries and officers that should be elected by the convention. Finally the convention proceeded to the election of the principal secretary. On the first ballot William H. English received forty-seven votes, Solon Turman twenty-seven, George L. Sites twenty, J. S. Buckles fourteen, with thirty-seven scattering; Biddle and Kent acting as tellers. No candidate having received a majority, a second ballot was taken, resulting in sixty-four votes for English, forty-one for Turman, fifteen for Sites, and twenty-five scattering. English was elected on the third ballot having received seventy-six votes to sixty-six for Turman with three scattering; seventy-three were needed to make a majority.[14] William H. English, as a historian and politician, was well qualified for the position.[15] At forty minutes past four o'clock the convention adjourned with its first day's work completed. All of the delegates, except four, had been present some time during the day; it is very doubtful if any succeeding day had as many members in attendance.[16] On the second day George L. Sites of Allen, Robert M. Evans of Fountain, and Harmon G. Barkwell of Perry were elected assistant secretaries by large majorities.[17] Read of Clark introduced resolutions calling for the election of Samuel McKinzie and Samuel J. Johnson as sergeant-at-arms and doorkeeper, which were accepted by the convention.[18] All of these minor officials were sworn in by Judge Blackford. Other officials were chosen from time to time as needed; and sometimes when not needed.[19] Arrangements were made by which the clergy of Indianapolis were to open each day with prayer. When no Indianapolis minister appeared the convention was often opened with prayer by one of the delegates; Badger of Putnam, Farrow of Putnam, and Crumbacker of Lake and Porter, were ministers and often served in this capacity.

The twelfth section of the act calling for the convention provided that the governor should appoint a stenographer to report the debates of the convention. In pursuance of this act Governor Joseph A. Wright appointed Harvey Fowler, of Washington City, to report the debates.[20] Milton Gregg of Jefferson, who constantly criticized the convention for lack of economy moved that it was inexpedient to publish the debates at the expense of the state and that the services of the stenographer should be respectfully declined.[21] Owen of Posey, perhaps the most widely known of the delegates, moved that the governor's appointment be accepted. A select committee of seven was appointed to study the question.[22] The committee recommended that Owen's resolution be accepted and the members of the convention adopted the report. The contest for the election of a printer to the convention was a very party one. J. P. Chapman of Marion (Democrat) contended that he was *ex officio* printer to the convention by virtue of his office as state printer. His contention was supported by the *Indiana Statesman*.[23] Austin H. Brown, of the *Indianapolis Sentinel*, had early announced his desire to be chosen printer to the convention;[24] the *Statesman* quoted from a letter which they claim Brown wrote to the delegates-elect soliciting their support.[25] The *Indiana State Journal* early noticed this rivalry between the two separate papers and wrote that "the *'Statesman'* and *'Sentinel'* have not yet settled which of the two establishments is to have the printing for the convention."[26] The fight was carried to the convention floor, the ultimate and final appeal, where a select committee was appointed to study the claim of Chapman and report to the convention. The *Statesman* contended that every member of the committee was unfriendly to them and accused the *Sentinel* of having made a bargain with the *Journal*.[27] They gave good evidence to support this charge. October 11 the committee, which had both Whig and Democratic members, reported that the state printer was not *ex officio* printer to the convention and had no legal claim to the office. One week later Austin H. Brown was elected printer to the convention; Brown received seventy-eight votes, Solon Turman thirty-five, Chapman six, with eleven scattering. Many delegates did not vote at all. The *Statesman* was furious at the result and from then on seems to have fared badly with the members of the convention.[28]

Framing and adopting rules was one of the easiest tasks of the convention. October 8 the rules of the House of Representatives were adopted as temporary rules, and the chair was authorized to appoint a committee to prepare permanent rules of the convention. The committee consisted of one from each of the thirteen judicial districts.[29] October 9, the committee was appointed and two days later reported rules and order to govern the deliberations of the convention; the committee report was laid upon the table and 150 copies were ordered to be printed. Five days later, on the eighth day of the session, the rules were adopted with minor amendments and changes. The rules followed the established parliamentary procedure used in the General Assembly and were not much changed during the labors of the convention. In general they permitted much freedom of debate and discussion, which prolonged the session but gave voice to all factions that wanted to speak.

Several plans were suggested for doing the work of the convention. John Pettit of Tippecanoe proposed that three major committees be appointed corresponding with the three major departments of government as recognized in the constitution.[30] Borden of Allen, who was perhaps the ablest parliamentarian of the convention, proposed that nineteen standing committees be appointed and suggested the committees which he thought would be needed.[31] This plan was modeled on that used by the Kentucky convention and was the essence of the plan ultimately adopted. Still another plan was discussed which would call for the consideration of the old constitution in the committee of the whole. The latter scheme being the most democratic of all was looked upon with favor by many of the delegates.[32] A much more simple plan was presented by Kilgore of Delaware which would have called for adjournment *sine die*.[33] At the same time these suggestions were proposed Read of Monroe, a professor in the state university, suggested that a select committee be appointed to prepare a plan of business for the convention. This latter suggestion was approved on the next day, and October 10 a committee was appointed to draft a plan.[34] October 11 the committee reported a plan providing for twenty-two standing committees, not counting a committee on elections and one on accounts; that report was adopted with a few minor changes on the next day. October 14 the president announced the appointment of the following standing committees:[35]

No. 1.—On the rights and privileges of the inhabitants of this State.—Messrs. Owen, Graham of Miami, Niles, Haddon, Prather, Coats, Murray, Chapman, and Berry.

No. 2.—On the legislative department.—Messrs. Bright, Smiley, Clark of Tippecanoe, Schoonover, Walpole, Edmonston, Duzan, Beach, and Miller of Gibson.

No. 3.—On the executive.—Messrs. Morrison of Marion, Stevenson, Beard, Sherrod, Gordon, Wolfe, Morgan, Bascom, and Barbour.

No. 4.—On state officers other than the executive and judiciary.—Messrs. Read of Clark, Moore, Bicknell, Bracken, Farrow, Mowrer, and Frisbie.

No. 5.—On the organization of the courts of justice.—1st circuit. Mr. Pettit; 2nd circuit, Mr. Thornton; 3rd circuit, Mr. Dunn of Jefferson; 4th circuit, Mr. Lockhart; 5th circuit, Mr. Nave; 6th circuit, Mr. Rariden; 7th circuit, Mr. Davis of Vermillion; 8th circuit, Mr. Biddle; 9th circuit, Mr. Anthony; 10th circuit, Mr. Terry; 11th circuit, Mr. McClelland; 12th circuit, Mr. Howe; 13th circuit, Mr. Smith of Ripley.

No. 6.—On matters pertaining to criminal law.—Messrs. Kent, Davis of Madison, Mooney, Hawkins, Chandler, Carter, and May.

No. 7.—On the practice of the law and law reform.—12th circuit, Mr. Borden; 1st circuit, Mr. Ristine; 2nd circuit, Mr. Gibson; 3rd circuit, Mr. Kelso; 4th circuit, Mr. Hall; 5th circuit, Mr. Wallace; 6th circuit, Mr. Newman; 7th circuit, Mr. Cookerly; 8th circuit, Mr. Kendall of Warren; 9th circuit, Mr. Mather; 10th circuit, Mr. Read of Monroe; 11th circuit, Mr. March; 13th circuit, Mr. Holman.

No. 8.—On special and local legislation, and uniformity of laws.—Messrs. Newman, Helmer, Miller of Gibson, Allen, Snook, Crumbacker, and Pepper of Crawford.

No. 9.—On impeachment and removals from office.—Messrs. Rariden, Biddle, Garvin, Mathes, and Brookbank.

No. 10.—On the elective franchise and the apportionment of representation.—4th circuit, Mr. Graham of Warrick; 1st circuit, Mr. Miller of Clinton; 2nd circuit, Mr. Smith of Scott; 3rd circuit, Mr. Pepper of Ohio; 5th circuit, Mr. Vanbenthusen; 6th circuit, Mr. Thomas; 7th circuit, Mr. Davis of Parke; 8th circuit, Mr. Harbolt; 9th circuit, Mr. Anthony; 10th circuit, Mr. Foster; 11th circuit, Mr. Clark of Hamilton; 12th circuit, Mr. Wunderlich; 13th circuit, Mr. Berry.

No. 11.—On county and township organization, powers, and officers.—3rd congressional district, Mr. Smith of Ripley; 1st district, Mr. Alexander; 2nd district, Mr. Prather; 4th district, Mr. Beeson; 5th district, Mr. Hendricks; 6th district, Mr. Gootee; 7th district, Mr. Barbour; 8th district, Mr. Clark of Tippecanoe; 9th district, Mr. Kendall of Wabash; 10th district, Mr. Hogin.

No. 12.—On currency and banking.—Messrs. Hamilton, Taylor, Dick, Mooney, Colfax, Dunn of Perry, Hardin, Helmer, Watts, Todd, and Shoup.

No. 13.—On corporations other than banking.—Messrs. Read of Monroe, Dobson, Kinley, Wiley, Gregg, Johnson, Sims, Badger, and Butler.

No. 14.—On state debt and public works.—Messrs. Hall, Milroy, Zenor, Ritchey, Maguire, Trembly, and Chenowith.

No. 15.—On finance and taxation.—11th circuit, Mr. Kilgore; 1st circuit, Mr. McFarland; 2nd circuit, Mr. Logan; 3rd circuit, Mr. Tannehill; 4th circuit, Mr. Hovey, 5th circuit, Mr. Hendricks; 6th circuit, Mr. Ballingall; 7th circuit, Mr. Bourne; 8th circuit, Mr. Miller of Fulton; 9th circuit, Mr. Niles; 10th circuit, Mr. Conduit; 12th circuit, Mr. Work; 13th circuit, Mr. Foley.

No. 16.—On the militia.—Messrs. Pepper of Ohio, Spann, Steele, Huff, and Kilgore.

No. 17.—On education.—Messrs. Morrison of Washington, Bryant, May, Hitt, Foster, Stevenson, Nofsinger, Milligan, and Blythe.

No. 18.—On future amendments of the Constitution.—Messrs. Ritchey, Crawford, Edmonston, Wheeler, and Murray.

No. 19.—On public institutions of the state.—Messrs. Wallace, Bryant, Colfax, Nofsinger, and Jones.

No. 20.—On salaries, compensation, and tenure of office.—Messrs. Dobson, Pettit, Howe, Bright, Lockhart, Miller of Gibson, Maguire, and Taylor.

No. 21.—On miscellaneous provisions.—Messrs. Walpole, Holliday, McLean, Hawkins, and Robinson.

No. 22.—On revision, arrangement, and phraseology.—Messrs. Owen, Bright, Morrison of Marion, Read of Clark, Pettit, Kent, Borden, Newman, Rariden, Graham of Warrick, Smith of Ripley, Hamilton, Read of Monroe, Hall, Kilgore, Pepper of Ohio, Morrison of Washington, Ritchey, Wallace, Dobson, and Walpole.

Committee on elections.—Messrs. Kelso, Shannon, Robinson, Fisher, and Cole.

Committee on accounts.—Messrs. Wheeler, Helm, Yocum, Bowers, and Tague.

As the work of the convention proceeded, various changes were made in the personnel of these committees. The real writing of the constitution was done in the committee meetings, although in most cases, they were merely trying to follow the wishes of the majority of the convention. Resolutions of inquiry and instruction were referred to appropriate committees to guide them in their work. The proposals of the committees were submitted to the convention for approval; at times these reports were sent back with instructions to be changed. Early in October, the old constitution had been referred to the standing committees section by section.[36]

The convention appointed many select committees. Some of these were used to avoid the discussion of troublesome issues on the convention floor; many performed other valuable services. More than twenty-five of these were appointed. Some of the leading ones were: on rules; to investigate legality of claim of state printer; on homestead exemption; in regard to geological survey of the state; in relation to Negroes and mulattoes; as to uniformity in assessments and taxation; on rights of married women; and the address to the electors of the state, referred to as, "Owens's Committee of Ten."

It is fortunate for the historian that fairly accurate and complete records were kept and have been preserved. There were those who opposed the keeping of records as being a needless waste of time and expense.[37] A resolution adopted October 21 made provision for both a journal and a record of debates.[38] Later resolutions provided for the printing and distribution of these primary sources. These documents were ordered to be distributed among the members of the convention, the surviving members of the convention of 1816, the clergymen who served as chaplains, to a county or public library in each county, and to the more important state officials. No doubt some of these were never distributed and if many of these books could talk they would probably have some stories to tell that would be of interest to Indiana historians, and typical of the method by which such records have been destroyed.

[1] *General Laws of the State of Indiana Passed at the Thirty-fourth Session of the General Assembly* (Indianapolis: John D. Defrees, 1850), 5; approved Jan, 19, 1850.

[2] Adopted January 21, 1850.

[3] *Journal of the Convention of the People of the State of Indiana to Amend the Constitution* (Indianapolis: Austin H. Brown 1851), 19-20, 45-47. From now on this "Convention Journal" will be referred to as "*Journal.*"

[4] December 25, 1850, the convention assembled in the Masonic Hall. See Jacob Piatt Dunn, *Indiana and Indianans* (Chicago: American Historical Society, 1919), 443.

[5] *Report of the Debates and Proceedings of the Convention for the Revision of the Constitution of the State of Indiana, 1850* (Indianapolis: A. H. Brown, 1850), 80-93.

[6] *Indiana Statesman*, 7 May 1851. This issue contains a copy of an article, in regard to the work of the convention, which was published in the *Northern Star*, 5 April 1851. The *Northern Star* was published in England. Special notice was made in the article of Owen's fight for the independent property rights of women.

[7] *Debates*, 1563. Pettit, in speaking against a night session, said: "In the night we have lectures, theatrical performances, shows, and every other kind of amusement here."

[8] Ibid., 3.

[9] Ibid., 4.

[10] Judge Blackford served on the Supreme Court bench of Indiana from 1817 to 1853, longer than any other judge in the history of the state. His "Reports" are very valuable source material.

[11] *Debates*, 5.

[12] *Madison Weekly Courier*, 16 October 1850, says that the Democrats met in the Supreme Court room the morning on which the convention assembled and "after looking over the whole ground determined to elect the Hon. George W. Carr as the presiding officer." Their Indianapolis correspondent wrote October 8 that, "Last night, we learned, the Democratic

caucus nominated Cap't. R. Evans, second clerk, Mr. Sites third, and Mr. Barkwell fourth clerk to the convention. The nominations will be confirmed as soon as the convention meets this morning." Also *Debates*, 8, notes Clark of Tippecanoe said: "He was willing to concur in the edict of these who had decided on three secretaries out of this body. . ."

[13] *Debates*, 7. They were Ritchey of Johnson, Colfax of St. Joseph, and Hovey of Posey.

[14] Ibid., 9, gives a tabulated statement of these votes.

[15] The Chicago University library has a collection of English papers, which from what little information has been learned about them, would probably give further light in regard to the work of the convention.

[16] All were present except: Jones of Bartholomew, Conduit of Morgan, Taylor of LaPorte, and Blythe of Vanderburgh.

[17] *Debates*, 9-13

[18] Ibid., 13.

[19] October 11 a resolution was adopted, "That the Doorkeeper be authorized to employ one assistant doorkeeper, one messenger, one attendant on the committee rooms, and one person to make fires in the Hall." A committee report showed that the Doorkeeper had already employed eight assistants. *Debates*, 46-47.

[20] *Journal*, 22. Robert Sutton, of Washington City, had been appointed but declined. Sutton had been stenographer for the Kentucky Convention. See *Indiana Statesman*, 4 September 1851.

[21] *Debates*, 30. Gregg of Jefferson: "But it may be argued that the publication of the debates of this convention will be found eminently useful for future reference, in order to explain the meaning of certain provisions of the Constitution, which, to some may be dark and ambiguous. Why, sir, I would as soon think of looking into the Koran of Mahomet, or of consulting the sublime and beautiful vision of John in the Isle of Patmos, for an elucidation of the meaning of the ten commandments—a code of morals that adapts itself to the capacity of every mind, and fully explains itself without the aid of a commentator. And so I trust will be with the instrument that may emanate from our hands."

[22] *Journal*, 23. The members were: Owen of Posey, Morrison of Washington, Maguire of Marion, Pepper of Ohio, Nofsinger of Parke, Clark of Tippecanoe, and Niles of LaPorte.

[23] *Indiana Statesman*, 11 September 1850.

[24] *Indiana Statesman*, 9 October 1850, quotes from the *Washington Democrat*.

[25] *Indiana Statesman*, 11 September 1850. The letter follows: "Indiana State Sentinel Office, Indianapolis, September 1, 1850, Sir: I take this method of informing you that I am a candidate for the office of printer to the convention. My establishment is complete, and the manner in which my paper is printed is deemed as sufficient recommendation as to my ability to execute any amount of printing the convention may require, and in a manner equal to any establishment in the country. I have invested the labor of several years, which is my all in this enterprise, and I have reduced the price of the paper to the lowest living rate. The printing for the Convention would naturally aid us. Your friendship toward me in this, my first application for official favor and patronage, will be duly appreciated. I am, very truly, your obedient servant, Austin H. Brown, Publisher, Indiana State Sent."

[26] *Indiana State Journal*, 28 September 1850. Ibid., 14 September 1850: "The Sentinel and Statesman seem to be anxious about the printing of the convention; the Statesman contending that it is entitled to is as the successor of J. P. Chapman, State Printer, and the Sentinel as the regular built organ of Democracy."

[27] *Indiana Statesman*, 20 November 1850. The members of this committee were: Milroy of Carroll, Dunn of Perry, Biddle of Howard and Cass, Logan of Washington, Thornton of Floyd, Lockhart of Posey and Vanderburgh, and Rariden of Wayne."

[28] *Indiana Statesman*, 20 November 1850: "Take it all in all, a more outrageous, highhanded, and unjustifiable act, was never committed by an legislative body anywhere, in our humble judgment, than was the action of the convention in the printing case."

[29] *Journal*, 21. The members were: Borden, twelfth circuit; Pettit, first; Read of Clark, second; Dunn of Jefferson, third; Hall, fourth; Wallace, fifth; Smiley, sixth; Stevenson, seventh; Biddle, eighth; Wheeler, ninth; Dobson, tenth; March, eleventh; Smith of Ripley, thirteenth.

[30] *Debates*, 13.

[31] Ibid., 13, 20. Pettit said of Borden's plan, "To undertake to dovetail together the action of nineteen different committees would be a more fatiguing task then to travel over the most old fashioned railroad in Indiana." And Pettit said this in 1850!

[32] Borden: "Could not the Convention take up the Constitution of Indiana and refer it to a committee of the Whole, and in that committee act upon it, in the same manner that the House of Representatives of the Union acts upon the President's message, and both branches of our State Legislature do upon the Governor's message?" Smith of Ripley: "They could take up the constitution, Article by Article, and it might be that they would agree upon those articles while in the committee of the whole, thus making short work of the labor before them. It was a false idea that every resolution and subject that had been discussed in the Convention of Kentucky, and Ohio, and New York had to be gone over again in the Convention of Indiana." Morrison of Marion: "He wished that the members of all parties should be heard in the discussion of the body, as he wanted to make the convention as democratic as possible—he wanted to make it a democratic Republican Whig convention." However, Morrison favored the use of several committees. Ibid., 15, 17, 20.

[33] Kilgore's motion, "WHEREAS, In the opinion of this Convention, the people of Indiana, under their present wholesome Constitution, have obtained an enviable position among the States of his Union, and now enjoy a degree of prosperity and general happiness, of which they may well be proud: AND WHEREAS, we are admonished by the elements by which we are surrounded, and which are apparent in our midst, that, there is a great danger in an effort to amend the organic law, of standing committees." *Debates*, 40.

[34] *Debates*, 41. The members were: first congressional district, Owen and Edmonston; second, Kent and Carr of Jackson; third, Berry and Holman; fourth Newman and Trembly; fifth, Tannehill and Maguire; sixth, Terry; seventh Cookerly and Davis of Parke; eighth, Bryant and Pettit; ninth, Miles and Miller of Fulton; tenth, Kilgore and May. Read of Monroe was chairman, making a total of twenty members.

[35] *Journal*, 52-54, the source from which these were copied. Committees are also given in *Debates*, 57-58.

[36] *Journal*, 90-94; *Debates*, 97-99

[37] *Debates*, 17. Smith of Ripley: "The idea that a large book must be made of their proceedings was absurd; and he could not but think that if those proceedings were to go entirely unreported, the term of their session would soon be brought to a close." This is typical of the view of many delegates.

[38] *Journal*, 107: "*Resolved*, That a record of the proceedings of this Convention shall be kept in the following manner, to-wit: All that class of legislative matter usually contained in the Journals of the Legislature shall be journalized under the direction of the Principal Secretary. He shall prepare, or cause to be prepared, a manuscript copy, to be deposited by the President and Secretary, in the office of the Secretary of State, in pursuance of the 14th section of the act, entitled, 'An act to provide for the call of convention of people of the State of Indiana to revise, amend, or alter the Constitution of said State.' There shall be kept a 'Journal of Debates', under the direction of the Stenographer; but said Journal of

Debates shall not contain that class of matter usually embraced in legislative journals further than may be actually necessary to give a correct understanding of the subject matter under discussion."

Photo Courtesy Indiana Historical Society

When the General Assembly convened in December 1850, delegates of the constitutional convention were required to relocate their sessions from the hall used by the House of Representatives. They chose the newly completed Masonic Hall, on Washington Street.

CHAPTER V

POLITICAL CHANGES

The convention made few important political changes. The General Assembly was deprived of much of its power but remained the most powerful organ of the government. The position of the governor was scarcely altered. County and township government was placed nearer to the people. The structure of the judicial department remained about as it was but all judges were made elective by the people. The most important political changes were: substitution of biennial sessions for annual sessions of the legislature; the almost complete prohibition of local and private legislation; popular election of all county officials, judges, and the heads of the administrative department; numerous changes in the tenure of office holding and the date of elections. The net result was to bring the government closer to the people, who were regarded as sovereign. The convention acted when Jacksonian Democracy was near its zenith in Indiana and it was considerably influenced by the philosophy of the frontier as expressed by Andrew Jackson.

The changes in the legislative department were made through the work of two committees. These committees, as were all of the other standing committees, were influenced and guided by resolutions of instruction and inquiry. M. G. Bright was chairman of the committee on the legislative department. This was one of the most important committees of the convention. October 31 this committee reported an article consisting of thirty-one sections:[1]

NUMBER 12.

Section 1. The legislative authority of this State shall be vested in a General Assembly, which shall be designated the General Assembly of the State of Indiana, and shall consist of a Senate and House of Representatives, and the enacting clause of every law shall be: "Be it enacted by the General Assembly of the State of Indiana."

Sec. 2. The Senate shall consist of not less than one third, nor more than one half of the number of the members of the House, and the House of Representatives shall consist of not less than sixty, nor more than seventy-five members—to be chosen by the qualified electors of their separate counties, or of the districts into which the State may from time to time be divided.

Sec. 3. Senatorial and Representative districts, when more than one county shall constitute a district, shall be composed of contiguous counties; and no county for representative purposes shall ever be divided.

Sec. 4. Senators shall be chosen for the term of four years, and Representatives for the term of two years from the next day after their general election, except that the term of service of one-half of the Senators first elected under this Constitution, or if the whole number be an uneven one, then the term of service of one less than half shall expire at the end of two years, and for the purpose of ascertaining whose term of service shall first expire, the Senators elect, at the first meeting of the General Assembly under the new Constitution, shall be divided by lot, into two equal classes, as near as may be; and the seats of the Senators of the first class shall be vacated at the expiration of two years, and of the second class at the expiration of four years, so that one half, as near as possible, shall be chosen biennially forever thereafter, and in case of increase of the number of Senators at any time, these shall be so annexed by lot to one or the other of the two classes, as to keep them as nearly equal as practicable.

Sec. 5. No person shall be a Senator or Representative who, at the time of his election, is not a citizen of the United States, and been an inhabitant of this State, for the two years next preceding his election, and the last year thereof of the county or district for which he may be chosen. Senators shall be at least twenty-five, and Representatives twenty-one years of age.

Sec. 6. No person holding any lucrative office under the United States, or this State, shall be eligible to a seat in either branch of the General Assembly: *Provided*, That officers in the militia to which there is attached no annual salary, and the office of post master when the compensation does not exceed five hundred dollars per annum, shall not be deemed lucrative.

Sec. 7. The sessions of the General Assembly shall be held biennially at the capital of the State, commencing on the first Monday after the first day of January, in the year of our Lord one thousand eight hundred and fifty-three, and on the same day of every second year thereafter, unless a different day or place be appointed by law. But if, in the opinion of the Governor, the public welfare at any time require it, he may by proclamation call a special session.

Sec. 8. Each House when assembled shall choose their own officers, (the President of the Senate excepted,) be the judges of the qualification and returns of their own members, determine the rules of their proceedings, and sit upon their own adjournment. But neither House shall, without the consent of the other, adjourn for more than three days, nor to any other place than that in which they may be sitting.

Sec. 9. Two-thirds of each House shall constitute a quorum to do business, but a smaller number may meet and adjourn from day to day, and compel the attendance of absent members. Two-thirds being in attendance, if no organization shall be effected in the first five days thereafter, the members of the House so failing shall be entitled to no compensation for services from the end of said five days until an organization is effected.

Sec. 10. Each House shall keep a journal of its own proceedings and publish the same, and the yeas and nays of the members on any question shall, on the request of——of them, be entered on the journal.

Sec. 11. Any member of either House shall have the right of protest, and of having his protest, with the reason of his dissent, entered on the journal.

Sec. 12. Either House may punish its members for disorderly behaviour, and, with the concurrence of two-thirds, expel a member, but not a second time for the same cause; and shall have all other powers necessary for a branch of the legislature of a free and independent State.

Sec. 13. Either House may punish by imprisonment during their session, any person not a member, who shall be guilty of any disrespect to the House by any disorderly or contemptuous behavior in their presence; but such imprisonment shall not, at any one time, exceed twenty-four hours.

Sec. 14. When vacancies happen in either branch of the General Assembly, the Governor shall issue writs of election to fill such vacancies.

Sec. 15. Senators and Representatives, in all cases except treason, felony, or breach of the peace, shall be privileged from arrest during the session of the General Assembly, and in going to and returning from the same; and shall not be subject to any civil process during the session of the General Assembly, or for fifteen days next before the commencement thereof.

Sec. 16. The doors of each House and of committees of the whole shall be kept open, except in such cases as, in the opinion of the House, may require secrecy.

Sec. 17. Bills may originate in either House, but may be altered, amended, or rejected in the other; except that bills for raising revenue shall originate in the House of Representatives.

Sec. 18. Every bill shall be read on three different days in each house, unless, in case of emergency, two-thirds of the House, when such bill may be depending, by a vote of yeas and nays, shall deem it expedient to dispense with this rule; and the vote on the final passage of every bill shall be taken by yeas and nays, and be entered on the journal. Every bill having passed both houses, shall be signed by the President and Speaker of their respective houses.

Sec. 19. Every bill which shall have passed both houses of the General Assembly shall, before its becoming a law, be presented to the Governor. If he approve, he shall sign it; but if not, he shall return it, with his objections, to the house in which it shall have originated, which shall enter his objections at large upon the journal and proceed to reconsider it. If after such reconsideration, it again pass both houses, by yeas and nays, by a majority of two-thirds of each house present, it shall become a law, notwithstanding the Governor's objections. If any bill shall not be returned by the Governor within five days (Sundays excepted) after it shall have been presented to him, it shall be a law in like manner as if he had signed it, unless the General Assembly, by adjournment, prevent such return, in which case it shall be a law, unless sent back within three days after their next meeting.

Sec. 20. Every resolution to which the concurrence of both houses may be necessary, shall be presented to the Governor, and before it shall take effect, be approved by him; or being disapproved, shall be repassed according to the rules and limitations prescribed in case of bills.

Sec. 21. All Elections by the General Assembly, or either branch thereof, shall be by a *viva voce* vote; and the vote shall be entered on the journal.

Sec. 22. No Senator or Representative shall, during the time for which he shall have been elected, be appointed to any civil office of profit under the State, which shall have been created, or the emoluments of which shall have been increased during such term, except such office as may be filled by elections of the people.

Sec. 23. No person who may hereafter be a collector or holder of public moneys, shall be eligible to a seat in either branch of the General Assembly, or to any office of trust or profit under this State, until he shall have accounted for and paid, as by law of this State required, all sums for which he may be liable.

Sec. 24. No law of the General Assembly, of a public nature, shall take effect until the same shall have been published in print and circulated in the several counties of the State, by authority, except in cases of emergency.

Sec. 25. No money shall be withdrawn from the treasury but in consequence of appropriations made by law, and an accurate statement of receipts and expenditures of the public moneys shall be attached to and published with the laws at every session of the General Assembly.

Sec. 26. The members of the General Assembly shall receive for their services a compensation to be fixed by law, and paid out of the public treasury; but no increase of compensation shall take effect during the session at which such increase may be made.

Sec. 27. No ex post facto law or laws, either impairing the obligation of contracts or giving effect to contracts otherwise void, shall ever be passed.

Sec. 28. The General Assembly shall have no powers to grant divorces or direct by special legislation, the sale of estates belonging to infants or other persons laboring under legal disabilities, but by general law, shall confer such favor on the courts of justice.

Sec. 29. No act of the General Assembly shall ever be revised or amended by reference to its title; but in such case the act revised or section amended, shall be re-enacted and published at full length.

Sec. 30. No special act, authorizing suit to be brought against the State, shall ever be passed.

Sec. 31. The assent of three fourths of each branch of the General Assembly shall be requisite to every bill, appropriating the public moneys or property for local or private purposes.

It is worthy of note that this article provided that senators should be chosen for four-year terms and representatives for two-year terms, biennial sessions of the legislature, authority to call special sessions vested in the governor, the General Assembly to assemble the first Monday after the first day in January unless a different date should be appointed by law, all elections in the

General Assembly to be *viva voce*, no divorces to be granted by General Assembly, a three-fourths vote of the Assembly required to appropriate money for local or private purposes, and the requiring of a two-thirds vote in each house to pass a bill over the governor's veto. Minor changes will be noted by comparison with the old constitution.

Walpole of Hancock and Madison submitted a minority report signed by Clark of Tippecanoe and Smiley of Fayette. This report called for giving the governor merely a suspensive veto. It was as follows:[2]

NUMBER 1—MINORITY.

Section 1. Every bill which shall have passed both Houses of the General Assembly shall be presented to the Governor, if he approve he shall sign it; but if not he shall return it with his objections to the House in which it shall have originated, which shall enter the objections at large upon the journals, and proceed to reconsider it. If after such reconsideration a majority of all the members elected to that House shall agree to pass the bill, it shall be sent, with the objections, to the other House, by which it shall likewise be reconsidered, and if approved by a majority of all the members elected to that House, it shall be a law; but in such cases the votes of both Houses shall be determined by yeas and nays, and the names of the persons voting for and against the bill, shall be entered upon the journals of each House respectively. If any bill shall not be returned by the Governor within five days (Sundays excepted) after it shall have been presented to him, it shall be a law in like manner as if he had signed it, unless the general adjournment prevents its return; in which case it shall be a law, unless sent back within three days after their next meeting.

Another minority report was submitted by Walpole and Edmonston of Dubois that, if adopted, would have made it possible for residents of the state to become senators or representatives without being citizens of the United States:[3]

NUMBER 2—MINORITY.

Section 4. No person shall be a Senator or Representative who is not a white male inhabitant of the State and resident therein, two years immediately preceding his election, and the last year thereof, in the county or district, for which he may have been chosen. Senators shall be at least twenty-five, and Representatives twenty-one years of age, and shall have paid a State and county tax.

There were many who favored a biennial session of the General Assembly as being more responsive to the wishes of the people. On the other hand, some favored triennial sessions.[4] Those who favored biennial sessions argued that the prohibition of local and private legislation would make annual sessions unnecessary and rid the state of constant turmoil and agitation caused by the passing of new laws each year. The savings made by having biennial sessions was estimated to be enough to pay for the expenses of a convention within a few years.[5] The clause providing for biennial sessions was passed by vote of 120 to five.[6] With much the same argument, the sessions of the General Assembly were limited to sixty days duration and special sessions were limited to forty days. The vote for *viva voce* elections was almost unanimous.[7]

The other standing committee that contributed to the work of the legislative department was the committee on local and special legislation, and the committee on uniformity of laws. The selection of a standing committee for this particular problem is a good indication of the insight with which the people viewed their past experience in this field of legislation. J. S. Newman of Wayne, a Whig, was chairman of this committee. November 8 Newman reported an article for the consideration of the convention:[8]

NUMBER 35.

Section. The General Assembly shall not pass any local or special laws in any of the following enumerated cases: that is to say,

Regulating the jurisdiction and duties of justices of the peace and constables.

For the punishment of crimes and misdemeanors.

Regulating the practice of law and in Chancery.

Providing for granting divorces and changing the venue in civil and criminal cases.

Changing the names of persons.

For laying out, opening, working on and repairing highways, and the election or appointment of supervisors.

Vacating roads, town-plats, streets, alleys, and public squares.

Regulating county and township business.

Regulating the election of county and township officers, and their compensation.

For the assessment and collection of taxes for State, county, township, or road purposes.

Providing for maintaining common schools and the preservations of school funds.

In relation to fees and salaries.

Providing for opening and conducting elections for State, county, or township officers, and where electors may vote.

Providing for the sale of real estate by executors, administrators, or guardians.

For the creation of private incorporations.

For the incorporation of colleges, seminaries, schools, churches, religious, scientific, or benevolent societies.

Providing for the incorporation of railroad, plank road, turnpike road, canal and bridge companies.

In relation to municipal corporations, such as congressional townships, school districts, cities, boroughs, towns, and villages.

And all laws in all cases shall be general and of uniform operation throughout the State.

This article shows the utter disgust of the people for the manner in which local and special legislation had been carried on. It passed, with alterations, by a vote of 116 to thirteen.[9] Article four, sections twenty-two and twenty-three of the present constitution shows the extent to which the report was adopted. The convention had three standing committees that framed articles dealing with the executive and administrative departments of the government. Morrison of Marion, a Democrat, was chairman of the committee on the executive. This committee reported article seventeen on November 1:[10]

NUMBER 17.

Section 1. The executive power shall be vested in a Governor, who shall hold his office for—years. A Lieutenant Governor shall be elected and hold this office for the same term of time.

Sec. 2. No person shall be eligible to the office of Governor, or Lieutenant Governor, who has not been five years a citizen of the United States, and a resident of the State of Indiana five years next preceding his election, nor shall any person be eligible to either of said offices, who has not attained the age of thirty years.

Sec. 3. The Governor shall be ineligible to any other office during the time for which he was elected.

Sec. 4. The Governor and Lieutenant Governor shall be elected at the time and places of choosing members of the General Assembly. The persons respectively having the highest number of votes for Governor and Lieutenant Governor shall be elected, but in case two or more shall have an equal and the highest number of votes for Governor or for Lieutenant Governor, the General Assembly shall, forthwith, by joint ballot, choose one of the said persons as having an equal and the highest number of votes as Governor or as Lieutenant Governor.

Sec. 5. In voting for Governor and Lieutenant Governor the electors shall distinguish whom they vote for as Governor and whom as Lieutenant Governor. The returns of every election for Governor and Lieutenant Governor, shall be sealed up and transmitted to the seat of government, directed to the Speaker of the House of Representatives who shall open them and publish them in the presence of both Houses of the General Assembly.

Sec. 6. The Governor shall be commander-in-chief of the military and naval forces, and may call out such forces to execute the laws, to suppress insurrections, and to repel invasions.

Sec. 7. He shall transact all necessary business with officers of government, and may require information in writing from the officers of the executive department, upon any subject relating to the duties of their respective offices.

Sec. 8. He shall take care that the laws be faithfully executed.

Sec. 9. He may convene the General Assembly on extraordinary occasions.

Sec. 10. He shall give to the General Assembly, and at the close of his official term, to the next General Assembly, information by message of the condition of the State, and recommend such measures to them as he shall deem expedient.

Sec. 11. He may convene the General Assembly at another place, should the seat of government become dangerous from disease or a common enemy.

Sec. 12. He shall issue writs of election to fill such vacancies as occur in the Senate and House of Representatives.

Sec. 13. He may grant reprieves, commutations and pardons after convictions, for all offenses except treason and cases of impeachment, upon such conditions and with such restrictions and limitations as he may think proper, subject to regulations provided by law, relative to the manner of applying pardons. Upon conviction for treason, he may suspend the execution of the sentence, until the case shall be reported to the General Assembly at its next session, when the General Assembly shall either pardon, or commute the sentence, or grant a further reprieve. He shall communicate to the General Assembly at each session, information of each case of reprieve, commutation or pardon granted, and the reasons therefor. He shall also have power to remit fines and forfeitures, and shall report to the General Assembly at its next session, the names of persons in whose favor such remittances are made, and the amount so remitted.

Sec. 14. No member of congress, or person holding any office under the United States, or this State, shall exercise the office of

Governor or Lieutenant Governor.

Sec. 15. The Governor shall, at stated times, receive for his services a compensation, which shall neither be increased nor diminished during the term for which he shall have been elected.

Sec. 16. The Lieutenant Governor shall, by virtue of his office, be president of the Senate, have a right, when in committee of the whole, to debate and vote on all subjects, and when the Senate are equally divided to give the casting vote.

Sec. 17. In case of impeachment of the Governor, his removal from office, death, refusal to qualify, resignation, or absence from the State, the Lieutenant Governor shall exercise all the powers and authority appertaining to the office of Governor, until another be duly qualified, or the Governor absent or impeached, shall return or be acquitted.

Sec. 18. Whenever the government shall be administered by the Lieutenant Governor, or he shall be unable to attend as president of the Senate, the Senate shall elect one of their own members as president for that occasion. And if, during the vacancy of the office of Governor, the Lieutenant Governor shall be impeached, removed from office, refuse to qualify, resign, die, or be absent from the State, the president of the Senate pro tem shall, in like manner, administer the government, until he shall be superceded by a Governor or Lieutenant Governor. The Lieutenant Governor, while he acts as president of the Senate, shall receive for his services the same compensation which shall, for the same period, be allowed to the Speaker of the House of Representatives, and no more: And during the time he administers the government, as Governor, shall receive the same compensation which the Governor would have received and been entitled to, had he been employed in the duties of his office, and no more.

Sec. 19. The president pro tempore of the Senate, during the time he administers the government, shall receive, in like manner, the same compensation which the Governor would have received, had he been employed in the duties of his office, and no more.

Sec. 20. If the Lieutenant Governor shall be called upon to administer the government, and shall, while in such administration, resign, die, or be absent from the State, during the recess of the General Assembly, it shall be the duty of the Secretary of State, for the time being, to convene the Senate for the purpose of choosing a president pro tempore.

Sec. 21. Vacancies that may happen in offices, the appointment of which is vested in the Governor, or in the General Assembly shall be filled by the Governor during the recess of the General Assembly, by granting commissions that shall expire at the end of the next session.

Sec. 22. Every bill which shall have passed both Houses of the General Assembly, shall be presented to the Governor: If he approve, he shall sign it; but if not he shall return it with his objections, to the House in which it shall have originated, who shall enter the objections at large upon their journals; and proceed to reconsider it. If, after such reconsideration, a majority of all the members elected to that House, shall agree to pass the bill, it shall be sent, with the objections to the other House, by which it shall likewise be reconsidered, and, if approved by a majority of all the members elected to that House, it shall be a law; but, in such cases, the vote of both Houses shall be determined by yeas and nays, and the names of persons voting for or against the bill, shall be entered on the journals of each House respectively. If any bill shall not be returned by the Governor within five days (Sundays excepted) after it shall have been presented to him, the same shall be a law, unless the general adjournment prevent its return; in which case it shall be a law.

Sec. 23. Every resolution to which the concurrence of both Houses may be necessary, shall be presented to the Governor, and before it shall take effect, be approved by him; or, being disapproved, shall be repassed by a majority of all members elected to both Houses, according to the rules and limitations prescribed in case of a bill.

Sec. 24. There shall be a seal of this State, which shall be kept by the Governor and used by him officially, and shall be called "the Seal of the State of Indiana."

Sec. 25. All commissions shall be in the name and by the authority of the State of Indiana, and sealed with the State seal and signed by the Governor, and attested by the Secretary of State.

This article is much like the corresponding portions of the first constitution. The governor still remained the chief executive with few real powers to act. The second committee which dealt with these departments was the committee on state officers other than the executive and judiciary. Read of Clark, a farmer, was chairman of the committee. This committee was the first to report an article to the convention for its consideration. Hence this article was designated as article number one:[11]

NO. 1. ARTICLE.

Section 1. A Secretary of State shall be chosen by the qualified electors, and be commissioned by the Governor for two years, until a new Secretary be elected and qualified: *Provided*, That no person shall be eligible to the office of Secretary of State more than four years in any term of six years. He shall keep a fair register and attest all the official acts and proceedings of the Governor; and shall, when required, lay the same and all papers, minutes, and vouchers relative thereto before either House of the General Assembly, and shall perform such other duties as may be enjoined upon him by law.

Sec. 2. There shall be chosen by the qualified electors, and commissioned by the Governor, a Treasurer and Auditor, whose powers and duties shall be prescribed by law, and who shall hold their offices for two years, and until their successors be elected and qualified; *Provided*, That no person shall be eligible to the office of Treasurer or Auditor more than four years in any term of six years.

These same administrative heads had existed under the old constitution. The important change this article proposed was in the tenure of office and the method of election. The third committee was on county and township organization powers and officers. Thomas Smith of Ripley, a Democrat, was chairman of this committee. October 29 this committee reported three articles for the consideration of the convention:[12]

NUMBER 5.

Section 1. There shall be elected in each county, by the qualified electors thereof, a sheriff, coroner, recorder, county auditor, county treasurer, and a clerk of the circuit court, at the time and place of holding elections for members of the General Assembly. The clerk, auditor and recorder shall each continue in office four years, and until their successors shall be chosen and qualified. But no person shall be eligible to the office of clerk, recorder or auditor more than eight years in any term of twelve years. The sheriff, coroner and treasurer shall each continue in office two years, and until their successors shall be chosen and qualified: *Provided*, That no person shall be eligible to the office of sheriff or treasurer more than four years in any term of six years.

Sec. 2. When the office of clerk of the circuit court of any county shall be vacant, the circuit court of such county or the judge thereof, shall appoint a clerk *pro tem*, who shall hold his office till the next general election, and until his successor shall be chosen and qualified.

Sec. 3. No person shall be eligible to the office of clerk of the circuit court, unless he shall first have obtained from one or more of the judges of the Supreme Court, or from one or more of the judges of the circuit courts, a certificate that he is qualified to execute the duties of the office of clerk of the circuit court.

Sec. 4. A competent number of justices of the peace shall be elected by the qualified electors in each township, and shall continue in office four years, if they so long behave well, whose powers and duties shall be prescribed by law.

NUMBER 6.

Section 1. Such other county and township officers as may be necessary, shall be appointed in such manner as may be prescribed by law.

Sec. 2. Vacancies in office, in this article not herein provided for, shall be filled in such manner as may be prescribed by law.

Sec. 3. No person shall be rendered ineligible to any office in this article provided, by reason of his appointment *pro tem*, to such office.

Sec. 4. All county, town and township officers shall reside within their respective towns, counties and townships, and shall keep their respective offices at such places therein, as may be directed by law.

NUMBER 7.

Section 1. No person shall be elected or appointed as a county officer within any county, who shall not have been a citizen and an inhabitant therein, one year next preceding his appointment, if the county shall have been so long erected; but if the county shall not have been so long erected, then within the limits of the county or counties out of which the same shall have been taken.

All county, town, and township officers may be impeached or removed from office in such manner as shall be provided by law.

Sec. 3. The General Assembly shall provide by law for a uniform mode of doing county and township business.

Sec. 4. The General Assembly shall reduce no county to a less content than four hundred square miles.

It is worthy of note that article five provided for the popular election of sheriff, recorder, auditor, treasurer, coroner, and a clerk of the circuit court in each county; the county auditor and treasurer had not been provided for under the old constitution. This article recommended the election of a competent number of justices of the peace for four-year terms. Articles six and seven were of a general nature, Gootee of Martin and Alexander of Pike submitted a minority report in the form of a protest; said protest being addressed to the president of the convention:[13]

The undersigned, a minority of the committee on "county and township organization," to whom was referred the 12th section of the 11th article of the Constitution of Indiana, most respectfully beg leave to dissent from the conclusion of the majority, as embodied in their report, for various reasons, amongst which are,

1. That it is anti-republican to deprive a clear majority of the people from dividing or arranging their counties as their interests or convenience may require.

2. That it is in its very nature a legislative matter, and ought not to find a place in the organic law of the land.

For these reasons and many others that might, with great force, be brought to bear against the expediency and utility of putting such a clause in the new Constitution, we most respectfully dissent from the report, and trust the Convention will not sanction such an anti-republican clause in the new Constitution.

We are of those who believe the people can be safely trusted with their own interest, and that there is no place where they can deposit power more secure that in their own hands.

We would therefore most respectfully recommend to the Convention so to amend the report of the majority "That a majority of all the voters of the county or counties of which a proposed new county is to be made, must first be had before any new county can be made."

All of which is most respectfully submitted.

THOMAS GOOTEE.
CHARLES ALEXANDER.

This minority was a strong appeal for local right and freedom in determining county lines. As finally adopted, the office of county surveyor was added to the list of county officials. Most of these other proposals were adopted in the new constitution. No specific provision is made to regulate city or town government; the largest city in the state at that time had less than 10,000 inhabitants.[14] The pardoning power of the governor was limited, his appointive power diminished, and the provision reenacted giving him authority to call special sessions in cases of emergency.

The work of the convention in regard to the judicial department is of questionable value. Under the old constitution the three Supreme Court judges were appointed by the governor with the consent of the Senate; the Supreme Court appointing its own clerk. The demands of the people that all judges be elected by popular vote was recognized by the delegates; the abolition of the old appointive system has been severely questioned. Pettit of Tippecanoe, a Democrat, who gained much attention by his persistent and determined opposition to the grand jury system, was chairman of the committee on the organization of the courts of justice. As a member of the United States Congress, Pettit had already obtained notoriety for his opposition to the appointment of chaplain in the House of Representatives. He was a "freak" but one of the ablest members of the convention. November 7 this committee submitted two articles for the consideration of the convention:[15]

NUMBER 29.

Section 1. The judicial power of this State shall be vested in one Supreme Court, in Circuit Courts, and in such other inferior Courts as the General Assembly may establish.

Sec. 2. The Supreme Court shall consist of five judges, three of whom shall form a quorum, who shall hold their office six years, if they so long behave well. The State shall be divided into five Supreme Court districts, of contiguous territory, as nearly equal in population as may be; but no county shall be divided in the formation of said districts, and a judge shall reside in, and be elected by, the electors of each district.

Sec. 3. The Supreme Court shall have jurisdiction in appeals from, and writs of error to, the Circuit and other courts, in such manner as shall be prescribed by law; and such original jurisdiction as the legislature may confer upon it.

Sec. 4. The Supreme Court shall appoint its own clerk, who shall hold his office for six years, if he shall so long behave well; and whose duty shall be prescribed by law.

Sec. 5. There shall be a reporter of the decisions of the Supreme

Court appointed by the same and removable at its will; but no judge shall be allowed to report the decisions of the Supreme Court.

Sec. 6. The Supreme Court shall appoint its own sheriff, who shall perform such duties as may be required by law.

Sec. 7. The State shall be divided into at least twenty circuits, and a circuit judge shall be elected by the electors in each circuit, and shall reside therein; and shall hold his office six years, if he shall so long behave well.

Sec. 8. The Circuit Court shall be composed of one judge only, who shall hold at least three courts every year, in each county in his circuit, and shall have such civil and criminal jurisdiction as may be prescribed by law.

Sec. 9. The Legislature may provide by law that the judge of one circuit may hold the courts of another circuit, in cases of necessity or convenience.

Sec. 10. There shall be a clerk of the Circuit Court elected by the electors in each county, who shall hold his office six years, if he shall so long behave well, and who shall perform such duties as may be prescribed by law.

Sec. 11. There shall be a competent number of justices of the peace elected by the electors in each township in the several counties, and who shall continue in office five years, if they shall so long behave well, whose powers and duties shall be regulated and defined by law.

Sec. 12. All judicial officers of this State shall be conservators of the peace in their respective jurisdictions.

NUMBER 30.

Section 1. There shall be elected by the qualified electors of the State, an attorney general, whose powers and duties shall be prescribed by law, and who shall hold his office for four years, and until his successor is elected and qualified.

Sec. 2. There shall be elected in each judicial circuit, by the electors thereof, a prosecuting attorney, who shall hold his office for two years, and until his successor is elected and qualified.

Pettit submitted a minority report signed by McClelland of Randolph (who was born in Ireland as his name might lead one to believe) and Howe of LaGrange:[16]

NUMBER 6—Minority.

Sec. —. The Supreme Court shall consist of five judges, three of whom shall form a quorum, who shall hold their office six years, if they so long behave well. The State shall be divided into five Supreme Court districts, of contiguous territory as nearly equal in population as may be; but no county shall be divided in the formation of said districts, and a judge shall reside in each district; but they shall all be elected at the same time by the electors of the whole State.

Sec. —. There shall be a clerk of the Supreme Court elected by the electors of the whole State, who shall hold his office six years, if he shall so long behave well, and whose duty shall be prescribed by law.

The committee on matters pertaining to criminal law reported a brief article defining treason and the method by which an individual may be convicted. This article was submitted November 4:[17]

NUMBER 23.

Section 1. Treason against the State shall consist in levying war against it, and in giving aid and comfort to its enemies.

Sec. 2. No person shall be convicted of treason, unless on the testimony of two witnesses to the same overt act, or on his confession in open court.

Kent of Floyd, a Democrat, was chairman of this committee, which reported the article in regard to treason. During the session of the convention, Kent received considerable publicity because of his "fight" with Hovey of Posey on the convention floor.[18] A third committee, which contributed to the work of framing an article for the judicial department was the committee on the practice of law and law reform. Borden of Allen, a Democrat, who was one of the ablest judges in the state, was made chairman of this committee. This committee made several reports to the convention:

NUMBER 27.[19]

Section 1. All prosecutions shall be carried on in the name of, and by the authority of this State; and the style of all process shall be "The State of Indiana."

NUMBER 33.[20]

Section 1. Every person who shall give or accept a challenge to fight a duel, or who shall knowingly carry to another person a challenge to fight a duel, or who shall agree to go out of the State to fight a duel, shall be ineligible to hold any office of trust or profit.

NUMBER 34.[21]

Section 1. The General Assembly at its first session after the adoption of this Constitution, shall provide for the appointment of three commissioners, whose duty it shall be to revise, reform, simplify, and abridge the rules and practice, pleadings, forms, and proceedings, both civil and criminal, of the Courts of this State. And they shall provide for the abolition of the distinct forms of actions at law now in use, and that justice may be administered in a uniform mode of pleading without reference to any distinction between law and equity. And the General Assembly may also make it the duty of said commissioners to reduce into a systematic code the General Statute Law of this State; and said commissioners shall, from time to time, report the result of their labors to the General Assembly, with such recommendations and suggestions as to abridgement and amendment as to said commissioners may seem necessary. Provision shall be made by law for filling vacancies, regulating the tenure of office, and the compensation of said commissioners.

Article thirty-four, quoted above, was not satisfactory to the entire committee and two minority reports were given:

NUMBER 7.[22]

Sec. —. The General Assembly, at its first session after the adoption of this Constitution, shall provide for the election, by the people, of three commissioners, whose duty it shall be to revise, reform, simplify, and abridge the rules and practice, pleadings, forms, and proceedings, both civil and criminal, of the courts of this State; and they shall provide for the abolition of the distinct forms of action at law now in use: and that justice may be administered in a uniform mode of pleading, without reference to any distinction between law and equity. And the General Assembly may also make it the duty of said commissioners to reduce into a written and systematic code, the whole body of the laws of this State, or so much and such parts thereof as said commissioners shall find practicable and expedient. They shall report the result of their labors, from time to time, to the General Assembly, for their modification and adoption.

Provision shall be made by law for filling vacancies, regulating the tenure of office and the compensation of said commissioners.

Article No. 8.[23]

Section 1. The General Assembly, at its first or some subsequent session after the adoption of this Constitution, may provide for the appointment of three commissioners, whose duty it shall be to revise, reform, and simplify the rules, practice, forms and proceedings, civil and criminal of the courts of this State. And the commissioners shall provide for the abolition of the distinct forms of action now in use. And they shall, from time to time, as their labors progress, report their proceedings to the General Assembly, with such suggestions and recommendations as to said commissioners may seem proper.

Sec. 2. The General Assembly may also make it the duty of said commissioners to reduce into a systematic code, the general statute laws of this State; and they shall, from time to time, report the results of their labors to the General Assembly, with such recommendations and suggestions as to abridgements and amendments as to said commissioners may seem necessary.

NUMBER 50.[24]

Sec. —. Tribunals of conciliation may be established with such powers and duties as shall be prescribed by law, or the powers and duties of such tribunals may be conferred upon any of the other courts of this State; but such tribunals and other courts, when sitting as such tribunals; shall have no power to render judgment to be obligatory on the parties, except they voluntarily submit their matters in difference, and agree to abide the judgment, or assent thereto, in the presence of such tribunals or court, in such cases as shall be prescribed by law.

The provision for the revision of law practice and pleadings was at the time considered to be one of the greatest achievements of the convention. The section in regard to tribunals of conciliation has remained almost a dead letter. Another article which has become famous as the "moral character" clause completes the work of the committee on law and law reform:[25]

NUMBER 59.

Section 1. Any person of good moral character and possessing the right of suffrage, shall be entitled to admission to practice in all Courts of the State.

One of the most interesting struggles of the whole convention came as a result of Pettit's persistent effort to abolish the grand jury system. Friends and opponents of the system gave a spirited defense of their positions.[26] Finally a compromise was reached whereby it was decided to insert the section, "The General Assembly may modify, or abolish, the Grand Jury System."[27]

Thus far this chapter has dealt with changes in the three departments of the government. Another group of political changes may be considered in the field of changes in the elective machinery and system of office holding. Three committees contributed most of the articles for these changes. The more important of these three committees was the committee on the elective franchise and the apportionment of representation. Graham of Warrick, a Democrat, was chairman of this committee. This committee made several reports to the convention:

NUMBER 13.[28]

Section 1. In all elections not otherwise provided for by this Constitution, every white male citizen of the United States, of the age of twenty-one years and upward, who has resided in the State six months immediately preceding such election, and every white male of foreign birth of the age of twenty-one years and upwards, having resided in the United States one year, and having declared his intention to become a citizen of the United States, conformably to the laws of the United States on the subject of naturalization, and having resided in this State six months immediately preceding such election, shall be entitled to vote in the township where he resides, except such as shall be enlisted in the army of the United States or their allies.

Sec. 2. All elections, not otherwise provided for in this Constitution, shall be by ballot.

Sec. 3. Electors shall, in all cases except treason, felony, or breach of the peace, be free from arrest in going to, during their attendance at, and in returning home from elections.

Sec. 4. The General Assembly shall have power to exclude from electing, or being elected, any person convicted of any infamous crime.

Sec. 5. No Person shall be deemed to have lost his residence in this State by reason of his absence on business of the United States, or of this State.

Sec. 6. Every person shall be disqualified from holding office for the term for which he shall have been elected; who shall have been convicted of having given or offered any bribe, threat, or reward to procure his election.

NUMBER 18.[29]

Section 1. All general elections shall be held on the first Tuesday in October, biennially.

NUMBER 21.[30]

Section 1. The Senate shall consist of thirty-four members, and the House of Representatives of one hundred, to be elected by the qualified electors of their respective counties, or by the districts into which the State may, from time to time, be divided.

Sec. 2. The General Assembly shall, every six years, after the adoption of this Constitution, make an equitable distribution of the above named number of Senators and Representatives among the several counties and districts: *Provided always*, That no county shall be divided for Senatorial or Representative purposes.

NUMBER 44.[31]

Section 1. The General Assembly shall at their first meeting after the adoption of this Constitution, and every six years thereafter, cause an enumeration to be made of all white male inhabitants above the age of twenty-one years.

Sec. 2. The number of Senators and Representatives shall at the several periods of making such an enumeration be fixed by law and apportioned among the several counties according to the number of white male inhabitants above twenty-one years of age in each: *Provided*, The first election of members of the General Assembly under this Constitution, shall be according to the apportionment made by the Legislature at its session of 1850-51.

In studying these reports it is noticed that it was recommended (and later adopted by the convention) that every white male of foreign birth of twenty-one years of age or above, having resided in the United States one year, be given the right to vote if he conforms to the naturalization laws in the United States and has declared his intention of becoming a citizen; all elections, unless otherwise provided, to be by ballot. The change to biennial elections was to be excepted if the General Assembly were to meet biennially.

Mr. Rariden of Wayne, a Whig, was chairman of the committee on impeachment and removal from office. His committee reported December 18:

NUMBER 46.[32]

Sec. —. All county and township officers shall be liable to be removed from office on indictment and conviction for any felony or misfeasance in office, in the Circuit Court of the county wherein they shall hold their office.

Sec. —. All State officers shall be liable to removal from office by impeachment by the House of Representative, to be tried by the Senate, for any crime or misdemeanor, and on conviction, shall be removed.

Sec. —. Any judge being convicted on indictment of any felony or corruption in office, may be removed from office by the judgment of the Supreme Court, on information in the name of the State.

Sec. —. Any State officer may removed from office by a joint resolution of the General Assembly, for incapacity or for general negligence of the duties of office; two-thirds of the members elect, of each branch, voting therefor.

Sec. —. The General Assembly shall pass laws regulating proceedings for the removal of officers from office, State, county, and township, pursuant to the foregoing provisions.

This process of impeachment and removal from office was designed to weaken the power the General Assembly had in such matters.

The old constitution had made provision for revision but not for minor amendments from time to time, unless such amendments could be made in a convention. The new constitution makes direct provision for amendment but no specific provision for a constituent convention. Ritchey of Johnson, a Democrat, was chairman of the committee on future amendments of the constitution. This committee made its report January 16, less than one month before the adjournment of the convention. It suggested the following article:[33]

NUMBER 53.
Amendments to the Constitution

Section 1. Whenever two-thirds of the members elected to each branch of the General Assembly shall think it necessary to call a Convention to alter or amend this Constitution, they shall recommend to the electors at the next election of members of the General Assembly to vote for or against a Convention; and if it shall appear that a majority of all the electors of the State voting for Representatives have voted for a Convention, the General Assembly shall, at its next session, call a Convention for the purpose of revising, altering or amending this Constitution.

Sec. 2. Any amendment or amendments to this Constitution may be proposed in either branch of the General Assembly, and if the same shall be agreed to by two-thirds of all the members elected in each of the two houses, such proposed amendment or amendments shall be referred to the next regular session of the General Assembly, and shall be published at least three months previous to the time of holding the next election for members of the House of Representatives; and if at the next regular session of the General Assembly after said election, a majority of all members elected in each branch of the General Assembly shall agree to said amendment or amendments, then it shall be their duty to submit the same to the people at the next general election for their adoption or rejection in such manner as may be prescribed by law; and if a majority of all the electors voting at said election for members of the House of Representatives shall vote for such amendment or amendments, the same shall become a part of the Constitution. If two or more amendments be submitted at the same time, they shall be submitted in such manner that the people shall vote for or against each of the amendments separately, and while an amendment or amendments which has been agreed upon by one General Assembly is awaiting the action of a succeeding Assembly, or undergoing the final consideration of the people, no additional amendment or amendments shall be proposed.

Most of the political changes of the convention were agreed upon in principle by a large majority of the delegates. There were often differences as to the proper method or means to be used in securing the desired end. In debates, party lines were not always regarded and many measures split across factions within the parties. The student of American history can see in these changes an index of the broader political changes of this period of American history.

[1] *Journal of the Convention of the People of the State of Indiana to Amend the Constitution* (Indianapolis: H. Fowler, A.H. Brown, 1851), 166-170; *Report of the Debates and Proceedings of the Convention for the Revision of the Constitution of the State of Indiana, 1850* (Indianapolis: A. H. Brown, 1850), 276.

[2] *Journal*, 170-171.

[3] Ibid.

[4] *Debates*, 96-97. Allen of Clinton and Carroll favored triennial sessions but was willing that biennial sessions be given a trial. *Debates*, 94-96, Read of Clark: "Whereas, if the sessions of the Legislature were biennial with proper limitations and restraints upon their powers, the laws would be better known and executed; and there would be saved a vast amount of the public money. But as it is not the Representatives danced and the public pay this fiddler." *Debates*, 94, Clark of Tippecanoe: "Where annual elections end, tyranny begins."

[5] *Journal*, 965. In the address to the electors of the state: "Thus, if no special session be called during five years, the saving in that period, by this provision alone, will overpay the entire expenses of the Convention."

[6] *Debates*, 1079.

[7] *Journal*, 481-482. The vote was 109 to four.

[8] Ibid., 216-217.

[9] Ibid., 767.

[10] Ibid., 177-180.

[11] Ibid., 129.

[12] Ibid., 149-151.

[13] Ibid., 151.

[14] Indianapolis, Madison, and New Albany were the three largest cities; the latter two were very jealous of the development being made at the State Capitol.

[15] Ibid., 207-209.

[16] Ibid., 208-209.

[17] Ibid., 192.

[18] There are several items about the "Kent vs. Hovey" fight in the newspapers of the period. It appears that actual blows were perhaps exchanged.

[19] *Journal*, 202.

[20] Ibid., 214.

[21] Ibid., 214-215.

[22] Ibid., 215. This report was signed by James W. Borden (chairman of the law reform committee), G. F. Cookerly, and Walter March.

[23] *Journal*, 216. This was advocated by Newman, Mather, and Kelso.

[24] Ibid., 553-554.

[25] Ibid., 796.

[26] *Debates*, 316, Read of Monroe: "For the first time in any American Constitutional Convention, or in any law making body having power over the subject, in any country of the world where the common law prevails, is it now, and in this body proposed to abolish the Grand Jury System." *Debates*, 139, Rariden of Wayne: "The grand jury system is but an auxiliary to the system of common schools, and churches, and Sabbath schools, and all institutions for the furtherance of good; morals, and the well-being of society." *Debates*, 162, speech of Gibson: "Blot out Grand Juries from our code, and you almost place woman out of the pale of the laws' protection." *Debates*, 166, Gibson quotes Jefferson as saying that no nation could be enslaved, "Between whose liberties and the sovereign stood Grand and Pettit Juries." *Debates*, 178, Biddle said: "Sir, this mixing up of temporal and spiritual things is not, in my judgment a very proper course; but if it be allowed to combine them together, or to illustrate the one by other, I have no hesitation whatever in saying, that had the Savior lived in any country in which the Grand Jury system prevailed, he would never have been crucified at all, because he had committed no crime. I speak, of course of the order of human events." *Debates*, 145, Petitt said: "For I protest that in this, as in every other notion here, I am guided only by that spirit so eloquently prayed for by the gentleman who has just addressed the Throne of Grace before us; and an earnest wish that we may do nothing here but what shall rebound to the glory of God, and the advantage of the people of the State of Indiana."

[27] Indiana Constitution, art. 7, sect. 17.

[28] *Journal*, 171-172.

[29] Ibid., 181.

[30] Ibid., 188-189.

[31] Ibid., 407.

[32] Ibid., 462.

[33] Ibid., 693.

Photo Courtesy Indiana State Library

Indiana poet laureate Sarah Bolton organized women statewide to honor Robert Dale Owen's efforts in securing married women some protection over their property. The topic received considerable attention from the delegates, but after its initial passage, the married women's property rights amendment was reconsidered and did not find its way into the final form of the Constitution. Nevertheless, Indiana women led by Bolton presented Owen with a silver pitcher in appreciation of his work.

CHAPTER VI

Economic And Social Changes

The Constitution of 1851 is an index to the social and economic changes that had been taking place in Indiana in the generation prior to 1850. The debates of the convention are a very excellent source for one who desires to view and understand the life of that period. Indiana, at that time, was almost solely an agricultural state; and most of the delegates were pioneer farmers. It was the era of the individualistic farmer and opposition toward anything which tended toward industrialization was regarded as a hallmark of true democracy. The strife between the agricultural and mercantile classes was in embryo.

The banking question was a subject that had been constantly agitated. Since 1834, Indiana had been designated by a state banking system. Public opinion on the question of banking was much unsettled and divided. The State Bank had been efficient but it was regarded as a monopoly that should be crushed. The philosophy of Andrew Jackson, in regard to banks and monopolies, was in accord with that of the frontier and his doctrines were often quoted on the floor of the convention. Read of Monroe, a professor in the state university, referred to him as "a man of as remarkable sagacity as ever lived."[1] President Jackson had warned the people that the destruction of the Federal Bank was not enough and that constant watch must be maintained to keep the monied monsters out of the states. There was no satisfactory experience to guide the delegates in setting up another banking system. The State Bank was not without its defenders; at the other extreme were those who wanted "Free Banks or No Banks." Many advocated some kind of a general banking system. The New York system, as adopted in their constitution of 1846, was often suggested as a model. The people expected a change but there was no uniform demand for any one proposed substitute. November 5 the committee on currency and banking reported an article providing for free banking.[2] Several minority reports were given; these expressed hostility toward the State Bank. Several sessions of the convention were taken for a thorough discussion of this subject. Resolutions of petition and inauguration were sent to the delegates from various public meetings over the state.[3] The *Indiana Statesman* early predicted that the work of the convention would be repudiated unless a section was adopted providing for free banking.[4] The system finally adopted was a compromise which was a victory for the proponents of a general banking system. The General Assembly retained the power to charter a bank but the convention dealt a death blow to the monopoly that the State Bank had exercised since its establishment in 1834. This bank, known as the Second State Bank, was allowed to continue its establishment until the expiration of its charter in 1859.

One of the most quoted clauses of the constitution is that in regard to the uniformity of assessment and taxation. The old system had been a "system of small systems" which was made to suit various localities. This clause had its origin in Pettit's proposal to add such a feature as an additional section to the article on the legislative department. Several amendments were offered to Pettit's plan and on motion of Hall of Gibson the section and pending amendments were referred to a select committee of five. This committee reported a section which, except for alteration in phraseology, was adopted by the convention without a vote on February 5. An amendment to provide for a state board of equalization was rejected. Making the tax and assessment laws of the state general and uniform was a decided step toward the centralization of power in the hands of the state government at the expense of local units.

When the convention was in the midst of its labors the *Indiana Statesman*, as the organ of liberal democracy in the state, called for a complete overthrow of the "entire system of monopoly." They expressed a feeling that monopolies had already reached dangerous proportions.[5] A meeting of citizens at Lafayette adopted a resolution denouncing all monopolies as social and political evils. November 29 the committee on corporations other than banking made a report for the consideration of the convention.[6] A few days later a second report was made. The first provided that corporations should not be created by special acts, and that they might be altered or repealed from time to time; this last provision was not adopted by the convention. The second article proposed made stockholders of a corporation liable in proportion to the value of their stock to that of the total stock of the corporation. The work of this committee was incorporated into sections thirteen and fourteen of article two of the present constitution. It met the demand of those who called for the abolition of local and private charters by legislative enactment.

The internal improvement "system" and other state expenditures had put the finances of the state in a sorry situation. There was widespread demand that the new constitution should furnish security against the recurrence of this condition. The discussion of the subject caused members of the convention to be afflicted with a "loss of their memories."[7] Men who had done logrolling on behalf of the internal improvements bill in 1836, which led to the state debt, were most earnest in defense of the movement to prevent such a situation from happening again. Kilgore of Delaware—a Whig—in a very frank speech, laid before the convention the manner in which the internal improvements bill had been adopted by the General Assembly. He showed that the measure had been supported by both political parties and by the people themselves. He even explained the part that several of the delegates had taken in securing the passage of the bill; most of these delegates were not urging a strict curb on the General Assembly to prevent future losses.[8] But as far as the people were concerned the placing of responsibility for the bill was a secondary matter. The important thing, as Smith of Ripley stated, was that the people wanted a constitutional provision that would "make it forever impossible that the scenes of 1836 should be re-enacted."[9] Owen contended:

> One generation of men have no right to impose burdens upon the succeeding. One generation of men have no moral right to contract a public debt so vast that the next generation, and perhaps that which follows it, shall be loaded down with taxes, to discharge the interest and repay the capital.[10]

This is a contention that the present generation can understand by comparison to the arguments now being used for the revision of World War debts. The provision as adopted, prohibiting a state debt except in very special cases, met the approval of a very large majority of the delegates.

The constitution of 1816 had outlined an education system in advance of others of that period. But it had practically remained a dead letter as far as legislative enactment was concerned. When the convention assembled, the common school movement was then attracting the chief attention in educational circles.[11] It was felt that the state should be responsible for giving every child an opportunity to have an elementary education. Secondary schools and colleges were frowned upon by people who had the lawmaking voice of the state. The press of the period devoted much space to the discussion of educational problems and needs. The committee on education was made up of men who were chosen because they were known to be friendly to the common social idea.[12] December 11 the thirty-fourth anniversary of the admission of Indiana into the Union, this committee reported an article for the consideration of the convention.[13] In framing this article, the committee inserted a section making it the duty of the state university to maintain a normal school "in order to furnish the common schools of the State with efficient and well qualified teachers." This article caused a spirited debate among the delegates. There were those who favored a state school system for elementary training to the exclusion of all other higher schools, unless supported by private resources. Others wanted to take the revenue from the Congressional school fund and divide it among the various colleges of the state under state administration; this movement was of questionable legality. There was another group who wanted to keep the state university intact and encourage its growth by affording it all possible facilities. As adopted, the article places much emphasis on common schools and none on higher education. The state university was not regarded with favor by the convention and its existence today cannot be justified by strict interpretation of the constitution. Another trend toward centralization is noted in the establishment of a state superintendent of public instruction. Morrison of Washington, Owen of Posey, May of Steuben, and Read of Monroe were leaders in striving to maintain educational standards. Daniel Read was in charge of the normal school, maintained as a part of Indiana University, established in 1852 until his leaving the university in 1856 when the school was discontinued.

The most picturesque struggle in the whole convention was that of Robert Dale Owen to secure independent property rights for women. That contest called forth the best talent of the convention in debate. The old law was based almost solely on the common law, which recognized the complete authority of the husband over the wife in property rights. In 1847 the legislature had passed an act that secured to married women limited property rights.[14] October 19 Owen introduced a resolution of inquiry on this subject, which was referred to the committee on rights and privileges of the inhabitants of the state, of which Owen was the chairman. January 16 the committee reported a provision that contained the substance of Owen's resolution of inquiry. February 14, when the section came up for passage, Owen moved to recommit the section to a select committee of one and to report a (less radical) section providing that "laws shall be passed for the security of the property rights of married women, of widows, and orphans."[15] The motion carried and Owen was appointed to the committee and made a report as instructed by the convention. Then the section was voted upon and passed with seventy-one voting for and sixty-one against.[16] It was then referred to the committee on revision, arrangement, and phraseology. Apparently the victory had been won but the next day the vote was reconsidered and the section was voted down by a vote of sixty-three for to sixty-eight against. The fight to secure a constitutional provision had been lost.

The debate over this question was very amusing. Those who favored the common law status spoke of the conditions in Mexico, Turkey, and France (with its horrors and brutal conditions!) as examples of what would happen if Indiana should overthrow the established order of the marriage contract. The ladies themselves took a hand in the debates and came to the convention hall to cheer Owen and hiss those who opposed them in their effort to secure property rights. Professor Read defended Owen's proposition and spoke of the shame and disgrace of the present conditions. John Pettit, a political friend of Owen, expressed a belief in Owen's sincerity but felt that it was not a proper step to give women independent property rights. Oliver Badger took an extreme view and offered to show in debate that the proposition was contrary to Christian scriptures.[17] Owen was willing, so he and Badger debated the question. Badger was a "New Light" preacher and quoted scripture, which proved beyond a doubt in his mind, that independent property rights were against the law of God. Owen, who never had any too much regard for the regular churchmen, was equal to the occasion. Badger attacked Owen as lacking in an appreciation and understanding of Christian virtues and standards. In answer to this attack, Owen quoted from "Abou Ben Adhem" as expressive of his creed.[18] Owen was defending a movement that was new and his opponents followed the usual conservative argument against changing the status quo. Owen failed in the convention but returned to the General Assembly where, in 1853, it made limited progress in securing property rights for women. The women of Indiana expressed their gratitude to Mr. Owen, for his work on their behalf, by presenting him with a beautiful silver pitcher after the convention had adjourned. Mrs. Sarah Bolton, the poetess, took a very active part in making this presentation possible. Professor William C. Larrabee delivered the address in presenting the pitcher.[19]

Before the convention assembled there had been agitation that a homestead exemption should be fixed by the constitution. The constitution of 1816 had asserted this principle and the statutory law had already made provision for some exemptions. October 29 the committee on the rights and privileges of the inhabitants of the state reported a section providing for an exemption of "a reasonable amount of property from seizure or sale." The section was referred to a select committee of one from each congressional district.[20] November 26 the section passed by a vote of one hundred seventeen to eleven. The *Indiana Statesman* suggested that it first thought a majority would probably oppose this provision as a change of the established custom, but that misfortunes are common to all and expressed approval of the principle.[21] It was in accord with the liberal thought of the time, and its adoption as a definite principle in the new constitution was another step away from the days of the first constitution.

From the present point of view one of the most useless debates of the convention was that which occurred over the rights and privileges of Negroes. Day after day was consumed in a discussion of this subject, and using Badger's estimate of cost, it was very expensive.[22] The Civil War soon wiped away the article that the convention wrote into the constitution. The delegates felt that they were facing a problem that was threatening their very civilization. Early in the discussion Read of Clark outlined three courses which the people of the state might take. Read stated his first as being "amalgamation—aye, sir, I repeat it, amalgamation;" the second would call for the giving of the state over to the black population;

"The third is, to prohibit the immigration of Negroes to the State, to give no encouragement to those that are already here that they can ever enjoy equal social or political privileges, and keep the State for ourselves and our descendents."[23] This latter method for solving the problem seems to have been favored by almost all of the delegates. To most of the delegates it was a matter of Negro exclusion or amalgamation, the latter unthinkable to them. The *Indiana State Sentinel* expressed this same view.[24] But some papers of the state gave feeble protest against the exclusion of Negroes and mulattoes from the state.[25] Robert Dale Owen, as defender of the rights of women and working people, might have been expected to have been friendly to this oppressed class but such was not the case.[26] His committee on the rights and privileges of the inhabitants of the state reported a section October 26 making it mandatory for the General Assembly, at its first session under the new constitution, to forbid Negroes or mulattoes from coming into the state. November 20 the question was referred to a select committee of ten with pending resolutions and amendments.[27] January 23, the committee reported the following article:[28]

NUMBER 51.

Section 1. No negro or mulatto shall come into and settle in this State after the adoption of this Constitution.

Sec. 2. All contracts made with negroes and mulattoes coming into this State, contrary to the provision of the first section of this article shall be void; and all persons who shall employ, or otherwise encourage such negroes or mulattoes to remain in this State shall be fined in any sum not less than ten, or more than five hundred dollars.

Sec. 3. There shall be an annual appropriation set apart by law for the gradual colonization of Negroes and their descendents, who may be in the State at the adoption of this Constitution.

Sec. 4. After the year 1860, no negro or mulatto shall acquire real estate, or any interest therein, otherwise than by descent.

Sec. 5. The General Assembly shall pass laws to carry out the provisions of the foregoing sections of this article if adopted by the people.

Sec. 6. This article shall be submitted to a separate vote of the people in this form: "Exclusion and Colonization of negroes and mulattoes?" aye or no.

With some changes each of these sections passed by large majorities. This article was probably submitted separately to gain more votes for the constitution among the Free Soil element. The delegates regarded the Negro as the biological, social, and political inferior of the white man. Dobson, of Owen and Green, stated that, "No pure negro has wishes and wants like other people," and that three-fourths of the people of the state would rather emigrate elsewhere than to remain in Indiana if Negro suffrage were granted.[29] May of Steuben was the only delegate who advocated Negro suffrage in any form.[30] He regarded the Negro as the social and intellectual inferior of the white but added that,

> Either the negro is a man constituted like ourselves by nature, or else he is only an animal—a mere brute. If the negro be but the mere brute, then, sir let us treat him as one in all respects. . . . But if we decide that the negro is a man—that he has the attributes of humanity—then let us for our own sake, if not for his, for consistency's sake ever recognize him as a man and treat him as a man.[31]

In a few years the Civil War and its revolutionary changes were to set aside all of this part of the organic law as being in conflict with the constitution and laws of the federal government.

The delegates considered the Negro problem in another form that had a very partisan coloring. November 30 Rariden of Wayne, a Whig, introduced a preamble and four resolutions giving a strong endorsement of the Compromise Measures of 1850. On motion of Mr. Pettit these resolutions were laid upon the table by a vote of sixty to fifty-seven.[32] After prolonged debate these resolutions were discarded and resolutions, proposed by Owen of Posey were adopted on December 3. Ninety-nine voted for Owen's resolutions; twenty-three voted against. Four delegates rose but refused to vote on the resolutions. Rariden was leader of the Whigs as was Owen of the Democrats. The Democrats were in control of the convention and apparently wanted the credit of having put the resolutions through. However the resolutions of Rariden were stronger in their support of the Compromise Measures of Congress than were those of Owen.[33] Several delegates did not wish to commit themselves on the issue and some of these pretended that they thought the convention was not a proper place to discuss such matters. Many of the leading newspapers of the state took the same view.[34] Indiana was not the only state whose constitutional convention adopted such resolutions. December 23 similar resolutions were received from the Maryland state constitutional convention and on motion Owen, as president, was authorized to acknowledge the receipt of the resolutions and send, in return, a copy of those approved by the Indiana convention. A reading of these debates over Negro exclusion and the Compromise Measures of 1850 make a very interesting study to show the extent to which the people of Indiana had become agitated over the slavery question by 1850.

It would be easy to be severe in criticizing the convention as having been lacking [innovation]. The homestead exemption had already been recognized in the statutory law and the convention merely gave constitutional status to it as a principle. Robert Dale Owen made no gains in his endeavor to secure independent property rights for women. No delegate seems to have had an adequate conception of how the Negro problem should be adjusted. No satisfactory solution of this problem has yet been found and it remains an issue that needs the cooperation and united wisdom of both races. The article on education is far less favorable to higher education than the corresponding article in the constitution of 1816. Without a strong public opinion being gradually established, higher education would have suffered much from the new constitution. Judged by present standards, the constitution of 1851 has many weaknesses. Viewed from the standards of 1851, it is a document worthy of those who made it. It was not an unusual document.

[1] *Report of the Debates and Proceedings of the Convention for the Revision of the Constitution of the State of Indiana, 1850* (Indianapolis: A. H. Brown, 1850), 221.

[2] *Journal of the Convention of the People of the State of Indiana to Amend the Constitution* (Indianapolis: A.H. Brown, 1851), 193-197.

[3] *Indiana Statesman*, 13 November 1850, speaks of a large meeting in Lafayette and gives resolutions adopted in favor of free banking. Ibid., 4 December 1850, adopted resolutions for free banks saying, "that we prefer no banks to our present system—one founded on monopoly and carried on for the benefit of the few at the expense of the many." Ibid., 20 November 1850, public meeting in Shelby County instructed Hendricks to "go for the State Bank, and not for Free Banks."

[4] Ibid., 13 November 1850.

[5] Ibid., 18 December 1850: "The time has come when the masses should speak out and demand the overthrow of the entire system of monopoly, and there can be no more fitting subject for the deliberations of the convention than this."

[6] *Journal*, 309.

[7] *Debates*, 676.

[8] Ibid., 676-680; Kilgore's discussion is very frank and complete. He had voted for the bill himself.

[9] Ibid., 679.

[10] Ibid., 674.

[11] The *Common School Advocate* had been established in 1846; in 1849 the oft-debated school referendum was held.

[12] Note the speeches, given in the appendix, made at the reunion of the survivors of the constitutional convention in 1885. See remarks of William McKee Dunn especially.

[13] *Journal*, 407-409.

[14] Jonathan Harvey introduced the act of 1847 which began the removal of these common law disabilities. Harvey was born in Wayne County in 1817, represented Hendricks County in the legislature several times as a Whig, was one of the founders of the Republican Party in Indiana, was a delegate to the Republican National Convention which nominated Fremont, and secretary of state from 1861-1863. Jacob Piatt Dunn, *Indiana and Indianans* (Chicago: American Historical Society, 1919), 454.

[15] *Journal*, 894.

[16] *Journal*, 897.

[17] *Debates*, 815-818, gives many quotations from the Bible.

[18] Ibid., 826: "When there is a question in regard to my religious opinions, be my reply this, that I adopt and endorse the sentiment of Leigh Hunt's beautiful parable."

[19] Presentation was made in May 1851. The testimonial is a magnificent silver pitcher, weighs forty-four ounces, and is valued at one-hundred and thirty dollars and has following inscription on it: "Presented to Hon. Robert Dale Owen, by the women of Indiana, in acknowledgement of his true and noble advocacy of the independent rights of [women]." *Indiana Statesman*, 21 May 1851.

[20] The members were: tenth district Mr. Murray, first district Mr. Hovey, second

district Mr. Prather, third district Mr. Bracken, fourth district Mr. Beeson, fifth district Mr. Chapman, sixth district Mr. Dick, seventh district Mr. Chenowith, eighth district Mr. Ristine, ninth district Mr. Colfax. *Journal*, 148.

[21] *Indiana Statesman*, 30 October 1850.

[22] Debates, 119: "And when they reflected that every speech of two minutes in length draws from the public treasury five dollars, it ought to admonish them that their words should be few and well ordered."

[23] *Debates*, 247.

[24] *Indiana State Sentinel*, 28 November 1850: "In the case of a wreck where two brothers seek safety by clinging to the same plank, if it is unable to sustain the weight of both, the law of self-preservation, which knows no sympathy, will justify the stronger to break the grasp of the weaker to save himself. Such is the case of the white and black races. They can never mingle or amalgamate. Such attempts would degrade the whites without elevating the black. They can never occupy the same domicile, or stand on the same level of equality. The great evil of African slavery is that the subject is of a distinct race."

[25] *Indiana Statesman*, 20 November 1850, says the members of the convention are contemplating prohibiting the ingress of free Negroes into the state "and the gradual reduction of barbarism of those already here." The *Statesman* speaks of the policies proposed and adds, "And this is the year of our Lord 1850, in a Christian land, in the free State of Indiana, in a body of intelligent men, who require the blessings of Almighty God to be daily invoked upon their labors, and many of who claim to be servants of the Most High...Heaven help us when such counsels prevail!" *Madison Weekly Tribune*, 2 May 1851, quoting from the *Perrysville Eagle*: "The arguments used are the arguments of expediency, the arguments of the strong against the weak, the arguments of despots over their prostrate subjects. They who use them have no appreciation of the split that dares to do right regardless of consequences, no heart to recognize those rights in others that they demand for themselves."

[26] *Debates*, 231: "They can never obtain political rights here. They can never obtain social rights here. And for these reasons, I think we ought not to have them amongst us."

[27] *Journal*, 271. The members were: Kent, Owen, Holman, Rariden, Maguire, Dobson, Stevenson, McFarland, Niles, and Howe.

[28] *Journal*, 652.

[29] *Debates*, 233.

[30] Ibid., 246. May said: "But I say that if the black man has not intelligence and discretion enough at the age of twenty-one to make him worthy the exercise of the elective franchise, then extend the prescribed age to thirty-one, or forty-one, or if need be to ninety-one."

[31] Ibid., 245.

[32] *Debates*, 857-858. Pettit said, "I am afraid, sir, that there is a cat in the meal tub, or a snake in the grass, and I move that the preamble and resolutions be laid upon the table."

[33] Both sets of resolutions may be found in the appendix.

[34] *Indiana State Journal*, 21 December 1850, "With exception of the State Sentinel and 'Rariden's Cambridge City mouthpiece,' every paper in the state that has spoken on the subject (and most of them have) has denounced their introduction as a useless waste of time and unwarranted expenditure of the people's money." *Indiana Statesman*, 11 December 1850, quoting from 1. *Indiana Courier*: "We think their time might be more profitably employed in attending to the business entrusted them." 2. *Richmond Jeffersonian*: Resolutions "ought to have been kicked out of that body with ceremony." ("That body" refers to the convention). 3. *New Albany Ledger*: "Convention not the place to discuss them." See also *Prairie Chieftain*, 10 December 1850.

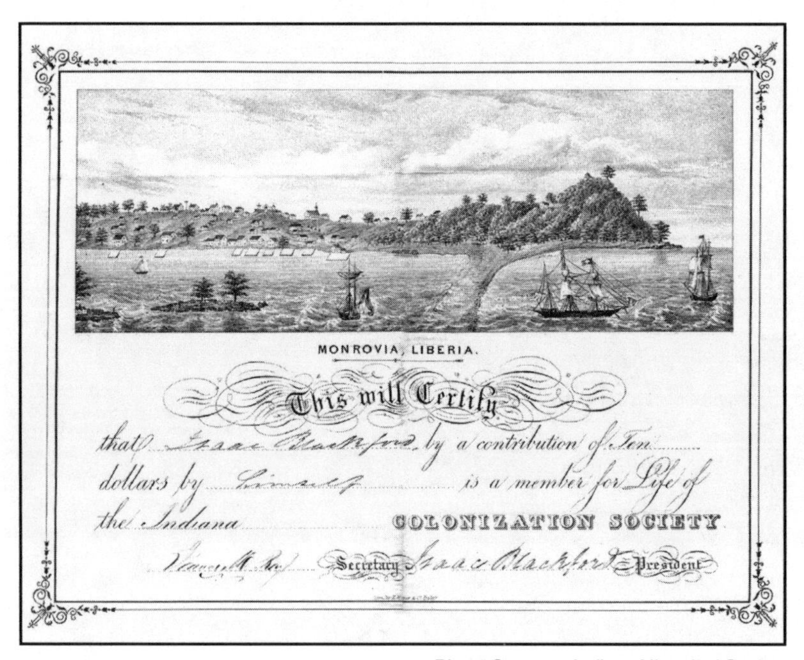

MONROVIA, LIBERIA.

This will Certify

that Isaac Blackford by a contribution of dollars by is a member for Life of the Indiana COLONIZATION SOCIETY.

Secretary Isaac Blackford President

Photo Courtesy Indiana Historical Society

Certificate of membership in the Indiana Colonization Society. Justice Isaac Blackford is listed as president of the society.

In 1850 the nation, not just Indiana, faced a looming crisis regarding slavery and the fate of free blacks. Many Hoosiers were ambivalent, or outright hostile, about the presence of black persons in Indiana, and the topic was heatedly debated by convention delegates. The delegates ultimately presented a separate constitutional provision for ratification prohibiting the immigration of free blacks into Indiana. Hoosier voters overwhelming approved the measure and it became Article 13 of the 1851 Indiana Constitution.

CHAPTER VII

The Constitution Before The People

The act calling for the election of delegates to the convention made it the duty of the General Assembly to submit the work of the convention to the people. This procedure was in accord with the political philosophy of the period and was accepted by the delegates as the proper step. The schedule, which is still printed as part of the constitution, indicates that the delegates expected the constitution to be voted upon by the people.[1] The convention left the procedure to be directed by the General Assembly. February 14, four days after the convention adjourned, Governor Joseph A. Wright approved an act of the General Assembly giving the people the right to approve or reject the new constitution at the approaching August election. February 25 the governor issued his official proclamation notifying the electors that a copy of the constitution had been deposited with the secretary of state and that a poll would be taken on the first Monday of August next. The constitution and the governor's proclamation were printed in papers all over the state. Some papers printed the constitution in several issues; often in successive issues.[2] The people were not kept in ignorance as to the content of the constitution.

The campaign for the ratification of the constitution may be said to have begun in the convention itself. January 21 Owen introduced a resolution calling for a committee of ten to consist of one delegate from each congressional district, to "prepare an address to the electors of the State, embodying brief statement of the changes proposed in the amended constitution, and such other matters in connection therewith, as may aid in securing its adoption." Walpole, a Whig of Hancock and Madison, was the only delegate to speak against this resolution. He expressed the opinion that the address would be one-sided, written by Owen and his associates (this was probably a very accurate charge), and that it would reflect upon the intelligence of the people as they could form their own opinions by reading the debates and newspaper accounts.[3] Owen's resolution was adopted and the committee was appointed four days later.[4] February 8, on the Saturday before the convention adjourned on Monday, this "Committee of Ten" as it came to be called, reported an address that had been accepted by all of the committee members present at the committee meeting.[5] The address was read to the convention by the secretary and "the report was unanimously concurred in."[6]

The address is clear and concise. It was probably the work of Owen.[7] This address is the best contemporary explanation of the changes made and is very important in showing what the convention considered as its most important changes. It was printed in newspapers all over the state, and was used as a campaign document. If its author deemed it necessary to secure ratification he was no doubt mistaken. On the other hand, the address was so worded that it was no doubt valuable in securing votes for the new constitution. The address may be found in the appendix.

The Democrats were wholehearted in support of the new constitution. The *Indiana State Sentinel* as early as December 15, 1850, when the convention was barely half through its labors, said: "The Constitution, we predict, when it comes from the hands of the convention, will be worthy of the people of our young and rising commonwealth, now numbering more than a million inhabitants." July 26 the *Sentinel* called attention to four of the most important provisions of the new constitution as being: provisions in favor of common schools; popular election of judges; restrictions against local and judicious guards for general legislation; and "above all" the measures to ensure reform in the practice of law. The *Indiana Statesman*, as exponent of liberal democracy in the state, regarded the adoption of the constitution "as a fixed fact."[8] The *Indiana State Journal* expressed conflicting views and had little to say during the campaign.[9] The press of the state was in favor of a constitution.[10] At a county convention, held at Lawrenceburg on April 12, 1851, the Democrats of Dearborn County adopted a resolution stating that they would use "every honorable exertion to secure the adoption of the new constitution" as conducive to the "prosperity and happiness" of the people of the state.[11] The files of the *Independent Press* show that the Lawrenceburg debating club debated various sections of the new constitution as compared to the old. It was decided that the giving of voting privileges to non-citizens was a mistake. There were many who disapproved of this clause. Even Senator Bright, a Democrat, rebuked the convention for inserting this clause.[12] There were those who denounced the Negro exclusion clause but they were not numerous.[13] Judge E. H. C. Chamberlain, whom the *Statesman* had supported for election as delegate, voted for the new constitution "as a mere choice of evils."[14] He was much disappointed at the failure of Owen's modified proposal to secure property rights for women; he expected the constitution to be adopted. Professor Larrabee, who gave the address in presenting Owen with the silver pitcher, said:

> As to the new Constitution, it is a medley of good, bad, and indifferent. The good is very good, the bad is very bad, and the indifferent is very indifferent. On the whole the good predominates, and the Constitution will be adopted by a vote so large, that the minority will not be worth counting.[15]

Ezra Ferris, who had been a member of the constitutional convention of 1816, was pleased with some parts of the new constitution but wrote against its adoption.[16] He wrote in defense of the existing state banking system. An interesting anecdote of the campaign explains how, on the morning of the general election, a clergyman called at the office of the *Indiana Statesman* to get some information in regard to what the new constitution said about capital punishment. He said that if the new constitution "prohibited capital punishment, it was contrary to the Bible, and he could not vote for it." He was assured that the constitution fully recognized "the virtues of hemp as a moral regenerator" and "departed with his heart considerably lightened."[17]

It was generally recognized that if the Negro exclusion clause were adopted it would not only prevent further immigration of blacks to Indiana but also so influence public opinion as to make conditions very unfavorable for those already in the state. There were about ten thousand free Negroes and mulattoes in the state, or about one black for every hundred whites. While the convention was in session numerous petitions were sent to the delegates on behalf of this class of inhabitants. Some of these petitions were signed by Negroes, and the Quakers were very active on their behalf. About the first of July 1851 a central committee, representing the colored people of the state, sent the following call:[18]

> There will be a State Convention held in the city of Indianapolis, on the first day of August next. The object in calling for a convention is to consult as to the propriety of emigration, and to elect delegates to a National Convention. We hope to see a large turn out on the part of the colored people on the occasion. We invite all to come. The time has come when every colored man in the State should consider his situation, we also hope that every county in the state, where there are any of our people, will hold meetings, and appoint their delegates and them to the Convention. Let us come together: We think it is high time that we take

> into consideration the oppressive laws that have so long opposed us, and are at the present time oppressing us. Let the word be Convention! Convention!!

This circular was signed by J. G. Britton, P. B. Delaney, John L. Johnson, W. M. Hanley, W. Franklin, W. Brown, W. T. Boyd, P. Bushrod, Rev. W. Douglas; with John L. Johnson as secretary to the committee. The *Indiana Sentinel* and *Indiana State Journal* both encouraged emigration as being the only solution to the problems of the two races.[19] The convention met August 1 in the old African Methodist Church in Indianapolis. The first day was spent largely in organization. There were representatives from the following counties in attendance: Marion, Vigo, Washington, Madison, Floyd, Clark, Bartholomew, Jefferson, Vanderburgh, Posey, Gibson, and Ohio. There were about sixty colored delegates in attendance at one time; many of these were ministers. John G. Britton of Marion was elected president of the convention. The delegates discussed the various places to which they might emigrate and the problems involved in each country. Canada was much discussed as affording them excellent opportunities. Other places considered were Jamaica, Mexico, South America, and Liberia. Many were not in favor of emigration at all; some wanted to petition Congress for a land grant to colonize. The *Indiana Statesman* says, "The Convention was highly respectable in its character, embodied much talent, and their proceedings were conducted with much talent and propriety."[20] Perhaps the true feeling of the convention is contained in the following quotations from the proceedings:[21]

> The British Government has made propositions to emigrate to the Island of Jamaica. We have already received a proposition for New Granada. Other South American Republics are ready to receive us, on terms of equality. But this is our country. We know no other. Her we love, and are ever willing to defend [her].

The convention probably had very little influence on the voting but it is very interesting because of the insight that it gives to the relation between the two races at the time. It is wondered if this was not the first such colored convention in the state.

Both the friends and enemies of the new constitution expected the people to adopt the new constitution. The *Madison Weekly Tribune*, edited by Milton Gregg who was a leading Whig member of the convention, predicted that the constitution would be adopted by a forty thousand majority, "And yet the Editor of the *State Sentinel* came near going into *conniptions* for fear the rascally Whigs would defeat it."[22] The general election at which the constitution was submitted was held August 4. The actual poll in favor of the "charter of the people's right," as the independent press called the new constitution, far exceeded the expectations of its warmest friends. The *Indiana Statesman* counted the election an "avalanche of victory for the Democracy of Indiana."[23] The August 8 issue of the *State Sentinel* shows that this orthodox leader of democracy was more than elected. Across their editorial page was the expression "Crow! Chapman, Crow!!" and beneath that the picture of a rooster. The Whigs reminded the *Sentinel* that they had their "coon" and that after the election of 1852 the "rooster would forever cease to crow!!"[24]

The total vote for the constitution was 113,230; the total vote against was 27,638. The thirteenth article, calling for the policy of Negro exclusion, was adopted by an even larger majority, or 113,828 votes for to 21,873 votes against.[25] Starke County gave a unanimous vote for the adoption of the constitution, with 104 votes cast. Porter, Lake, Pulaski, and Benton each polled less than ten votes against the constitution. Ohio County was the only county to give an adverse vote, being 315 for to 438 against the constitution. The vote in Switzerland and Vanderburgh Counties, both bordering on the Ohio River, was very close. A study of the map shows that the northern tier of the counties gave larger votes, proportionally, than did those along the Ohio River. Just the opposite is true in case of Negro exclusion. Four counties voted against Negro exclusion. These were Elkhart, LaGrange, Steuben, and Randolph; the first three of these counties bordered the state of Michigan. The vote in St. Joseph County was very close. All of the counties along the Ohio River gave very decisive votes for the adoption of article thirteen excluding Negroes. Dubois County gave 739 votes for to two against exclusion. It is not surprising to find those nearest Kentucky casting larger majorities for Negro exclusion, for these were more acquainted with the problem. The vote cannot be called a truly sectional one for the state as a whole voted the same way; it is a ruse that the northern counties were more in favor of the constitution and less in favor of Negro exclusion. The difference was merely one of degree.

September 3 Governor Joseph A. Wright issued his proclamation giving the official election returns and declaring the new constitution to be adopted by the people of the state.[26] November 1, 1851 the new constitution went into effect. In his message to the General Assembly on December 2, Governor Wright spoke to the members in regard to the peaceful revolution that had taken place and said:

> On the first day of November last, the Constitution, under which you have assembled, went into operation. On that day we passed from the old to the new. That Constitution under which, for more than a third of a century, we have grown from a handful to a million inhabitants, secured and protected in all of the rights of freemen, has passed away and a new instrument taken its place. The change is radical in some of the most essential parts of our organic law, but it has been affected without strife, continuation, or bloodshed, and without affecting, in the slightest degree, the uniform and peaceful pursuits of our people.

[1] Indiana Constitution (1851), schedule secs. 13 and 14.

[2] The three Indianapolis newspapers—the *Indiana State Sentinel*, the *Indiana State*

Journal, and the *Indiana Statesman* each have several issues containing both the new constitution and the governor's proclamation. See files for February and March 1851. See also: *Madison Weekly Courier*, 28 February 1851, *Independent Press*, 28 March 1851, and other local papers of the state.

[3] *Report of the Debates and Proceedings of the Convention for the Revision of the Constitution of the State of Indiana, 1850* (Indianapolis: A. H. Brown, 1850), 1732. Such an address would be "a libel upon the judgment and understanding of the people."

[4] *Journal of the Convention of the People of the State of Indiana to Amend the Constitution* (Indianapolis: Austin H. Brown, 1851), 780. The members were: first district Owen, second district Carr, third district Berry, fourth district Smiley, fifth district Maguire, sixth district Helmer, seventh district Davis of Vermillion, eighth district Bryant, ninth district Colfax, tenth district Bascom. Owen was chairman; Miles was later selected to take the place of Colfax.

[5] Niles of LaPorte was not present.

[6] *Debates*, 2046.

[7] Ibid. Owen said: "I will state to the Convention that I have been compelled to draw up this address in a hasty manner. . . ."

[8] *Indiana Statesman*, 12 March 1851, quoting from the *Fort Wayne Sentinel*, lists the chief reforms as: "Biennial sessions of the legislature with sessions limited to 61 days, every bill must be read throughout before its passage and the vote taken, special legislation abolished so far as possible, all incorporations are to be made by a general law, laws and court practice to be codified and simplified, strict supervision over legislature in regard to State Debt, popular election of officials, suffrage to foreigners who have been in State one year and have declared intention of becoming citizens, homestead exception, provision that the legislature may abolish or modify the Grand Jury system, right of jury trial in all cases, general banking law, and article in regard to negroes to be submitted separately." For other changes see *Independent Press*, 1 August 1851.

[9] *Indiana Daily Journal*, 10 May 1851: "So far as we are concerned, immediately upon reading the new Constitution, we declared that we should not vote for it." *Indiana (Weekly) State Journal*, 22 February 1851: "In our opinion, while it contains much that is objectionable, there are so many redeeming features in it that we shall give our vote in favor of its adoption, trusting to time and experience to correct the errors it contains, in the mode which it prescribes for its future amendment."

[10] *Madison Weekly Courier*, 19 February 1851: "We are for the new constitution." *New Albany Weekly Ledger*, 19 February 1851: "But if the friends of that instrument—the friends of reform—do their duty, all will be well." *Indiana State Sentinel*, 26 July 1851: "In our estimation it is far superior" to the old one.

[11] *Independent Press*, 18 April 1851.

[12] *Indiana Daily Journal*, 12 July 1851. Bright said: "I am opposed to the clause allowing foreigners to vote, and am sorry it is there. Both parties tried to see how far they could go to get foreign votes."

[13] *Indiana (Weekly) State Journal*, 22 February 1851; *Indiana State Journal*, 30 April 1851.

[14] *Indiana Statesman*, 19 March 1851. Also *Madison Weekly Tribune*, 20 August 1851. Chamberlain said: "No matter how cruelly the instrument may [suppress] the spirit of progress. . .it will be adopted."

[15] *Prairie Chieftain*, 1 April 1851.

[16] *Independent Press*, 27 June 1851.

[17] *Indiana Statesman*, 21 July 1852.

[18] *Indiana State Sentinel*, 3 July 1851.

[19] Ibid. "It gives us great pleasure to publish the following call for a State Convention of colored persons. Let them meet together and consult on their future prospects. The question with them is truly a question of slavery or freedom. If they determine to emigrate to Liberia, they determine in favor of their own freedom and the independence of their posterity. If they determine to remain in this country, they decide in favor of slavery and degradation. In name they may be free, but what is that freedom worth to them, with the prejudices of color and caste which will exist as long as white man treads the earth. Let them return to the land of their fathers where, under the approving smile of Heaven, they may be free indeed. We trust that a liberal appropriation may be made by the Legislature of the State, and by action of the General Government, to aid all such as desire to emigrate. It is a great work and one which we can enter into with heart and soul, and one upon which we love to dwell." *Indiana Daily Journal*, 6 May 1851: "It is the right move for them, and we hope they may not fail entering into it heartily."

[20] *Indiana Statesman*, 27 August 1851.

[21] Ibid.

[22] *Madison Weekly Tribune*, 13 August 1851.

[23] *Indiana Statesman*, 13 August 1851.

[24] *Indiana State Journal*, 7 October 1851.

[25] See map in regard to the results for a further study and for the sources from which this material was obtained.

[26] See appendix for this proclamation.

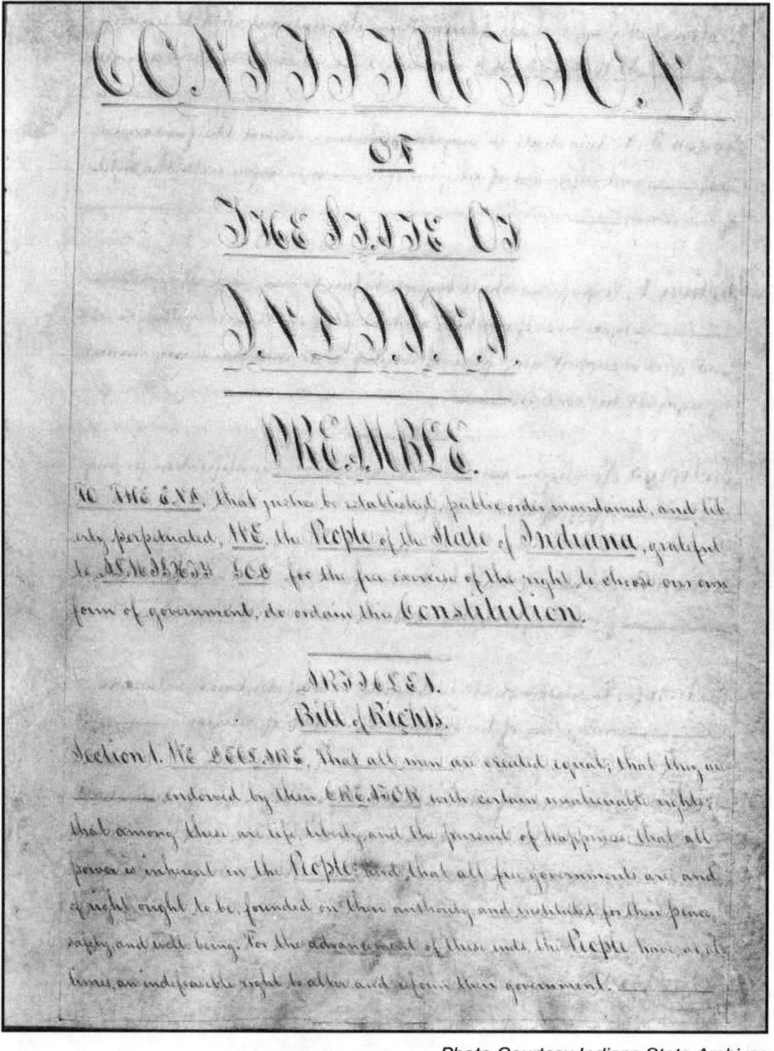
CONSTITUTION

OF

THE STATE OF

INDIANA.

PREAMBLE.

TO THE END, that justice be established, public order maintained, and liberty perpetuated; WE, the People of the State of Indiana, grateful to ALMIGHTY GOD for the free exercise of the right to choose our own form of government, do ordain this Constitution.

ARTICLE I.

Bill of Rights.

Section 1. WE DECLARE, That all men are created equal; that they are endowed by their CREATOR with certain unalienable rights; that among these are life, liberty and the pursuit of happiness; that all power is inherent in the People; and that all free governments are, and of right ought to be, founded on their authority, and instituted for their peace, safety and well being. For the advancement of these ends, the People have, at all times, an indefeasible right to alter and reform their government.

Photo Courtesy Indiana State Archives

This image is of one of the original handwritten copies of the Indiana Constitution as completed in 1851. The constitution is on display in the Statehouse rotunda each year during the legislative session.

CHAPTER VIII

The Changes Made: Conclusion

In referring to the alterations made in the organic law Robert Dale Owen, chairman of the "Committee of Ten" and perhaps author of the address to the people, said: "The changes are numerous. Even we who have made them would be somewhat puzzled to sit down and enumerate them."[1] For the most part, the more important changes are discussed in the "Address to the People," printed in the appendix. A brief review of these changes and additions will be helpful in giving a better understanding of the work of the convention.

When the standing committees of the convention were appointed the president selected a committee "on revision, arrangement, and phraseology." Owen was made chairman of this committee.[2] Many of the most prominent delegates were chosen to assist him. The conciseness and clearness of the present constitution, as being superior to the first, is due to the work of this committee.

The preamble of the new constitution is much more brief than in that of the old. It is interesting to note that it contained recognition of God not found in the first constitution. Pettit of Tippecanoe was the only member of vote against this recognition.

The first article is the Bill of Rights. It differs very little from that of the old constitution and many parts are repeated verbatim. However, some new items are included. One is that "no person shall be rendered incompetent as a witness, in consequence of his opinions on matters of religion." Another that "no money shall be drawn from the treasury, for the benefit of any religious or theological institution." Both of these provisions were in the contemporary constitutions of Michigan and Wisconsin.[3] Still another new provision is that "the General Assembly shall not grant to any citizen, or class of citizens, privileges or immunities, which upon the same terms, shall not be equally open to all citizens." Provision is also made that the right of eminent domain, except in case of the state, shall not be given except when property has been "first assessed and tendered." The principle of a homestead exemption is recognized but no fixed amount is asserted. The right of jury trial is secured in all cases, under the old constitution this right was not given in prosecution for petit misdemeanors and in cases where the amount in controversy was less than twenty dollars. This article was made much longer.

The second article deals with suffrage and elections. This was article six under the old constitution. The first constitution provided that every white male, twenty-one years of age and over, who had resided in the state for one year could vote. The new constitution shortened the residence requirement to six months for citizens of the United States, and in addition, gave the right of suffrage to:

> every white male, of foreign birth, of the age of twenty-one years and upwards, who shall have resided in the United States one year, and shall have resided in the State during the six months immediately preceding such election, and shall have declared his intention to become a citizen of the United States. . . .

The address to the people stated that this "liberal provision will undoubtedly tend to increase the wealth and population of our State by attracting emigrants toward it."[4] A new provision was inserted making anyone who takes part in a duel, either directly or indirectly, "Ineligible to any office of trust or profit." Negroes and mulattoes were denied the right of suffrage. It was provided that all elections by the people must be by ballot; all elections by the General Assembly, or either branch thereof, must be *viva voce*. Pluralism in office holding, except in a few special instances, was forbidden. The date of general elections was changed from August to the second Tuesday in October.[5] This date was regarded as one of "much greater leisure to farmers."

Article three is the shortest article in the constitution. It contains but one section. It provides for a distribution of power among the legislative, judicial, and executive departments of the government. It is an index of the political theory of the age which regarded "separation of powers" and checks and balances as necessary to prevent tyranny in government. This article contains no new theory but was completely reworded.

The changes in article four, regarding the General Assembly, were numerous. The new constitution provided that: senators shall be chosen for a term of four years; representatives for two years;[6] regular legislative sessions to be held bi-annually, and limited to sixty-one days; special sessions to be called by the governor and limited to forty days; the General Assembly to make an enunciation of all the white male inhabitants over twenty-one years of age every six years; no county should ever be divided for senatorial apportionment; senators and representatives must be inhabitants of the district which they represent; compensation of the members of the General Assembly to be fixed by law; and all laws to be uniform and general. The two most important changes were the adoption of biennial sessions and the requirement that "all laws shall be general, and of uniform operation throughout the State," in so far as practicable. It was estimated that biennial sessions alone would save enough money to pay the expenses of the convention, within five years time, if no special sessions were called.[7] The "Address to the Electors" lists still other changes on this department.

Article five deals with the executive department of the government.

"The changes in this department are unimportant. . . ."[8] The governor's term of office is increased from three to four years "to correspond to biennial sessions of the Legislature."[9] He is not eligible to succeed himself but may be reelected again after having been out one term. No individual has ever served a second term under the present constitution. The qualifications for being governor were [altered], the previous requirement that a candidate must be a citizen of the United States for ten years was reduced to a five-year citizenship requirement. A minor change in the "suspensive" vote power makes it impossible for the governor to hold a bill over from one session of the legislature to another. The pardoning power of the governor was limited in the new constitution. The lieutenant governor, except for presiding over the Senate and voting in case of a tie, has nothing of importance to do. He has potential powers which are exercised only if he succeeds to the office of governor. Abolition of this office would not greatly curtail the safety of the commonwealth.[10]

The old constitution united the provisions in regard to the executive and administrative branches into one article. The new constitution has an article for each of these. This is one of the best evidences we have to show that state government was becoming more centralized and complex at that time. Article six, on administration, consists of ten sections. The new constitution makes the secretary, treasurer and auditor of state elected by the electors, depriving the General Assembly of its former power to appoint these officials. Under the first constitution the secretary of state held office for four years, the auditor and treasurer for three years. None of those officials are eligible to office more than "four years in any term of six years." In counties, the voters are called upon to elect "a clerk of the Circuit Court, auditor, recorder, treasurer, sheriff, coroner, and surveyor." The clerk, auditor, and recorder serve for four-year terms and are not eligible to office more than eight years in any term of twelve years. The treasurer, sheriff, coroner, and surveyor, serve for two years and are not eligible to office more than four years in any period of six years. The old constitution had provided for the election of but two county officials: the sheriff and the corner. Township organization is not outlined by the constitution. However, the General Assembly was given power to establish "such other county and township officers as may be necessary."

Several alterations were made in article seven dealing with the judicial department.[11] The new constitution calls for the popular election of all judges; even the clerk of the Supreme Court was made dependent upon the vote of the people. The Supreme Court may consist of from three to five judges, each elected from a separate district but chosen by the people at large. The tenure of office, for judges, is reduced from seven to six years. The people of each judicial circuit elect a prosecuting attorney who holds office for two years. The voters in each township are authorized to elect "a competent number of Justices of the Peace" for four-year terms. In response to the contest for the abolition of the grand jury the constitution provides that "the General Assembly may modify, or abolish the Grand Jury system;" the grand jury system was guaranteed by the old constitution. The practice of law was thrown wide open to "every voter of good moral character" and this has been one of the most condemned clauses of the constitution. The legislature may establish "tribunals of conciliation" but these courts cannot render obligatory judgment unless the parties concerned agree to do so before a case is submitted. The convention regards the provision and simplification of law procedure and forms as one of its chief labors, if the "Address to the People," adopted unanimously, is a reflection of their attitude.[12] The press of the state was wholehearted in praise of this section.

Perhaps the article which suffered most at the hands of the convention was the article in regard to education, article eight, and yet, judged by the needs of the people in the 1850s one wonders if it wasn't probably very superior to the provisions in the old constitution in regard to this same subject. The first constitution made it the duty of the General Assembly "to provide, by law, for a general system of Education, ascending a regular gradation, from township schools to a state university, wherein, tuition shall be gratis, and equally open to all." The article in the second constitution makes it the duty of the General Assembly "to provide, by law, for a general and uniform system of common schools, wherein tuition shall be without charge, and equally open to all." A common school fund was created to "remain a perpetual fund, which may be increased, but shall never be diminished," and the interest of this fund can only go to the use of common schools. This fund was made to consist of the congressional township fund, surplus revenue fund, saline fund, bank tax fund, county seminary fund, and other revenues from fines and forfeitures. Besides this was the provision made for taxes on corporations. A new feature was added in the establishment of another elective office: the state superintendent of public instruction. A study of the article indicates that both the letter and spirit of the article is unfriendly to higher or college education. The county seminaries were abolished.

Article nine has three sections in regard to institutions; it is merely an enlargement of section four of article nine in the old constitution. In very general terms it provides for care of the deaf and dumb, blind, insane, asylums for the poor, and an institution of correction for juvenile offenders. It is brief but very elastic.

Article ten reflects the utter disgust of the people with the conditions of state finances for the generation preceding the calling of the convention. A state debt was forbidden except to meet causal deficits in the revenues, pay interest on state debt, suppress insurrection, or to provide for the public defense.[13] The first section made it mandatory for the General Assembly to provide "for a uniform and equal rate of assessment and taxation." This is the section to which many farmers today object.

Article eleven deals with corporations, which had not even begun to develop as they are now known. The General Assembly was given authority to establish a general banking law and a bank with branches under specified conditions; the state was never to be a stockholder in any bank. The restrictions on banking were very severe and were similar to those in the New York constitution under which "not a dollar had been lost."[14]

Article twelve provides for the organization and equipping of the militia of the state. It excuses those from bearing arms who are conscientiously opposed to such service. The whole article has been shortened.

Article thirteen has since been removed by constitutional amendment and replaced by an article on municipal corporations.[15] The original article dealt with the subject of Negroes and mulattoes. "No additional disability, not found in the old Constitution, is imposed by the new, on Negroes or Mulattoes or their descendants, who may be in the State at the time of the adoption of the amended Constitution."[16] Perhaps the new constitution performed the valuable service of collecting all of the sections of the old, which had discriminated against the Negro, into one article, for the convenience of the Negroes and mulattoes who could not read! This article reflects the deep conviction on the part of the delegates that separation of the two races was the only possible solution.

Article fourteen states the boundaries of the state. It is binding only because it agrees with the boundary fixed by Congress.

Article fifteen deals with miscellaneous sections. The last section made it the duty of the General Assembly to provide "for the permanent enclosure of preservation of the Tippecanoe Battle Ground."

Article sixteen provides for a rigid and lengthy process of amendment. No provision is made for constitutional amendment; such power is usually considered to come from the Bill of Rights. The old constitution had provided for a convention but no amending process; the new does just the opposite. The present constitution has been amended nine times.

The distinctive features of the constitution of 1851 may be summarized as follows:

- Tenure of office was made short and rotation made necessary by restricting the tenure of office.
- Almost all offices were made elective by the people.
- The power of the General Assembly was much curbed.
- The machinery of government was enlarged and made more complex.

- County government was made more democratic; seven elective county offices were provided.
- Suffrage was extended to aliens without becoming citizens of the United States.
- A tedious process of amendment was provided; no direct provision made for convention.
- In the field of education, emphasis was placed upon common schools.
- Sessions of the General Assembly were to be held biennially with regular sessions limited to sixty-one days.
- Salaries not fixed but left to be determined by law.
- Pluralism in office holding strictly guarded against.
- Laws and regulations to be uniform and general wherever possible.
- Further immigration of Negroes or mulattoes into the State was denied. Those already here were denied the right of suffrage and service in the militia.
- The date of general elections changed from August to October.
- Practice of law opened to all voters of "good moral character."
- Revision of laws and simplification of court procedures made mandatory on the next General Assembly.
- State debt was forbidden except in very special cases.
- Free or general banking provided for; no further connection between government and banks.
- Made it possible to abolish the grand jury.
- Noticeable absence of provisions in regard to municipal government.
- The constitution, for the most part, was not cluttered up with "statutory" regulations.
- The constitution is clear and concise in its style.
- It shows a decided development in the centralization of authority at the State Capitol.

[1] *Report of the Debates and Proceedings of the Convention for the Revision of the Constitution of the State of Indiana, 1850* (Indianapolis: A. H. Brown, 1850), 1729.

[2] The others were: Carr, Berry, Smiley, Maguire, Helmer, Davis of Vermillion, Bryant, Colfax, Bascom. *Journal of the Convention of the People of the State of Indiana to Amend the Constitution* (Indianapolis: H. Fowler, A.H. Brown, 1851), 780.

[3] *Debates*, 2042.

[4] *Debates*, 2642. "Address to the Electors."

[5] *Debates*, 2045. "Address to the Electors." In 1881, Governor Albert Porter, an Indiana Civil War general, issued a proclamation declaring in effect an amendment that changed the date of the general election to "the first Tuesday after the first Monday in November."

[6] Under the old constitution, senators were chosen for three-year terms and representatives for one year.

[7] *Debates*, 2043. "Address to Electors."

[8] Ibid., 2043.

[9] Ibid.

[10] Before the adoption of the seventeenth amendment to the federal constitution the lieutenant governor often became governor to succeed the governor who was often elected to the senate by the General Assembly.

[11] The constitution of 1816 made the supreme and circuit judges. The former appointed by the governor and confirmed by the senate; the later chosen by joint ballot of the two houses of the General Assembly.

[12] *Debates*, 2044. "Address to Electors."

[13] *Debates*, 2044. "Address to Electors:" "Had this provision, brief and simple as it is, been inserted in the Constitution of 1816, it would have saved the State from a loss of six millions of dollars."

[14] Ibid., 2045.

[15] The constitution of Indiana as usually published is not the original; but has all amendments inserted.

[16] *Debates*, 2045. "Address to Electors."

APPENDIX I

THE CONSTITUTION OF 1851[1]

Preamble[2]

TO THE END, that justice be established, public order maintained, and liberty perpetuated; WE, the PEOPLE of the State of Indiana, grateful to ALMIGHTY GOD for the free exercise of the right to choose our own form of government, do ordain this Constitution.

ARTICLE I: Bill of Rights

Section 1. WE DECLARE, That all men are created equal; that they are endowed by their Creator with certain inalienable rights; that among these are life, liberty, and the pursuit of happiness; that all power is inherent in the People; and that all free governments are, and of right ought to be, founded on their authority, and instituted for their peace, safety, and well-being. For the advancement of these ends, the People have, at all times, an indefeasible right to alter and reform their government.

Sec. 2. All men shall be secured in the natural right to worship Almighty God, according to the dictates of their own consciences.

Sec. 3. No law shall, in any case whatever, control the free exercise and enjoyment of religious opinions, nor interfere with the rights of conscience.

Sec. 4. No preference shall be given, by law, to any creed, religious society, or mode of worship; and no man shall be compelled to attend, erect, or support, any place of worship, or to maintain any ministry, against his consent.

Sec. 5. No religious test shall be required as a qualification for any office of trust or profit.

Sec. 6. No money shall be withdrawn from the treasury for the benefit of any religious or theological institution.

Sec. 7. No person shall be rendered incompetent as a witness, in consequence of his opinions on matters of religion.

Sec. 8. The mode of administering an oath or affirmation, shall be such as may be most consistent with, and binding upon, the conscience of the person to whom such oath or affirmation may be administered.

Sec. 9. No law shall be passed restraining the free interchange of thought and opinion, or restricting the right to speak, write, or print, freely, on any subject whatever: but, for the abuse of that right, every person shall be responsible.

Sec. 10. In all prosecutions for libel, the truth of the matters alleged to be libelous, may be given in justification.

Sec. 11. The right of the people to be secure in their persons, houses, papers, and effects, against unreasonable search or seizure, shall not be violated; and no warrant shall issue, but upon probable cause, supported by oath or affirmation, and particularly describing the place to be searched, and the person or thing to be seized.

Sec. 12. All courts shall be open; and every person, for injury done to him in his person, property, or reputation, shall have remedy by due course of law. Justice shall be administered freely, and without purchase; completely, and without denial; speedily, and without delay.

Sec. 13. In all criminal prosecutions, the accused shall have the right to a public trial, by an impartial jury, in the county in which the offense shall have been committed; to be heard by himself and counsel; to demand the nature and cause of the accusation against him, and to have a copy thereof; to meet the witnesses face to face, and to have compulsory process for obtaining witnesses in his favor.

Sec. 14. No person shall be put in jeopardy twice, for the same offense; and no person, in any criminal prosecution, shall be compelled to testify against himself.

Sec. 15. No person arrested, or confined in jail, shall be treated with unnecessary rigor.

Sec. 16. Excessive bail shall not be required. Excessive fines shall not be imposed. Cruel and unusual punishments shall not be inflicted. All penalties shall be proportioned to the nature of the offense.

Sec. 17. Offenses, other than murder or treason, shall be bailable by sufficient sureties. Murder or treason shall not be bailable, when the proof is evident, or the presumption strong.

Sec. 18. The penal code shall be founded upon the principles of reformation, and not of vindictive justice.

Sec. 19. In all criminal cases whatever, the jury shall have the right to determine the law and the facts.

Sec. 20. In all civil cases, the right of trial by jury shall remain inviolate.

Sec. 21. No man's particular services shall be demanded, without just compensation. No man's property shall be taken by law, without just compensation; nor, except in case of the State, without such compensation first assessed and tendered.

Sec. 22. The privilege of the debtor to enjoy the necessary comforts of life, shall be recognized by wholesome laws, exempting a reasonable amount of property from seizure or sale, for the payment of any debt or liability hereafter contracted: and there shall be no imprisonment for debt, except in case of fraud.

Sec. 23. The General Assembly shall not grant to any citizen, or class of citizens, privileges or immunities, which, upon the same terms, shall not equally belong to all classes.

Sec. 24. No *ex post facto* law, or law impairing the obligation of contracts, shall ever be passed.

Sec. 25. No law shall be passed, the taking effect of which shall be made to depend upon any authority, except as provided in this constitution.

Sec. 26. The operation of the laws shall never be suspended, except by the authority of the General Assembly.

Sec. 27. The privilege of the writ of *habeas corpus* shall not be suspended, except in case of rebellion or invasion; and then, only if the public safety demand it.

Sec. 28. Treason against the State shall consist only in levying war against it, and in giving aid and comfort to its enemies.

Sec. 29. No person shall be convicted of treason, except on the testimony of two witnesses to the same overt act, or upon his confession in open court.

Sec. 30. No conviction shall work corruption of blood, or forfeiture of estate.

Sec. 31. No law shall restrain any of the inhabitants of the State from assembling together in a peaceable manner, to consult for their common good; nor from instructing their representatives; nor from applying to the General Assembly for redress of grievances.

Sec. 32. The people shall have a right to bear arms, for the defense of themselves and the State.

Sec. 33. The military shall be kept into strict subordination to the civil power.

Sec. 34. No soldier shall, in time of peace, be quartered in any house, without the consent of the owner; nor, in time of war, but in a manner to be prescribed by law.

Sec. 35. The General Assembly shall not grant any title of nobility, nor confer hereditary distinctions.

Sec. 36. Emigration from the State shall not be prohibited.

Sec. 37. There shall be neither slavery, nor involuntary servitude, within the State, otherwise than for punishment of crimes, whereof the party shall have been duly convicted. No indenture of any Negro or Mulatto, made and executed out of the bounds of the State, shall be valid within the State.

ARTICLE II: Suffrage and Elections.

Section 1. All elections shall be free and equal.

Sec. 2. In all elections, not otherwise provided for by this Constitution, every white male citizen of the United States, of the age of twenty-one years and upwards, who shall have resided in the State during the six months immediately preceding such election; and every white male, of foreign birth, of the age of twenty-one years and upwards, who shall have resided in the United States one year, and shall have resided in this State during the six months immediately preceding such election, and shall have declared his intention to become a citizen of the United States, conformably to the laws of the United States on the subject of naturalization; shall be entitled to vote, in the township or precinct where he may reside.

Sec. 3. No soldier, seaman, or marine, in the army or navy of the United States, or of their allies, shall be deemed to have acquired a residence in the State, in consequence of having been stationed within the same; nor shall any such soldier, seaman, or marine, have the right to vote.

Sec. 4. No person shall be deemed to have lost his residence in the State, by reason of his absence, either on business of this State or of the United States.

Sec. 5. No Negro or Mulatto shall have the right of suffrage.

Sec. 6. Every person shall be disqualified from holding office, during the term for which he may have been elected, who shall have given or offered a bribe, threat, or reward, to procure his election.

Sec. 7. Every person who shall give or accept a challenge to fight a duel, or who shall knowingly carry to another person such a challenge, or who shall agree to go out of the State to fight a duel, shall be ineligible to any office of trust or profit.

Sec. 8. The General Assembly shall have power to deprive of the right of suffrage, and to render ineligible, any person convicted of an infamous crime.

Sec. 9. No person holding a lucrative office or appointment, under the United States or this State, shall be eligible to a seat in the General Assembly; nor shall any person hold more than one lucrative office at the same time, except as in this Constitution expressly permitted: *Provided*, that offices in the militia to which there is attached no annual salary, and the office of Deputy Postmaster where the compensation does not exceed ninety dollars per annum, shall not be deemed lucrative: *And provided, also*, that counties containing less than one thousand polls, may confer the office of Clerk, Recorder, and Auditor, or any two of said offices, upon the same person.

Sec. 10. No person who may hereafter be a collector, or holder of public moneys, shall be eligible to any office of trust or profit, until he shall have accounted for, and paid over, according to law, all sums for which he may be liable.

Sec. 11. In all cases in which it is provided that an office shall not be filled by the same person more than a certain number of years continuously, an appointment *pro tempore* shall not be reckoned a part of that term.

Sec. 12. In all cases, except treason, felony, and breach of the peace, electors shall be free from arrest, in going to elections, during their attendance there, and in returning from the same.

Sec. 13. All elections by the people shall be by ballot; and all elections by the General Assembly, or by either branch thereof, shall be *viva voce*.

Sec. 14. All general elections shall be held on the second Tuesday in October.

ARTICLE III: Distribution of Powers.

Section 1. The powers of the Government are divided into three separate departments; the Legislative, the Executive including the Administrative, and the Judicial; and no person, charged with official duties under one of these departments, shall exercise any of the functions of another, except as in this Constitution expressly provided.

ARTICLE IV: Legislative.

Section 1. The Legislative authority of the State shall be vested in a General Assembly, which shall consist of a Senate and a House of Representatives. The style of every law shall be: "Be it enacted by the General Assembly of the State of Indiana;" and no law shall be enacted, except by bill.

Sec. 2. The Senate shall not exceed fifty, nor the House of Representatives one hundred members; and they shall be chosen by the electors of the respective counties or districts, into which the State may, from time to time, be divided.

Sec. 3. Senators shall be elected for the term of four years, and Representatives for the term of two years, from the day next after their general election: *Provided, however*, that the Senators elect, at the second meeting of the General Assembly under this Constitution shall be divided, by lot, into two equal classes, as nearly as may be; and the seats of Senators of the first class shall be vacated at the expiration of two years, and of those of the second class at the expiration of four years; so that one-half, as nearly as possible, shall be chosen biennially forever thereafter. And in case of increase in the number of Senators, they shall be so annexed, by lot, to one or the other of the two classes, as to keep them as nearly equal as practicable.

Sec. 4. The General Assembly shall, at its second session after the adoption of this Constitution, and every sixth year thereafter, cause an enumeration to be made of all the white male inhabitants over the age of twenty-one years.

Sec. 5. The number of Senators and Representatives shall, at the session next following each period of making such enumeration, be fixed by law, and apportioned among the several counties, according to the number of white male inhabitants above twenty-one years of age, in each: *Provided*, that the first and second elections of members of the General Assembly, under this Constitution, shall be according to the apportionment last made by the General Assembly, before the adoption of this Constitution.

Sec. 6. A Senatorial or Representative district, where more than one county shall constitute a district, shall be composed of contiguous counties; and no county, for Senatorial apportionment, shall ever be divided.

Sec. 7. No person shall be a Senator or Representative who, at the time of his election, is not a citizen of the United States; nor any one who has not been, for two years next preceding his election, an inhabitant of this State, and, for one year next preceding his election, an inhabitant of the county or district, whence he may be chosen. Senators shall be at least twenty-five, and Representatives at least twenty-one years of age.

Sec. 8. Senators and Representatives, in all cases except treason, felony and breach of the peace, shall be privileged from arrest, during the session of the General Assembly, and in going to and returning from the same; and shall not be subject to any civil process, during the session of the General Assembly, nor during the fifteen days next before the commencement thereof. For any speech or debate in either House, a member shall not be questioned in any other place.

Sec. 9. The sessions of the General Assembly shall be held biennially at the capital of the State, commencing on the Thursday next after the first Monday of January, in the year one thousand eight hundred and fifty-three, and on the same day of every second year thereafter, unless a different day or place shall have been appointed by law. But if, in the opinion of the Governor, the public welfare shall require it, he may, at any time, by proclamation, call a special session.

Sec. 10. Each House, when assembled, shall choose its own officers, (the President of the Senate excepted,) judge the elections, qualifications, and returns of its own members, determine its rules of proceeding and sit upon its own adjournment. But neither house shall, without the consent of the other, adjourn for more than three days, nor to any place other than that in which it may be sitting.

Sec. 11. Two-thirds of each House shall constitute a quorum to do business; but a smaller number may meet, adjourn from day to day, and compel the attendance of absent members. A quorum being in attendance, if either House fail to effect an organization within the first five days thereafter, the members of the House so failing, shall be entitled to no compensation, from the end of the said five days until an organization shall have been effected.

Sec. 12. Each House shall keep a journal of its proceedings, and publish the same. The yeas and nays, on a question, shall, at the request of any two members, be entered, together with the names of the members demanding the same, on the journal: *Provided*, that on a motion to adjourn, it shall require one-tenth of the members present to order the yeas and nays.

Sec. 13. The doors of each House, and of Committees of the Whole, shall be kept open, except in such cases as, in the opinion of either House, may require secrecy.

Sec. 14. Either House may punish its members for disorderly behavior, and may, with the concurrence of two-thirds, expel a member; but not a second time for the same cause.

Sec. 15. Either House, during its session, may punish, by imprisonment, any person not a member, who shall have been guilty of disrespect to the House, by disorderly or contemptuous behavior, in its presence; but such imprisonment shall not, at any one time, exceed twenty-four hours.

Sec. 16. Each House shall have all powers necessary for the branch of the legislative department of a free and independent State.

Sec. 17. Bills may originate in either House, but may be rejected or amended in the other, except that bills for raising revenue shall originate in the House of Representatives.

Sec. 18. Every bill shall be read, by sections, on three several days, in each House; unless, in case of emergency, two-thirds of the House where such bill may be depending, shall, by vote of yeas and nays, deem it expedient to dispense with this rule; but the reading of a bill by sections on its final passage, shall, in no case, be dispensed with; and the vote on the passage of every bill or joint resolution shall be taken by yeas and nays.

Sec. 19. Every act shall embrace but one subject and matters properly connected therewith; which subject shall be expressed in the title. But if any subject shall be embraced in an act, which shall not be expressed in the title, such an act shall be void only as to so much thereof as shall not be expressed in the title.

Sec. 20. Every act and joint resolution shall be plainly worded, avoiding, as far as practicable, the use of technical terms.

Sec. 21. No act shall ever be revised or amended by mere reference to its title; but the act revised, or section amended, shall be set forth and published at full length.

Sec. 22. The General Assembly shall not pass local or special laws, in any of the following enumerated cases, that is to say:

Regulating the jurisdiction and duties of Justices of the Peace and of Constables;

For the punishment of crimes and misdemeanors;

Regulating the practice in courts of justice;

Providing for changing the venue in civil and criminal cases;

Granting divorces;

For laying out, opening, and working on, highways, and for the election or appointment of supervisors;

Vacating roads, town plats, streets, alleys, and public squares;

Summoning and empanelling grand and petit juries, and providing for their compensation;

For the assessment and collection of taxes for State, county, township, or road purposes;

Providing for supporting common schools, and the preservation of school funds;

In relation to fees or salaries;

In relation to interest on money;

Providing for opening and conducting elections of State, county, or township officers, and designating the places of voting;

Providing for the sale of real estate belonging to minors or other persons laboring under legal disabilities, by executors, administrators, guardians, or trustees.

Sec. 23. In all cases enumerated in the preceding section, and in all cases where a general law can be made applicable, all laws shall be general, and uniform operation through out the State.

Sec. 24. Provision may be made, by general law, for bringing suit against the State, as to all liabilities originating after the adoption of this Constitution; but no special act authorizing such suit to be brought, or making compensation to any person claiming damages against the State shall ever be placed.

Sec. 25. A majority of all members elected to each House, shall be necessary to pass every bill or joint resolution; and all bills and joint resolutions so passed shall be signed by the Presiding Officers of the respective Houses.

Sec. 26. Any member of either House shall have the right to protest, and to have his protest, with his reasons for dissent, entered on the journal.

Sec. 27. Every statute shall be a public law, unless otherwise declared in the statue itself.

Sec. 28. No act shall take effect until the same shall have been published and circulated in the several counties of the State, by authority, except in cases of emergency, which emergency shall be declared in the preamble or in the body of the law.

Sec. 29. The members of the General Assembly shall receive, for their services, a compensation to be fixed by law; but no increase of compensation shall take effect during the session at which such increase may be made. No session of the General Assembly, except the first under this Constitution, shall extend beyond the term of sixty-one days, nor any special session beyond the term of forty days.

Sec. 30. No Senator or Representative shall, during the term for which he may have been elected, be eligible to any office, the election to which is vested in the General Assembly; nor shall he be appointed to any civil office of profit, which shall have been created, or the emoluments of which shall have been increased during such term; but this latter provision shall not be construed to apply to any office elective by the People.

ARTICLE V: Executive.

Section 1. The executive power of the State shall be vested in a Governor. He shall hold his office during four years, and shall not be eligible more than four years, in any period of eight years.

Sec. 2. There shall be a Lieutenant Governor, who shall hold his office during four years.

Sec. 3. The Governor and Lieutenant Governor shall be elected at the times and places of choosing members of the General Assembly.

Sec. 4. In voting for Governor and Lieutenant Governor, the electors shall designate for whom they vote as Governor, and for whom as Lieutenant Governor. The returns of every election for Governor and Lieutenant Governor shall be sealed up and transmitted to the seat of government, directed to the speaker of the House of Representatives, who shall open and publish them in the presence of both houses of the General Assembly.

Sec. 5. The persons, respectively, having the highest number of votes for Governor and Lieutenant Governor, shall be elected; but in case two or more persons shall have an equal and the highest number of votes for either office, the General Assembly shall, by joint vote, forthwith proceed to elect one of the said persons Governor or Lieutenant Governor as the case may be.

Sec. 6. Contested elections for Governor or Lieutenant Governor, shall be determined by the General Assembly, in such manner as may be prescribed by law.

Sec. 7. No person shall be eligible to the office of Governor or Lieutenant Governor, who shall not have been five years a citizen of the United States, and also a resident of the State of Indiana during the five years next preceding his election; nor shall any person be eligible to either of the said offices, who shall not have attained the age of thirty years.

Sec. 8. No member of Congress, or person holding any office under the United States or under this State, shall fill the office of Governor or Lieutenant Governor.

Sec. 9. The official term of the Governor and Lieutenant Governor shall commence on the second Monday of January, in the year one thousand eight hundred and fifty-three; and on the same day every fourth year thereafter.

Sec. 10. In case of the removal of the Governor from office, or of his death, resignation, or inabilities to discharge the duties of the office, the same shall devolve on the Lieutenant Governor; and the General Assembly shall by law, provide for the case of removal from office, death, resignation, or inability, both of the Governor and Lieutenant Governor, declaring what officer shall then act as Governor; and such officer shall act accordingly, until the disability be removed, or a Governor shall be elected.

Sec. 11. Whenever the Lieutenant Governor shall act as Governor, or shall be unable to attend as President of the Senate, the Senate shall elect one of its own members as President for the occasion.

Sec. 12. The Governor shall be commander-in-chief of the military and naval forces, and may call out such forces, to execute the laws, or to suppress insurrection, or to repel invasion.

Sec. 13. He shall, from time to time, give to the General Assembly information touching the condition of the State, and recommend such measures as he shall judge to be expedient.

Sec. 14. Every bill which shall have passed both Houses of the General Assembly, shall be presented to the Governor; if he approve, he shall sign it; but if not, he shall return it, with his objections, to the House in which it shall have originated, which House shall enter the objections, at large, upon its journals, and proceed to reconsider the bill. If, after such reconsideration, a majority of all the members elected to that House shall agree to pass the bill, it shall be sent, with the Governor's objections, to the other House, by which it shall likewise be reconsidered; and, if approved by a majority of all of the members elected to that House, it shall be a law. If any bill shall not be returned by the Governor within three days (Sundays excepted) after it shall have been presented to him, it shall be a law in like manner as if he had signed it, unless the general adjournment shall prevent its return, in which case it shall be a law, unless the Governor, within five days next after such adjournment, shall file such bill, with his objections thereto, in the office of Secretary of State, who shall lay the same before the General Assembly, at its next session, in like manner as if it had been returned by the Governor. But no bill shall be presented to the Governor, within two days next previous to the final adjournment of the General Assembly.

Sec. 15. The Governor shall transact all necessary business with the officers of government, and may require information in writing from the officers of the administrative department, upon any subject relating to the duties of their respective offices.

Sec. 16. He shall take care that the laws be faithfully executed.

Sec. 17. He shall have the power to grant reprieves, commutations, and pardons, after conviction, for all offenses except treason and cases of impeachment, subject to such regulations as may be provided by law. Upon conviction for treason, he shall have power to suspend the execution of the sentence, until the case shall be reported to the General Assembly, at its next meeting; when the General Assembly shall either grant a pardon, commute the sentence, direct the execution of the sentence, or grant a further reprieve. He shall have power to remit fines and forfeitures, under such regulations as may be prescribed by law, and shall report to the General Assembly, at its next meeting, each case of reprieve, commutation, or pardon granted, and also the names of all persons in whose favor remission of fines and forfeitures shall have been made, and the several accounts remitted: *Provided, however*, that the General Assembly may, by law, constitute a council to be composed of officers of State, without whose advice and consent the Governor shall not have power to grant pardons, in any case, except such as may, by law, be left to his sole power.

Sec. 18. When, during a recess of the General Assembly, a vacancy shall happen in any office, the appointment to which is vested in the General Assembly; or when at any time a vacancy shall have occurred in any other State office, or in the office of Judge of any court, the Governor shall fill such vacancy, by appointment, which shall expire when a successor shall have been elected and qualified.

Sec. 19. He shall issue writs of election to fill such vacancies as may have occurred in the General Assembly.

Sec. 20. Should the seat of government become dangerous from disease or a common enemy, he may convene the General Assembly at any other place.

Sec. 21. The Lieutenant Governor shall, by virtue of his office, be President of the Senate; have a right, when in committee of the whole, to join in debate, and to vote on all subjects; and, whenever the Senate shall be equally divided, he shall give the casting vote.

Sec. 22. The Governor shall, at stated times, receive for his services a compensation, which shall neither be increased nor diminished during the term for which he shall have been elected.

Sec. 23. The Lieutenant Governor, while he shall act as President of the Senate, shall receive, for his services, the same compensation as the Speaker of the House of Representatives; and any person acting as Governor, shall receive the compensation attached to the office of Governor.

Sec. 24. Neither the Governor nor Lieutenant Governor shall be eligible to any other office, during the term for which he shall have been elected.

ARTICLE VI: Administrative.

Section 1. There shall be elected, by the voters of the State, a Secretary, an Auditor, and a Treasurer of State, who shall, severally, hold their office for two years. They shall perform such duties as shall be enjoined by law, and no person shall be eligible to either of said offices more than four years in any term of six years.

Sec. 2. There shall be elected, in each county by the voters thereof, at the time of holding general elections, a Clerk of the Circuit Court, Auditor, Recorder, Treasurer, Sheriff, Corner, and Surveyor. The Clerk, Auditor, and Recorder shall continue in office four years, and no person shall be eligible to the office of Clerk, Recorder, or Auditor more than eight years in any period of twelve years. The Treasurer, Sheriff, Coroner, and Surveyor, shall continue in office two years, and no person shall be eligible to the office of Treasurer or Sheriff, more than four years in any period of six years.

Sec. 3. Such other county and township officers as may be necessary, shall be elected, or appointed, in such manner as may be prescribed by law.

Sec. 4. No person shall be elected, or appointed, as a county officer, who shall not be an elector of the county, nor any one who shall not have been an inhabitant thereof during one year next proceeding his appointment, if the county shall have been so long organized; but if the county shall not have been so long organized, then within the limits of the county or counties, out of which the same shall have been taken.

Sec. 5. The Governor, and the Secretary, Auditor, and Treasurer of State, shall, severally, reside and keep the public records, books, and papers, in any manner relating to their respective offices, at the seat of government.

Sec. 6. All county, township, and town officers, shall reside within their respective counties, townships, and towns; and shall keep their respective offices at such places therein, and perform such duties, as may be directed by law.

Sec. 7. All State officers shall, for crime, incapacity, or negligence, be liable to be removed from office, either by impeachment by the House of Representatives, to be tried by the Senate, or by a joint resolution of the General Assembly; two-thirds of the members elected to each branch voting, in either case, therefor.

Sec. 8. All State, county, township, and town officers, may be impeached, or removed from office, in such manner as may be prescribed by law.

Sec. 9. Vacancies in county, township, and town offices, shall be filled in such manner as may be prescribed by law.

Sec. 10. The General Assembly may confer upon the board, doing county business in the several counties, powers of a local, administrative character.

ARTICLE VII: Judicial.

Section 1. The Judicial power of the State shall be vested in a Supreme Court, in Circuit Courts, and in such inferior Courts as the General Assembly may establish.

Sec. 2. The Supreme Court shall consist of not less than three, nor more than five Judges; a majority of whom shall form a quorum. They shall hold their offices for six years, if they so long behave well.

Sec. 3. The State shall be divided into as many districts as there are Judges of the Supreme Court; and such districts shall be formed of contiguous territory, as nearly equal in population, as, without dividing a county, the same can be made. One of said Judges shall be elected from each district, and reside therein; but said Judges shall be elected by the electors of the State at large.

Sec. 4. The Supreme Court shall have jurisdiction, co-extensive with the limits of the State, in appeals and writs of error, under such regulations and restrictions as may be prescribed by law. It shall also have such original jurisdiction as the General Assembly may confer.

Sec. 5. The Supreme Court shall, upon the decision of every case, give a statement in writing of each question arising in the record of such case, and the decision of the Court thereon.

Sec. 6. The General Assembly shall provide, by law, for the speedy publication of the decisions of the Supreme Court, made under this Constitution; but no Judge shall be allowed to report such decisions.

Sec. 7. There shall be elected by the voters of the State, a Clerk of the Supreme Court, who shall hold his office four years, and whose duties shall be prescribed by law.

Sec. 8. The Circuit Courts shall each consist of one Judge, and shall have such civil and criminal jurisdiction as may be prescribed by law.

Sec. 9. The State shall, from the time to time, be divided into judicial Circuits; and a Judge for each Circuit, shall be elected by voters thereof. He shall reside within the Circuit, and shall hold his office for the term of six years, if he so long behave well.

Sec. 10. The General Assembly may provide by law, that the Judge of one Circuit may hold the Courts of another Circuit, in case of necessity or convenience; and in case of temporary inability of any Judge, from sickness or other cause, to hold the Courts in his Circuit, provision may be made, by law, for holding such courts.

Sec. 11. There shall be elected, in each Judicial Circuit, by the voters thereof, a Prosecuting Attorney, who shall hold his office for two years.

Sec. 12. Any Judge or Prosecuting Attorney, who shall have been convicted of corruption or other high crime, may, on information in the name of the State, be removed from office by the Supreme Court, or in such other manner as may be prescribed by law.

Sec. 13. The Judges of the Supreme Court and Circuit Courts shall, at stated times, receive a compensation, which shall not be diminished during their continuance in office.

Sec. 14. A competent number of Justices of the Peace shall be elected, by the voters in each township in the several counties. They shall continue in office four years, and their powers and duties shall be prescribed by law.

Sec. 15. All judicial officers shall be conservators of the peace in their respective jurisdictions.

Sec. 16. No person elected to any judicial office, shall, during the term for which he shall have been elected, be eligible to any office of trust or profit, under the State, other than a judicial office.

Sec. 17. The General Assembly may modify, or abolish, the Grand Jury system.

Sec. 18. All criminal persecutions shall be carried on, in the name, and by the authority, of the State; and the style of all process shall be: "The State of Indiana."

Sec. 19. Tribunals of conciliation may be established, with such powers and duties as shall be prescribed by law; or the powers and duties of the same may be conferred upon other Courts of justice; but such tribunals or other Courts when sitting as such, shall have no power to render judgment to be obligatory on the parties, unless they voluntarily submit their matters of difference, and agree to abide by the judgment of such tribunal or Court.

Sec. 20. The General Assembly at its first session after the adoption of this Constitution, shall provide for the appointment of three commissioners, whose duty it shall be to revise, simplify, and abridge, the rules, practice, pleadings and forms, of the Courts of justice. And they shall provide for abolishing the distinct forms of action at law, now in use; and that justice shall be administered in a uniform mode of pleading, without distinction between law and equity. And the General Assembly may, also, make it the duty of said Commissioners to reduce into a systematic code, the general statue law of the Sate; and said Commissioners shall report the result of their labors to the General Assembly, with such recommendations and suggestions, as to abridgement and amendment, as to said Commissioners may seem necessary or proper. Provision shall be made, by law, for filling vacancies, regulating the tenure of office, and the compensation of said Commissioners.

Sec. 21. Every person of good moral character, being a voter, shall be entitled to admission to practice law in all Courts of justice.

ARTICLE VIII: Education.

Section 1. Knowledge and learning, generally diffused throughout a community, being essential to the preservation of a free government; it shall be the duty of the General Assembly to encourage, by all suitable means, moral, intellectual, scientific, and agricultural improvement; and to provide, by law, for a general and uniform system of Common Schools, wherein tuition shall be without charge, and equally open to all.

Sec. 2. The Community School fund shall consist of the Congressional Township fund, and the lands belonging thereto;

The Surplus Revenue fund;

The Saline fund and the lands belonging thereto;

The Bank Tax fund, and the fund arising from the one hundred and fourteenth section of the charter of the State Bank of Indiana;

The fund to be derived from the sale of County Seminaries, and the moneys and property heretofore held for such Seminaries; from the fines assessed for breaches of the penal laws of the State; and from all forfeitures which may accrue;

All lands and other estate which shall escheat to the State for the want of heirs or kindred entitled to the inheritance;

All lands that have been, or may hereafter be, granted to this State, where no special purpose is expressed in the grant, and the proceeds of the sales thereof; the net proceeds of the sales of the Swamp Lands, granted to the State of Indiana by the act of Congress of 28th September, 1850, after deducting the expense of selecting and draining the same;

Taxes on the property of corporations, that may be assessed by the General Assembly for Common School purposes.

Sec. 3. The principal of the Common School fund shall remain a perpetual fund, which may be increased, but shall never be diminished; and the income thereof shall be inviolably appropriated to the support of Common Schools, and no other purpose whatever.

Sec. 4. The General Assembly shall invest, in some safe and profitable manner, all such portion of the Common School fund, as have not heretofore been entrusted to the several counties; and shall make provision, by law, for the distribution, among the several counties, of the interest thereof.

Sec. 5. If any county shall fail to demand its proportion of such interest, for Common School purposes, the same shall be re-invested, for the benefit of such county.

Sec. 6. The several counties shall be held liable for the preservation of so much of the said fund as may be entrusted to them, and for the payment of the annual interest thereon.

Sec. 7. All trust funds, held by the State, shall remain inviolate, and be faithfully and exclusively applied to the purposes for which the trust was created.

Sec. 8. The General Assembly shall provide for the election, by the voters of the State, of a State Superintendent of Public

Instruction; who shall hold his office for two years, and whose duties and compensation shall be prescribed by law.

ARTICLE IX: State Institutions.

Section 1. It shall be the duty of the General Assembly to provide, by law, for the support of Institutions for the education of the Deaf and Dumb, and of the Blind; and also, for the treatment of the Insane.

Sec. 2. The General Assembly shall provide Houses of Refuge, for the correction and reformation of juvenile offenders.

Sec. 3. The county boards shall have power to provide farms, as an asylum for those persons, who, by reason of age, infirmity, or other misfortune, may have a claim upon the sympathies and aid of society.

ARTICLE X: Finance.

Section 1. The General Assembly shall provide, by law, for a uniform and equal rate of assessment and taxation; and shall prescribe such regulations as shall secure a just valuation for taxation for all property, both real and personal, excepting such only for municipal, educational, literary, scientific, religious, or charitable purposes, as may be specially exempted by law.

Sec. 2. All the revenues derived from the sale of any of the public works belonging to the State, and from the net annual income thereof, and any surplus that may, at any time, remain in the Treasury, derived from taxation for general State purposes, after the payment of the ordinary expenses of the government, and of the interest on bonds of the State, other than Bank bonds; shall be annually applied, under the direction of the General Assembly, to the payment of the principal of the Public Debt.

Sec. 3. No money shall be drawn from the Treasury, but in pursuance of appropriations made by law.

Sec. 4. An accurate statement of the receipts and expenditures of the public money, shall be published with the laws of each regular session of the General Assembly.

Sec. 5. No law shall authorize any debt to be contracted, on behalf of the State, except in the following cases: to meet annual deficits in the revenue; to pay the interest on the State Debt; to repel invasion, suppress insurrection, or if hostilities are threatened, provide for the public defense.

Sec. 6. No county shall subscribe for stock in any corporated company, unless the same be paid for at the time of such subscription; nor shall any county loan its credit to any incorporated company, nor borrow money for the purpose of taking stock in any such company; nor shall the General Assembly ever, on behalf of the State, assume the debts of any county, city, town, or township; nor of any corporation whatever.

ARTICLE XI: Corporations.

Section 1. The General Assembly shall not have power to establish, or incorporate, any bank or banking company, or moneyed institution, for the purpose of issuing bills of credit, or bills payable to order or bearer, except under the conditions prescribed in this Constitution.

Sec. 2. No banks shall be established other than under a general banking law, except as provided in the fourth section of this article.

Sec. 3. If the General Assembly shall enact a general banking law, such law shall provide for the registry and countersigning, by an officer of the State, of all paper credit designed to be circulated as money; and ample collateral security, readily convertible into specie, for the redemption of the same in gold or silver, shall be required; which collateral security shall be under the control of the proper officer or officers of State.

Sec. 4. The General Assembly may also charter a bank with branches, without collateral security as required in the proceeding section.

Sec. 5. If the General Assembly shall establish a bank with branches, the branches shall be mutually responsible for each other's liabilities upon all paper credit issued as money.

Sec. 6. The stockholders in every bank or banking company shall be individually responsible, to an amount over and above their stock, equal to their respective shares of stock, for all debts or liabilities of said bank or banking company.

Sec. 7. All bills or notes issued as money shall be, at all times, redeemable in gold or silver; and no law shall be passed, sanctioning, directly or indirectly, the suspension by any bank or banking company, of specie payments.

Sec. 8. Holders of bank notes shall be entitled, in case of insolvency, to preference of payment over all other creditors.

Sec. 9. No bank shall receive, directly or indirectly, a greater rate of interest than shall be allowed, by law, to individuals loaning money.

Sec. 10. Every bank or banking company shall be required to cease all banking operations within twenty years from the time of its organization, and promptly thereafter to close its business.

Sec. 11. The General Assembly is not prohibited from investing the Trust Funds in a bank with branches; but, in case of such investment, the safety of the same shall be guarantied by unquestionable security.

Sec. 12. The State shall not be a stockholder in any bank, after the expiration of the present bank charter: nor shall the credit of the State ever be given, or loaned, in aid of any person, association, or corporation; nor shall the State hereafter become a stockholder in any corporation or association.

Sec. 13. Corporations, other than banking, shall not be created by special act, but may be formed under general laws.

Sec. 14. Dues from corporations, other than banking, shall be secured by such individual liability of the corporators, or other means, as may be prescribed by law.

ARTICLE XII: Militia.

Section 1. The militia shall consist of all able-bodied white male persons, between the ages of eighteen and forty-five years, except such as may be exempted by the laws of the United States, or of this State; and shall be organized, officered, armed, equipped, and trained, in such manner as may be provided by law.

Sec. 2. The Governor shall appoint the Adjutant, Quartermaster, and Commissary Generals.

Sec. 3. All militia officers shall be commissioned by the Governor, and shall hold their offices not longer than six years.

Sec. 4. The General Assembly shall, by law, determine the method of dividing the militia into divisions, brigades, regiments, battalions, and companies, and fix the rank of all staff officers.

Sec. 5. The militia may be divided into classes of sedentary and active militia, in such manner as shall be prescribed by law.

Sec. 6. No person, conscientiously scrupulous of bearing arms, shall be compelled to do militia duty; but such person shall pay an equivalent for exemption; the amount to be prescribed by law.

ARTICLE XIII: Negroes and Mulattoes.

Section 1. No Negro or Mulatto shall come into, or settle in the State, after the adoption of this Constitution.

Sec. 2. All contracts, made with any Negro or Mulatto coming into this State contrary to the provision of the foregoing section, shall be void; and all persons who shall employ such Negro or Mulatto, or otherwise encourage him to remain in the State, shall be fined in any sum not less than ten dollars, nor more than five hundred dollars.

Sec. 3. All fines which may be collected for a violation of the provisions of this article, or of any law which may hereafter be passed, for the purpose of carrying the same into execution, shall be set apart and appropriated for the colonization of such Negroes and Mulattoes and their descendants, as may be in the State at the adoption of this Constitution, and may be willing to emigrate.

Sec. 4. The General Assembly shall pass laws to carry out the provisions of this article.

ARTICLE XIV: Boundaries.

Section 1. In order that the boundaries of the State may be known and established, it is hereby ordained and declared, that the State of Indiana is bounded, on the East, by the meridian line, which forms the western boundary of the State of Ohio; on the South, by the Ohio river, from the mouth of the Great Miami river to the mouth of the Wabash river; on the East, by the line drawn along the middle of the Wabash river, from its mouth to a point where a due north line, drawn from the town of Vincennes, would last touch the north-western shore of said Wabash river; and, thence, by a due north line, until the same shall intersect an east and west line, drawn from a point ten miles north of the southern extreme of Lake Michigan; on the North, by said east and west line, until the same shall intersect the first mentioned meridian line, which forms the western boundary of the State of Ohio.

Sec. 2. The State of Indiana shall possess jurisdiction and sovereignty co-extensive with the boundaries declared in the preceding section; and shall have concurrent jurisdiction, in civil and criminal cases, with the State of Kentucky on the Ohio river, and with the State of Illinois on the Wabash river, so far as said rivers form the common boundary between this State and said States respectively.

ARTICLE XV: Miscellaneous.

Section 1. All officers, whose appointment is not otherwise provided for in this Constitution, shall be chosen in such manner as now is, or may hereafter be, prescribed by law.

Sec. 2. When the duration of any office is not provided for by this Constitution, it may be declared by law; and, if not so declared, such office shall be held during the pleasure of the authority making the appointment. But the General Assembly shall not create any office, the tenure of which shall be longer than four years.

Sec. 3. Whenever it is provided in this Constitution, or in any law which may be hereafter passed, that any officer, other than a member of the General Assembly, shall hold his office for any given term, the same shall be construed to mean, that such officer shall hold his office for such term, and until his successor shall have been elected and qualified.

Sec. 4. Every person elected or appointed to any office under this Constitution, shall, before entering on the duties thereof, take an oath or affirmation, to support the Constitution of this State, and of the United States, and also an oath of office.

Sec. 5. There shall be a Seal of State, kept by the Governor for official purposes, which shall be called the Seal of the State of Indiana.

Sec. 6. All commissions shall issue in the name of the State, shall be signed by the Governor, sealed with the State Seal, and attested by the Secretary of State.

Sec. 7. No county shall be reduced to an area less than four hundred square miles; nor shall any county under that area, be further reduced.

Sec. 8. No lottery shall be authorized; nor the sale of lottery tickets be allowed.

Sec. 9. The following grounds owned by the State in Indianapolis, namely: the State House Square, the Governor's Circle, and so much of out-lot numbered one hundred and forty-seven, as lies north of the arm of the Central Canal, shall not be sold or leased.

Sec. 10. It shall be the duty of the General Assembly, to provide for the permanent enclosure and preservation of the Tippecanoe Battle Ground.

ARTICLE XVI: Amendments.

Section 1. Any amendment or amendments to this Constitution, may be proposed in either branch of the General Assembly; and, if the same shall be agreed to by a majority of the members elected to the two Houses, such proposed amendment or amendments shall, with the yeas and nays thereon, be entered on their journals, and referred to the General Assembly to be chosen at the next general election; and if, in the General Assembly so next chosen, such proposed amendment or amendments shall be agreed to by a majority of all the members elected to each house, then it shall be the duty of the General Assembly to submit such amendment or amendments to the electors of the State; and if a majority of said electors shall ratify the same, such amendment or amendments shall become a part of this Constitution.

Sec. 2. If two or more amendments be submitted at the same time, they shall be submitted in such manner that the electors shall vote for or against each of such amendments separately; and while an amendment or amendments, which shall have been agreed upon by one General Assembly, shall be awaiting the action of a succeeding General Assembly, or of the electors, no additional amendment or amendments shall be proposed.

SCHEDULE.

This Constitution, if adopted, shall take effect on the first day of November, in the year one thousand eight hundred and fifty-one, and shall supersede the Constitution adopted in the year one thousand eight hundred and sixteen. That no inconvenience may arise from the change in the government, it is hereby ordained as follows:

First. All laws now in force, and not inconsistent with this Constitution, shall remain in force, until they shall expire or be repealed.

Second. All indictments, prosecutions, suits, pleas, plaints, and other proceedings, pending in any of the courts, shall be persecuted to final judgment and execution; and all appeals, writs of error, certiorari, and injunctions, shall be carried on in the several courts, in the same manner as is now provided by law.

Third. All fines, penalties, and forfeitures, due or accruing to the State, or to any county therein, shall inure to the State, or to such county, in the manner prescribed by law. All bonds executed to the State, or any officer, in his official capacity, shall remain in force, and inure to the use of those concerned.

Fourth. All acts of incorporation for municipal purposes shall continue in force under this Constitution, until such time as the General Assembly shall, in its discretion, modify or repeal the same.

Fifth. The Governor, at the expiration of the present official term, shall continue to act, until his successor shall have been sworn into office.

Sixth. There shall be a session of the General Assembly, commencing on the first Monday of December, in the year one thousand eight hundred and fifty-one.

Seventh. Senators now in office and holding over, under the existing Constitution, and such as may be elected at the next general election, and the Representatives then elected, shall continue in office until the first general election under this Constitution.

Eighth. The first general election under this Constitution, shall be held in the year one thousand eight hundred and fifty-two.

Ninth. The first election for Governor, Lieutenant Governor, Judges of the Supreme Court and Circuit Courts, Clerk of the Supreme Court, Prosecuting Attorneys, Secretary, Auditor, and Treasurer of State, and State Superintendent of Public Instruction, under this Constitution, shall be held at the first general election in the year one thousand eight hundred and fifty-two; and such of said officers as may be in office when this Constitution shall go into effect, shall continue in their respective offices, until their successors shall have been elected and qualified.

Tenth. Every person elected by popular vote, and now in office which is continued by this Constitution, and every person who shall be so elected to any such office before the taking effect of this Constitution (except as in this Constitution otherwise provided), shall continue in office until the term of which such person has been, or may be elected, shall expire: *Provided*, that no such person shall continue in office, after the taking effect of this Constitution, for a longer period than the term of such office in this Constitution prescribed.

Eleventh. On the taking effect of this Constitution, all officers thereby continued in office, shall, before proceeding in the further discharge of their duties, take an oath or affirmation to support this Constitution.

Twelfth. All vacancies that may occur in existing offices, prior to the first general election under this Constitution, shall be filled in the manner now prescribed by law.

Thirteenth. At the time of submitting this Constitution to the electors, for their approval or disapproval, the article numbered thirteen, in relation to Negroes and Mulattoes, shall be submitted as a distinct proposition, in the following form: "Exclusion and Colonization of Negroes and Mulattoes," "Aye" or "No." And should a majority of the votes cast be in favor of said article, then the same shall form a part of this Constitution; otherwise it shall be void, and form no part thereof.

Fourteenth. No Article or Section of this Constitution shall be submitted, as a distinct proposition: to a vote of the electors, otherwise than as herein provided.

Fifteenth. Whenever a portion of the citizens of the counties of Perry and Spencer, shall deem it expedient to form, of the contiguous territory of said counties, a new county, it shall be the duty of those interested in the organization of such new county, to lay off the same, by proper metes and bounds, of equal portions as nearly as practicable, not to exceed one-third of the territory of each of said counties. The proposal to create such new county shall be submitted to the voters of said counties, at a general election, in such manner as shall be subscribed by law. And if a majority of all the votes given at said election, shall be in favor of the organization of said new county, it shall be the duty of the General Assembly to organize the same, out of the territory thus designated.

Sixteenth. The General Assembly may alter or amend the charter of Clarksville, and make such regulations as may be necessary for carrying into effect the objects contemplated in granting the same; and the funds belonging to said town shall be applied, according to the intention of the grantor.

[1] *Report of the Debates and Proceedings of the Convention for the Revision of the Constitution of the State of Indiana, 1850* (Indianapolis: A. H. Brown, 1850), 2066–2077; this copies from this source. There are two original copies of the constitution in handwriting. One copy is preserved in the vault of the Indiana History section of the State Library. The second copy, along with a copy of the Constitution of 1816, is preserved in the private office of the secretary of state. Copies of the constitution may also be found in the issues of the *Indiana State Journal, Indiana State Sentinel,* and *Indiana Statesman* published in several issues after the adjournment of the convention on February 10.

[2] In copying the constitution whole words have been written in capital letters only when they were so used in the *Debates.*

APPENDIX II

ADDRESS TO THE PEOPLE

January 21 Owen introduced a resolution calling for a committee of ten to consist of one from each congressional district to, "Prepare an address to the electors of the State, embodying a brief statement of the changes proposed in the amended Constitution, and such other matters in connection therewith, as may aid in securing its adoption." Walpole, a Whig, was the only delegate to speak against this resolution. He expressed the opinion that the address would be one-sided, written by Owen and his associates (this was probably a very accurate charge), and that it would reflect upon the intelligence of the people as they could form their own opinions by reading the debates and newspaper accounts.[1] Owen's resolution was adopted and the committee appointed four days later. The members were Owen, Carr of the second district, Berry, Smiley, Maguire, Helmer, Davis of Vermillion, Bryant, Colfax, and Bascom. Owen was the chairman. Later Niles of LaPorte was appointed to take the place of Colfax. This committee was not chosen among the real leaders of the convention and Owen probably was the one who did the real work assigned to the group.[2] February 8, on the Saturday before the convention adjourned on Monday, this "Committee of Ten," as it came to be called, reported the address to the convention. The address was read to the convention by the secretary and "the report was unanimously concurred in."

The address is the best contemporary explanation of the changes made by the new constitution. It takes occasion to show several ways in which the new constitution would save the people money—an appeal that was very near to the desires of the electors. It is not well written but is most valuable for its content. The address can be found in some of the contemporary newspaper accounts.

Address To The Electors[3]

MR. PRESIDENT:—The select committee appointed to prepare an address to the electors of the State, embodying a brief statement of the changes proposed in the amended Constitution, and such other matters in connection therewith as may aid in securing its adoption, have had the subject under consideration, and have unanimously instructed me to report, for adoption by the Convention, the following address to the people of the State of Indiana:[4]

Chosen by the electors of the State of Indiana for the purpose of considering the present Constitution, and of proposing, for adoption or rejection, by the people, an amended Constitution, embodying such changes as we may deem proper, we have completed the task assigned us, and now lay before you the result of our labors.

The chief amendments which we have thought useful to make, are, briefly stated, as follows:

In addition to the guaranties which find a place in the old Constitution, to secure the rights of conscience and prevent the imposition, on the citizen, of any tax to support any ministry or mode of worship against his consent, it is provided, that no person shall be rendered incompetent as a witness in consequence of his opinions in matters of religion; and that no money shall be drawn from the treasury for the benefit of any religious or theological institution. Both of these provisions are found in the Constitutions of Michigan, Wisconsin, and others of recent date.

In the old Constitution the provision as to taxing private property for public use, is that it shall not be taken "without just compensation being made therefor;" but is not declared whether or not this property shall be assessed and paid for before it is taken. The provision in the new Constitution is, that when property is then taken, (except in case of the State) compensation shall be "first assessed and tendered." This is an important change. As the law now stands, an incorporated company, constructing a railroad or other public improvement, may take a man's property first and pay for it afterwards. The change proposed requires that, before taking any property, a tender should first be made of its assessed value. If that tender be rejected by the owner, and he seek his remedy by appeal, the property may be taken; so that one man may not be able, by unreasonable obstinacy, to arrest, for months or years, a work of public importance.

The principle of exempting a reasonable amount of the property of the debtor from seizure or sale, is asserted, but without specifying any amount. There is no provision of this kind in the old Constitution; though the present law, usually called the "hundred and twenty-five dollar law," is based upon the principle thus proposed to be permanently established.

The Legislature is authorized to continue, modify, or abolish the Grand Jury system. Under the old Constitution, provision for retaining it was imperative.

The right of trial by Jury is secured in all cases, civil and criminal. By the old Constitution, where the amount in controversy was less than twenty dollars, and also in prosecutions for petit misdemeanors, this right was not secured.

It is provided that "the General Assembly shall not grant to any citizen or class of citizens, privileges or immunities, which, upon the same terms, shall not equally belong to all citizens." This important provision is new.

As To Suffrage and Election.

By the old Constitution, citizens of the United States were entitled to vote. Under the new, foreigners who have been in the United States one year, and in this State six months immediately before any election, and who shall have declared, under oath, their intention to become citizens, have the right of voting. This liberal provision will undoubtedly tend to increase the wealth and population of our State by attracting emigrants toward it.

Post Masters, if their annual compensation be ninety dollars or less, but not otherwise, may be elected members of the Legislature, in counties with less than a thousand polls, but not in others, the offices of Clerk, Recorder, and Auditor, may be conferred on the same person. Both of these are new provisions.

No one who gives or accepts a challenge, or carries to another a challenge to fight a duel, shall be eligible to any office of trust or profit. This is also new.

In The Legislative Department.

The provision in regard to the number of Senators and Representatives remains unchanged. It is not to exceed a hundred in the House and fifty in the Senate, but that number may at any time be reduced by law.

The regular sessions of the Legislature are to be held once only in two years; but the Governor, if he thinks the public welfare requires it, may call special sessions. No regular session is to be longer than sixty-one days; nor any special session longer than forty days.

As the entire expense of the sessions of our General Assembly, including printing of laws and journals, have averaged, for the last ten years, upwards of forty thousand dollars annually, the saving by the change to biennial sessions may be set down at twenty thousand dollars a year. Thus, if no special sessions be called during five years, the saving, in that period, by this provision alone, will overpay the entire expenses of the Convention. This will also be afforded some opportunity to become acquainted with the laws of one session, before they are followed by the amendments of the next.

The following provisions, tending to check and regulate the legislative branch of government, are not found in the old Constitution:

First. Every bill is to be read throughout on three several days, unless two-thirds, under ayes and noes, suspend the rule.

Second. On the final passage of a bill, it is forbidden, under any circumstances, to dispense with its reading by sections.

Third. A majority of all the members elected to either branch shall be necessary to pass a law. The present Constitution permits a majority of those present (which may be a bare majority of a quorum) to pass a law.

Fourth. No law is permitted to be revised or amended by mere reference to its title, but the law so revised or amended must be set forth at full length. Great abuses have arisen for lack of such a provision. Amendments have been made, of which the House which enacted them knew the character only by some brief verbal statement from a member interested in their passage.

Fifth. No law is to embrace more than one subject and matters properly connected therewith; and the subject is to be expressed in the title. The tendency of the rule is to prevent what is familiarly termed "log-rolling." Two provisions having no proper connection with each other, may, under the present Constitution, be embraced in the same bill, and be carried by a combination of their respective friends, though neither, in itself, has merit or strength enough to obtain a majority, and would fail, as it ought, if voted upon singly.

Sixth. No law is allowed to pass, except under the ayes and noes, entered on the journals. This is one of the most effectual safeguards against hasty and inconsiderate legislation; and secures, under all circumstances, the responsibility of members of the Legislature, to their constituents.

Seventh. All elections by the General Assembly are by a *viva voce* vote, recorded on the journals.

Eighth. The most important restriction imposed upon the legislative branch, is that which provides that, in a variety of enumerated cases, (as the jurisdiction of Justices of the Peace, the mode of doing county and township business, the fees of county and township officers, road laws, common school laws, and so forth,) and in all cases where a general law can be made applicable, no special law shall be passed. It is an estimate much within the truth, that more than two-thirds of all the laws enacted in this State since her admission into the Union, have been of the character here forbidden. More than two-thirds of our legislation, therefore—and the most confusing and most mischievous portion of it—is cut off by this single provision. Independently of the intrinsic benefits of such a change, the saving thereby affected of expense, both as regards the time of the Legislature and the cost of printing our laws, will be great.

Ninth. By general law, provision may be made for sueing the State, but no special act authorizing suit to be brought against the State, or allowing damages against the State, is permitted. This will remove to courts of justice, where they properly belong, numerous claims which cannot be urged through a legislative body without temptation to demoralizing influences.

Tenth. The Legislature is prohibited from granting divorces.

Eleventh. Representatives hold their offices two years, serving one regular session; Senators hold their offices four years, serving two regular sessions.

Twelfth. The general elections, instead of being held, as now, on the first Monday in August, are to be held on the second Tuesday of October, of each year. This latter period is one of much greater leisure to farmers than the former.[5]

In The Executive Department.

The changes in this department are unimportant, being chiefly these:

The Governor and Lieutenant Governor are elected for four instead of three years, to correspond to the biennial sessions of the Legislature.

Neither of these officers is eligible more than four years in any period of eight years, nor to any other office, during the term for which he has been elected. These provisions are not in the old Constitution.

There is a slight change in regard to the veto power. If a bill is presented to the Governor within three days of the close of the session and he fail to return it, it shall be a law, unless, he file the bill, together with its objections, in the office of the Secretary of State, within five days after the adjournment. By the old Constitution, he might hold it over until the next session, and then return it with his objections.

As To State and County Officers.

The Secretary of State, Auditor of State, and Treasurer of State, who were elected, under the old Constitution, by the Legislature, are now elective by the people. The Secretary held his office for four years, and the Auditor and Treasurer theirs for three years; now, the term of office of all these officers, is two years only; and they are not eligible more than four years, in any period of six years.

In the counties, the term of service of the Clerk, Auditor, and Recorder, is put in the new Constitution, at four years; and they are not eligible more than eight years, in any period of twelve years. The Sheriff and Treasurer hold their office for two years, and are not eligible more than four years in any term of six years.

In The Judicial Department.

The Supreme and Circuit Judges, heretofore chosen, the former by the appointment of the Governor, confirmed by the Senate, and the latter, by a joint vote of both Houses, are, by the new Constitution, made elective by the people. There are to be no less than three nor more than five Supreme Judges; each to reside in, and be elected from, his own district; but all to be chosen by the votes of the people at large. Each Circuit Judge is chosen by the vote of the electors of the Circuit.

A Judge is rendered ineligible, during the term for which he may have been elected, to any other than a judicial office. This provision is new.

There is to be elected, by the people, a Prosecuting Attorney for each Judicial Circuit.

As To Law Reform.

The General Assembly is required, at its first session, to appoint three Commissioners, whose duty is shall be, to revise and simplify the practice and forms of the courts. They are to abolish the separate forms of action now in use; and to provide for a uniform mode of pleading, without distinction between law and equity. The Legislature may also cause these Commissioners to reduce, into a systematic code, the general Statute law.

Every person of good moral character, who is a voter, is entitled to admission to practice law in any of the Courts of this State.

These reforms are of an important character: Calculated to diminish the cost, and to correct the delay of law proceedings. As the law now is, a man may prosecute a perfectly just claim, but if he commence suit on what an arbitrary rule calls the wrong side of the court, he cannot recover. So, also, a man may have various demands for money against a neighbor, all of which could naturally and conveniently be set forth in the same declaration; but ancient practice has declared, that there are some ten or twelve different forms of action; and he may have to bring a separate suit, with its separate expenses, for each demand, though varying very slightly in their character. A remarkable example is this. If a man hold two promissory notes against another, payable in current bank paper the one being sealed and the other being not sealed, he must bring a separate suit upon each. No reason but a purely arbitrary one, founded upon antiquated usage, can be given for such vexatious and cost increasing distinction.

The Legislature is authorized to establish Courts of Conciliation, for the speedy decision of cases that may be voluntarily submitted to them, without the tedious and expensive process of law.

Education and State Institutions.

The principal change in this department, is the abolition of county seminaries, and the application of the funds to common schools. It is also provided, that the Legislature shall establish a uniform system of common schools, wherein tuition shall be free.

The swamp lands recently granted by Congress, and which, it is supposed, may be worth half a million of dollars, are added to the common school fund.

A Superintend[ent] of Public Instruction is to be elected by the people, his term of office being two years. The large amount of the school fund, scattered all over the State, and the important interests involved, demand the undivided attention of a competent officer.

The counties are responsible for such portions of the common school fund as may be entrusted to them. This incorporates into the Constitution a provision for the security of that fund, which has long been the statute law of the State.

The Institutions which the benevolence of Indiana has reared for the blind, the deaf and dumb, and the insane, are perpetuated by constitutional provision.

The Legislature is instructed to establish Houses of Refuge, for the correction and reformation of juvenile offenders.

PUBLIC DEBT.

The Legislature is prohibited from incurring any debt, except to meet casual deficits in the revenue, to pay the interest on the present State Debt, or to repel invasion, or suppress insurrection.

Had this provision, brief and simple as it is, been inserted in the Constitution of 1816, it would have saved the State from a loss of six millions of dollars. Upon that end we are now paying, without any return, some three hundred thousand dollars of interest, annually; that is, about eight hundred dollars a day; more than enough to maintain, in perpetual session, year after year, with all of its expenses of reporting and printing, such a Convention as that which has been engaged for the last four months, in framing a constitution, which shuts out, for the future, a possibility of similar folly.

No county is allowed to subscribe stock to any incorporated company, unless the same be paid at the time of subscription. The State is prohibited from assuming the debt of any town or county.

As To Banking and Corporations.

The Legislature may, or may not, establish banks in this State. If they establish banks, it is to be under the following restrictions:

No bank shall be created, otherwise than by general law, except one branch with branches.

If the Legislature decide to enact a general banking law, all banks thereby created, are to give ample collateral security, such as may be readily converted into money, for the redemption of all their notes in gold and silver; and this security is to be lodged in the hands of some officer of State. No such security has heretofore been demanded of banks in this State.

If the Legislature decide to charter a bank with branches, the branches are to be actually responsible, as the branches of our present State Bank now are.

The State is not hereafter to be a stockholder in any bank or other corporation.

All banks are required to redeem their notes, at all times, in gold and silver; and the Legislature is prohibited from ever authorizing a suspension of specie payments.

The stockholders, in all banks, are to be held individually responsible, to an amount over and above their stock, equal to the amount of their stock.

In case of insolvency, holders of bank notes are to have preference of payment over all other creditors.

No bank is to receive a higher rate of interest, than is allowed to individuals loaning money.

Every bank is to cease banking operations within twenty years from the time it is organized, and promptly thereafter to close up its business.

These restrictions on banking, not imposed in the former constitution, will not, it is believed, prohibit banking, under a safe system, by responsible associations. The restrictions on banking under a general law are similar to those of the New York system, as amended according to the provision of the new constitution of that State. Under that amended system, not a dollar has been lost to the bill-holders. As to the principle of making the branches of a bank, if established with branches, responsible for each other's liabilities, it has worked so well in the charter of our present State Bank, that it is believed a large majority of the people approve it.

In addition to the above restrictions, applying especially to banks, it is proved, as to corporations generally, that they shall not be created by special act, but may be formed under general laws.

Negroes and Mulattoes.

The article in regard to Negroes and Mulattoes is to be submitted separately to the people, It provides,

First. That no Negro or Mulatto shall come into, or settle in, this State, after the adoption of the new Constitution.

Second. That all contracts made with Negroes or Mulattoes who may come into the State, contrary to the foregoing provision, shall be void, and all persons who shall employ any such Negro or Mulatto, shall be fined in any sum not less than ten, nor more than five hundred dollars.

Third. That all fines collected for any breach of this article, shall be applied to the colonization of so many of the Negroes and Mulattoes, now in this State, as may desire to emigrate.

As to any further provision for colonization, it is left to future Legislation. A majority of the Convention were of the opinion, that the true interests alike of the white citizens of the State and of its colored inhabitants demanded the ultimate separation of the races; and that, as the Negro cannot obtain, among us, equal social and political rights, it is greatly to be desired that he should find a free home in other lands, where public opinion imposes upon color neither social disabilities nor political disfranchisement.

No additional disability, not found in the old Constitution, is imposed by the new, on Negroes or Mulattoes or their descendants, who may be in the State at the time of the adoption of the amended Constitution.

Mode of Amending The Constitution.

Amendments to the Constitution may be proposed in the Senate or House of Representatives. If passed by a majority of all members elected to either branch, they are referred to the next regular session of the Legislature, to be held two years thereafter. If passed by them, a second time, they are then, at the next general election, to be submitted the People; and if they pass this final ordeal, they become a part of the Constitution.

In this way, there will always occur a general election of members of the Legislature, during the canvass for which, the amendments that they may have been proposed at the previous session, can be brought in issue: and nearly three years must intervene, from the time an amendment is first proposed, before it can be finally adopted.

There was provided, in the old Constitution, no mode of submitting to the People separate amendments. The advantage of the provision is, that, without the expense of a Convention, the new Constitution, if found faulty or deficient in any of its parts, may be amended and perfected.

With this brief explanatory statement of the more important alterations embodied in the new Constitution, we place our work in the hands of our constituents, who alone can give it vitality.

Those who desire to examine arguments for or against he various charges that have been made, will find them spread at large, throughout the Debates of the Convention; officially reported, in accordance with the law which provided for the call of a Convention, by a corps of stenographers. Of the two volumes in which these Debates are embraced, three copies will be deposited in the Clerk's office of each county throughout the State.

[1] *Report of the Debates and Proceedings of the Convention for the Revision of the Constitution of the State of Indiana, 1850* (Indianapolis: A. H. Brown, 1850), 1732. Such an address, Walpole said, would be "a libel upon the judgment and understanding of the people."

[2] Ibid., 2046. Owen said: "I will state to the Convention that I have been compelled to draw up this address in a hasty manner. . ." A comparison of the phraseology of this address with the speeches of Owen will bring out likenesses; however, the evidence is not conclusive.

[3] Ibid., 2042-2046. The various titles used herein are from the sources. The various titles used herein are those used in the *Debates* as appropriate to the context.

[4] Ibid., 2042. Niles of LaPorte was not present when the committee voted on this instruction as Owen explained to the convention.

[5] The words herein underlined are printed in italics in the *Debates*.

Photo Courtesy Indiana Historical Society

This is an image of the Indianapolis Circle prior to construction of the Soldier's and Sailor's Monument. The English Opera House, viewable on the right, hosted the 1885 reunion of convention delegates. William English collected information about each delegate from friends, family members, and colleagues in preparation for this reunion. His material, held by the Indiana Historical Society, provides the most extensive collection of information about the delegates and the convention itself.

APPENDIX III

SOURCES RELATIVE TO THE UNION OF SURVIVING MEMBERS IN 1885

THE MEN OF 1850[1]

The meeting this week of the survivors of the Constitutional Convention of 1850, and of the antecedent Legislatures, as well as of the one which first assembled under its provisions, will be an event of great interest, not so much because of the work really performed by those bodies, but because of the natural interest centering about an assemblage of men who have lived so long, and seen so much of the progress and development of the State and Nation. We cannot feel that there will be any special occasion for rejoicing or felicitation over what was done in the constitutional convention; the resultant organic law was not one to particularly challenge the admiration of mankind, either then or now. But the meeting will serve the purpose of showing how far the State and country have outstripped the petting prejudices and narrow bigotries of that day, some of which found expression in the Constitution, and have always been a reproach to the Commonwealth; and it will, in addition, give the opportunity for reminiscence and personal reunion, that cannot fail to be to the last degree pleasant to the older generation of men, and of deepest interest to the younger generation that has grown up within the last third of a century. The men composing the convention and the Legislature were, of course, prominent in their several localities. Many of them have since that date risen to high distinction, and occupied places that brought them before the eyes not only of the country but of the world. Two Vice-presidents of the United States were of the body, Colfax and Hendricks, and one other, English, a candidate for that place. Others have been somewhat less conspicuous, but probably none the less useful in their day, and generation. Naturally, many have died; there are more survivors, relatively, of the Legislature than of the convention, for the reason that the latter body was composed of men of maturer years, on the average. It is to be noted that neither a member of the convention nor of the first Legislature, from Marion county, survives, David Wallace, J. P. Chapman, Douglass Maguire and A. F. Morrison, members of the convention, and Nicholas McCarty, Henry Brady, and Isaac Smith, of the first Legislature are all dead. There will be many facts of interest brought out by the meeting, and the Journal hopes the veterans will have a pleasant and enjoyable week. They will certainly be received with the honor and respect due them, and will find the hand and heart of the capital city of the State ready and warm in their welcome.

THE LAW MAKERS OF 1850[2]

A Gathering Of Men Notable In The History of the Commonwealth.

The Survivors of the Constitutional Convention of Thirty-Five Years Ago Indulge in Their First Reunion.

List of Those Who Responded to the Secretary's Call of the Roll.

Addresses by Hon. William H. English, Vice-President Hendricks, General William McKee Dunn and Col. Taylor.

The surviving members of the Constitutional Convention, the men who framed the present Constitution of Indiana, met yesterday afternoon, at 2 o'clock, at English's Opera-house, the gathering together of these law-makers being the work of Hon.

Wm. H. English, the principal secretary of that memorable convention. Wm. McKee Dunn, upon the meeting being called to order, moved that George W. Carr, the president of the convention of 1850, be called upon to preside over the present body, which was carried unanimously, and the president was conducted to the chair by Hon. Wm. S. Holman, of Dearborn, and Cromwell W. Barbour, of Vigo.

Mr. Carr, thanking the convention for this expression of regard, said: "It is a gratification to meet the surviving members of the constitutional convention of 1850, and exchange friendly greetings with each other once more. But, when I look over this meeting, and see so many vacant seats; when I miss so many familiar faces from our presence, and realize that fact that those faces are passed, and have gone beyond the shores of time; have passed over the river, and entered upon the unknown, and these faces will be seen here no more, this seems to me to be an occasion of solemnity and sadness. I trust one of the results of this meeting will be to strengthen and perpetuate the good feelings and respect we should have for one another, until, we, too, are called to meet our colleagues beyond the shores of time."

William H. English was chosen secretary, and immediately proceeded to call the roll of the members of the Constitutional Convention of 1850, with the names of the counties they represented, and the following responded as present: Oliver P. Badger, Putnam; Cromwell W. Barbour, Vigo; Othniel Beeson, Wayne; Horace P. Biddle, Cass, Howard, etc.; Alexander B. Conduit, Morgan; William McKee Dunn, Jefferson; James B. Foley, Decatur; John A. Graham, Miami; Jefferson Helm, Rush; Thomas A. Hendricks, Shelby; William S. Holman, Dearborn; Phineas M. Kent, Floyd; Beattie McClelland, Randolph; Samuel Pepper, Crawford; James Ritchey, Johnson; E. D. Taylor, LaPorte; Henry G. Todd, Hendricks; George W. Carr, Lawrence.

Those who are living but not in attendance are: Hiram Allen, Carroll and Clinton; Walter E. Beach, Elkhart; George Berry, Franklin; Wm. Bracken, Rush; Benjamin F. Brookbank, Union;

Oliver P. Davis, Parke and Vermillion; Christopher C. Graham, Warrick; Franklin Hardin, Johnson; Alvin P. Hovey, Posey; Wilson Huff, Spencer; John Mathes, Harrison; Cornelius J. Miller, Clinton; Robert H. Milroy, Carroll; W. F. Sherrod, Orange; Alex. C. Stevenson, Putnam; Elias S. Terry, Daviess; Amzi L. Wheeler, Marshall; Robert Work, Dekalb.

The roll-call showed thirty-three members known to be alive, of whom nineteen were present. Mr. Stevenson, the secretary explained, was unable to attend. He was the oldest living member of the Indiana Legislature, his service beginning in 1831.

Elder O. P. Badger then asked the Divine blessing upon the meeting.

James Ritchey moved that a recess of five minutes be taken that the members present might shake hands and look into each others faces. The motion was carried. When the five minutes had elapsed the president, calling the convention to order, produced an old fashioned silver watch with which he said he had timed the speeches of the convention of 1850, and which had kept good time ever since.

Letters were read from surviving members of the Constitutional Convention who were unable to attend. One of these letters was from Christopher C. Graham, now at Red Wing, Minn. An extract from it reads as follows: "In looking over the names of the framers of the Constitution of 1850, many who have risen to prominent stations, eminent as statesmen, jurists, scientists and scholars, and who have performed their trusts so nobly, wisely and honestly, I rejoice to have been one, though an humble one, in forming the Constitution that has guided the noble State, amid all its trying hours, to wealth and prosperity. Many who have been members of this convention have by continued service contributed in creating, developing and controlling public opinion and originating, molding and fostering the spirit that has led to the growing greatness and prosperity of the State. As the years roll away the veneration of a prosperous and happy people for them will be more lasting than 'storied urn or monumental bust.'"

A letter from Gen. R. H. Milroy read as follows: U.S. Indian Service, Yakima Agency, Ft. Simcoe, W. T., Sept. 18, 1885.

Hon. W. H. English:

My Dear Sir—received a few days ago from you the printed announcement of the thirty-fifth anniversary meeting of the surviving members of the Indiana Constitutional Convention of 1850 with the surviving members of the first Legislature under that Constitution, to be held at Indianapolis, on the 5th, 6th and 7th prox., with a few friendly lines in your own handwriting, directed to me at Delphi, Ind., which place I left over thirteen years ago, and have been residing in this Territory continuously since then. I can assure you that it would give me much enjoyment to meet the remnant of my colleagues of "auld lang syne," but time and other circumstances forbid. The term of my office being cut short, I am engaged in transferring it to my Democratic successor, preparatory to returning to my home at Olympia. Perhaps, should these reunions be continued, I may be spared to attend some future one, though being near three-score and ten it is uncertain. We will all soon be "over the river," where we will have a grand reunion of our whole convention. Remember me kindly to fellow members who may be present. Accept for yourself the best regards of

Your long-lost friend, R. H.

An Interesting Posthumous Paper

An interesting paper showing how the provision in Article VIII of the Constitution, entitled "Education," came to be prepared by the committee on education, and to be presented to the convention, was next read. It is a fragment of the inside history of the Constitutional Convention, written by the late John I. Morrison, and was found among his papers by his daughter after his death, and by her sent to Mr. English:

Nearly thirty years have elapsed since the convention met that formed the present Constitution of the State of Indiana.

Of the 150 delegates who composed that body, but a mere

remnant has been spared to the present hour. To notice the many reforms grafted into the policy of the State by the new Constitution is not proposed at present. This may be done at another time.

All that will be attempted now is to refer briefly to some of the provisions in Article 8, entitled "Education" and to give a little of its inside and unwritten history as it was molded by the committee on education, before it was reported to the convention and adopted as a part of the new Constitution.

The standing committee on education, selected by the president, chiefly on account of their well-known sentiments in favor of free schools and liberal education, was announced in the following order: Messr. Morrison of Washington, Bryant, May, Hitt, Foster, Stevenson, Nofsinger, Milligan and Blythe.

This committee went to work immediately, elected Col. James R. M. Bryant, of Warren, secretary, and resolved to hold meetings weekly, and daily when necessary, to compare views, collect information and take action upon all subjects of special reference by the convention.

Without exaggeration it may be added that every member was fully impressed with the deep sense of the heavy responsibility that rested upon him, and long and earnest were the conflicts before the general principles were settled, which should be embodied in the final report of the committee.

Indeed the first section of the article, which in the plain was copied from the old Constitution, gave rise to many warm and exciting discussions. A close comparison, however, will reveal differences, vitally important to the success and efficiency of the whole scheme. By the new Constitution a general and uniform system of common schools is established, wherein tuition shall be without charge and equally open to all. Under the old Constitution, all was chaos and uncertainty, and the Legislature was authorized to act "as soon as circumstances will permit."

By the new, every provision is mandatory. The system cannot remain inert; it must be put in active operations; it must have motion; it must move everywhere and at all times, and it must be uniform. While every word in this first section was submitted to the severest scrutiny, there is none that was canvassed with more care and diligence than the word "uniform." One member of the committee contended with great zeal and pertinacity that "equitable" was the proper word, but a wiser and better judgment preponderated, and this term was allowed to stand.

The second section, which particularizes what the principal of the common school fund shall consist of, was adopted in committee after much labor and paintaking, especially the clause which makes the funds to be derived from the sale of county seminaries and the fines assessed from breaches of the penal laws of the State, and all forfeiture that may secure, a part of the principal of the common school fund.

It was earnestly contended that all money arising from such sources should be regarded as so much annual income, and be applied as fast as it accrued to defray the current expenses of tuition. But a majority of the committee would entertain no proposition which did not contemplate a constant addition to the appropriation to the support of common schools, "and to no other purpose whatever." Although the retention of this phrase was said to be in deference to the wishes of the chairman, yet, in the light of experience, its necessity has been fully vindicated, and it is believed no true friend of common schools, can be found, at the present day, so hypocritical as to extract, if he could, this clincher from the Constitution.

The sixth section, which held the several counties liable for so much of the fund as may be entrusted to them, and for the payment of the annual interest thereon, met with very formidable opposition when first suggested in committee; but when it was shown that this section was an exact copy of the law already on the statute books, all opposition was withdrawn. This section has done its full share in preserving the integrity of the principal and securing the payment in full of all the accruing interest.

For the seventh section, which makes all trust funds remain inviolate, the state is indebted to the late Hon. John Pettit, not a member of the committee, but one of the ablest delegates of the convention.

For the eighth section, which provides for the election of the State Superintendent of Public Instruction, the chairman of the committee must alone be held responsible. By a majority vote in the committee this section was stricken from the final report. The potent argument used to defeat the measure was the creation of an additional State officer and the consequent expense of maintaining such an office.

The news of the decision of the committee in rejecting the section was received with very great alarm by its friends on the floor of the convention. It was regarded as a fatal blow against the State undertaking to educate the children of the State without a sentinel to guard the public funds from pillage and misappropriation, as well as a head to guide the general system and mold it into proper form. It was believed that the whole system would soon become a wreck as certainly as the richly laden vessel when deprived of a captain to keep its reckoning and control its helm. In the midst of general despondency the chairman, having found a few sympathizing friends who proffered their support, determined to submit the rejection to the tender mercies of the convention.

To his great relief, after a somewhat stormy debate, the additional section was adopted and ordered to be engrossed by a vote of 78 to 50, and added to the new Constitution.

We satisfy any regrets that the term of office was not made four years instead of two, it may suffice to add that the aid referred to was promised on the express condition that the term of office should be limited to two years.

The Meeting then adjourned for the afternoon.

THE EVENING SESSION.

The meeting was called to order at half-past seven by the president, and the Central Glee Club sang "Auld Lang Syne." Vice-President Hendricks was then presented to the meeting and spoke as follows:

The several States of our Union are endowed with all the powers that may be exercised by free and independent communities, which are not prohibited by their own constitutions, nor by the constitution of the United States, and which are consistent with their relations to each other and to the Federal Union.

The work of revising a State constitution consists mainly in declaring the rights of the people, in limiting and defining the powers intended to be exercised, and in prohibiting powers not intended to be exercised, rather than in creating rights or conferring powers not possessed.

It will be observed, therefore, that the amendments made by the convention of 1850-1 consist mainly in providing additional protection to natural rights, in removing restrictions therefrom, and in regulating the exercise of powers already recognized as existing.

The Legislative department exercises a discretion in its action far beyond that permitted to either of the other departments, even extending their control in important respects, and therefore the amendments affecting it and its mode of proceeding were of special importance.

As briefly as possible, I will endeavor to review a recollection of the amendments made by the convention.

Under the old Constitution the sessions of the Legislature were annual. The laws were then subject to constant modification and repeal. Biennial sessions were substituted, with the authority on the part of the Governor to call extra sessions to provide for special emergencies. Experience has shown the wisdom of the change. Legislation had been more carefully conducted; the laws have become more stable; and the people have been able better to know what the laws are.

It was also provided that no regular session should exceed sixty-one days in length, nor any special session forty days. At the time of its adoption this limitation was not, perhaps, too great, but experience now shows that it prevents the constantly increasing subjects of legislation. This provision may be readily modified under the clause providing for amendments.

To promote care and integrity in legislation, provisions were made requiring every bill to be read throughout on three several days, unless the rule be suspended on the call of the ayes and noes; but on the final passage the rule can not be suspended; and a majority of all the members elected to each branch, voting on the ayes and noes, shall be necessary to pass a bill.

No law may be amended by reference to its title; but the amended law must be set forth at its full length. Under the decisions of the courts the last provision is of but modified value. It is often difficult to tell what is amended and what is amendment.

The provision that no law shall embrace more than one subject is useful and important. It has stopped "log-rolling" in legislation: a meritorious measure can not now be made to carry one that has neither merit nor strength.

Among the best reforms of the new constitution was that which forbade special legislation, where general law can be made applicable. Under it special privileges have given way to public right, under general legislation.

The provision authorizing the Legislature to provide for suing the State does not appear to have been demanded by public sentiment. The Legislature has uniformly declined to exercise the power conferred.

The amendments affecting the executive department of the State were less important. The official terms of the Governor and Lieutenant-Governor were changed from three to four years, so as to correspond with the biennial sessions of the Legislature, and those officers were made ineligible for more than four years in any period of eight years and to any other State office during the term of office. The Judges of the Supreme Court were formerly chosen by appointment of the Governor and confirmation by the Senate, and the Judges of the Circuit Court by the joint vote of the two branches of the Legislature. By the new constitution they are made elective, the former by the people of the State, and the latter by the people of the circuit.

They are ineligible to any other than judicial offices during the term for which they are elected.

The Judges of the Supreme Court are required upon the decision of every case, to give a statement in writing of each question arising in the record, and to make a decision thereon. The repeal of that provision would relieve that Court of great labor without, as I believe, any hurt to the public interest. Such regulation may be safely left to legislative discretion.

The limitation upon the legislative power to confer original jurisdiction upon the Supreme Court, in the Constitution of 1816, is removed by the provision in Art. 7 of the new Constitution, and the Legislature is allowed entire discretion on that subject.

The duty was imposed upon the Legislature to provide for law reform, and promptly and faithfully was discharged. The importance and value of the reform is felt in the rapid dispatch of business in the courts, in the relief from vexations and bewildering technicalities, and in the increased certainty that justice will be done. Experience has shown the reform to be much more valuable than at the time was supposed. The Indiana code does honor to the convention that imposed the duty to revise and simplify the practice and forms of the courts: to the Commissioners who bestowed patient labor, great learning and excellent judgment upon its production, and upon the Legislature for its prompt approval and enactment.

The benevolent institutions of the State, the cause of education and the security of the common school fund were wisely and permanently provided for.

By the wise provision of the new constitution our State and county authorities have been prohibited from contracting any serious indebtedness, and the influence of that provision has been most salutary. Enterprise and development have advanced, and the people have seen wealth, relieved of the fear and danger of crushing taxation. Systems of State and free banking were provided for, and a well regulated State Bank was established, which for some years contributed largely to the success of our trade and commerce, but its currency has been wholly superseded by that of the National Banks. The provisions on the subject of banking are substantially obsolete.

An article prohibiting the further settlement of negroes and mulattoes in the State was submitted to the people, separately from the other parts of the Constitution, and was adopted by a large vote. After the adoption of the amendments to the constitution of the United States, the provisions of that article were inconsistent in spirit with the rights of the colored race, and the article was stricken from the constitution of the State, by an amendment subsequently adopted.

By the old Constitution the right to vote was restricted to citizens of the United States. Under the new constitution that right was extended to foreigners resident in the United States for one year, and in the State six months immediately before any election, and who shall have declared, under oath, their intentions to become citizens.

The mode of electing some of the State officers was so changed as to make them elective by the people, and changes were also made in their terms of office, and also in the terms of some of the county officers.

Important additions were made to the bill of rights in favor of individual right, and the right of conscience.

1. No person shall be held incompetent as a witness in consequence of his opinion in matters of religion.

2. No money shall be drawn from the treasury for the benefit of any religious or theological institution.

3. The assessed value of private property shall be tendered before such property be taken, except in the case of the State.

4. A reasonable amount of the debtor's property shall be exempt from seizure and sale.

5. The right of trial by jury is extended.

6. Privileges and immunities shall not be granted to one citizen, or class of citizens, which, upon the same terms, shall not equally belong to all citizens.

The new constitution provides the mode in which it may be amended. Any proposed amendment shall be considered by the Legislature at two separate sessions, and if agreed to at both sessions, it shall be submitted to the electors of the State, and if ratified by them, it shall become a part of the constitution. The people are made secure against hasty amendments. No proposition can pass these ordeals without being thoroughly considered and well understood. Future amendments, that experience may indicate, can be made in the manner provided without much delay, without cost to the people, and with every assurance that it is wisely and well done.

The amendments made by the convention of 1851 extended to every department, and have influenced every branch of the public service. The convention "builded better than it knew." Its work has borne the hard test of experience. We may judge somewhat of its excellence by the fact that during the thirty-four years that have since elapsed, but few amendments have been required, in all, I believe, but nine, and those mostly because of changes that have since taken place. Three of the later amendments related to the change in the legal status and condition of the colored race, made by the amendments to the constitution of the United States. Another of the amendments was required to make the time of our general election agree with the time fixed by Congress for the election of members of Congress. The increased population of the State made it necessary, in order to defeat illegal voting, to fix by constitutional amendment a period of residence in the voting precinct, before the right to vote should be exercised. The increasing disparity in the fees and salaries of public officers made an amendment necessary so as to permit special legislation on that subject. It seems also to have been thought necessary to modify the language used in defining the judicial power. The last of the amendments was useful, but it did not relate to matters of interest to the State. It was a provision limiting the amount of taxation in cities and municipal corporations.

In scarcely a single instance have the late amendments become necessary because of any defective or incomplete work on the part of the convention of 1851. The constitution then adopted stands almost without change or modification. Under its provisions the people have maintained local self-government in its highest excellence. In peace and in war it has guarded their rights, protected their interests, and promoted their welfare and prosperity.

By an amendment adopted in 1873 the Legislature is prohibited ever to recognize any liability of the State to pay the Wabash and Erie Canal bonds. Thereby that question was forever put to rest.

I congratulate you who are living, and I honor the memories of the delegates who are dead, for the perfect work done by the convention.

Hon. William H. English was the next speaker. He spoke as follows:

The history of the men who framed a Constitution which has already existed over the third of a century, and under which a State has grown to be great and prosperous ought to be a subject of interest to its citizens.

To me, whatever pertains to the rise and progress of governments, and especially of my own State and Nation, is interesting. Certainly the progress which has been made by the State of Indiana ought to be satisfactory and gratifying to her citizens; and, as to the Nation at large, I do not know of any country, in ancient or modern times, that has grown in prosperity and greatness with the rapidity of the United States of America. The mind can scarcely comprehend this Nation's wonderful progress.

What a vast and glorious country it is, stretching from ocean to ocean over thousands and thousands and thousands of miles of as good a country as the sun of Heaven shines upon, and with over fifty-five millions of self-governed peoples, possessing greater privileges and advantages, and real prosperity and happiness, than any on earth!

And have you ever thought in what a brief period this greatness has been attained?

When some of the members of this reunion were born there were only about 300,000 white people in this country west of the Allegheny Mountains.

There are, no doubt, persons now living who were born before the adoption of our Federal Constitution. Just think what grand results have come in the span of a single life.

I do not feel that I am a very old man myself, and yet I have seen every President of the United States but the first five. Incidentally, I may say, that, although I was quite young when I saw General Jackson, I have a very distinct recollection of the personal appearance of the old hero.

I also remember distinctly the personal appearance of Martin Van Buren, even to the way he was dressed. I saw him at the residence of Governor William Hendricks, in the city of Madison. I can not fix the date exactly, but I think it was after the expiration of his term as President, and that he visited this city during the same tour.

I saw General Harrison about 1840, and in 1844 I went to Washington, where I frequently saw John Tyler, who was then in the Presidential chair. I had been Postmaster of my native village under his administration, the first office I ever held.

Ex-President John Quincy Adams was then a member of the United States House of Representatives. I saw him often, and was in Washington the day he died in the Speaker's room of the old Capitol, with the memorable words on his lips, "This is the last of earth."

I remained in Washington an humble office-holder in one of the Departments during the administration of James K. Polk, and was a member of Congress during the entire terms of Franklin Pierce and James Buchanan, so that I saw more of these three presidents than any of the others, but I have seen them all from Jackson to Cleveland.

For nearly half a century I have been a pretty close observer of our public men, and of the legislative assemblies of our State and Nation.

If you were to ask me to name the strongest body of men I have ever seen, I should not hesitate to answer the Senate of the United States in 1850.

If you were to ask me to name the strongest body I have ever seen assembled in Indiana, some might think it invidious for me to designate, but the general judgment of the public would, no doubt, be the convention which framed the present Constitution of the

State. And this would be no disparagement of the Legislatures of the State, which, in my judgment, favorably compare with the Legislatures of any State in the Union; besides, many members of the Convention had served in previous Legislatures, and over a dozen served in the long and important legislature of 1851-2, which was an exceedingly strong body, and in the matter of remodeling the government to conform to the new constitution and in revising and simplifying the whole code of laws, performed a work of greatest importance to the people and the State.

I think it will be universally conceded that the convention was composed of a high order of men—men of whom any country might justly feel proud—and my object on this occasion will be to say something of the convention and its members.

A majority decided to call a convention. There were two bills introduced at the session of the General Assembly 1848-9 , both on the 15th of December—one in the House by Thomas A. Hendricks, then representing Shelby County, and one in the Senate by John I. Morrison, a Senator from Washington County. I presume the bills were the like import—probably duplicates as to which Mr. Hendricks may possibly remember. The Senate bill passed the Senate January 2, 1849, by a vote of 34 to 12, and in looking over the vote to-day I was glad to find the name of my honored father, Major Elisha G. English, then a Senator from Scott and Jackson, recorded in favor of the passage of the bill. The same bill seems to have passed the House January 13, 1849, all the members voting for it but two, and this was the origin of the convention. The body was composed of 150 members, of which fifty were elected from Senatorial Districts, and one hundred from Representative Districts, but they all sat as one body.

As a matter of local history, it may be stated that the convention met at the capital of the State, in the old hall of the House of Representatives, on the first Monday of October the 7th, 1850, and adjourned February 10, 1851. It was, consequently, in session 127 days, and this is the 35th anniversary of its meeting. The convening of the Legislature of 1850, in December of that year made a change of the place of meeting of the convention necessary, and the sessions there after were held in Masonic Hall, in this city, then just completed.

The members were paid $3 per day for their services, and allowed the usual legislative mileage. The entire cost of the Convention was only $85,683.05.

Observe, this was the total expense of a body composed of 150 members, in a session of 127 days. The Legislature has the same number of members, and for the regular session of only sixty-one days, costs now nearly $100,000 per sessions—sometimes more—the average for the last ten years being about $95,000. I refer to this to show, first, that the convention was an economical as well as an able body and cost less than half as much as our Legislatures cost now for the same length of service; and second, to show that, in the one item of changing the sessions of the Legislature from annual to biennial, the convention has saved the people up to this time certainly over a million of dollars.

In the matter of limiting the creation of public debt, an amount has, no doubt, been saved that is simply incalculable. My purpose, however, is not to speak of these things, but more particularly of the personnel of the convention.

Of the 150 members all were natives of the United States but six. These six were, to say the least, fully up to the general average. They were James Dick, G.H. Ballingall and Robert Dale Owen, born in Scotland, and Allen Hamilton, Dixon Milligan and Beattie McClelland, born in Ireland.

With the first five named, "life's fitful fever is over," and they are sleeping in honored graves. My venerable friend, Judge Beattie McClelland, whom I am glad to see is now present, is the only one of the six who now survives. Of the 144 born in the United States, 74 were born in Northern States, and 70 in Southern, distributed as follows: Kentucky heads the list with 22 members; next come Pennsylvania and Virginia, each with 19 members; then Ohio with 17 and New York with 16; Indiana follows with 13; North Carolina with 10; Maryland and Tennessee with 7 each; Massachusetts and

South Carolina with 4 each; Connecticut, 2; and 1 each from Delaware, New Hampshire, Vermont and New Jersey, so that as far as nativity is concerned, no less than sixteen States and two foreign countries were represented.

An examination as to their occupations in life shows as great diversity as their nativity, but I think there was a greater proportion of farmers than I have ever seen in any other legislative body, there being no less than sixty-two. The lawyers stand next on the list, the number being thirty-nine; next the physicians, numbering sixteen; then the merchants and traders, numbering eleven; then teachers, manufactures and surveyors, two each. There was one tanner, one carpenter, one millwright, one bricklayer, one County Recorder, one accountant, one miller, one editor and one banker, and as to the occupations of others I have no information.

As to politics, in that day the two great parties were the Whig and Democratic. Ninety-four members of the convention were classed as Democrats and fifty-three as Whigs.

William Steele, of Wabash County, classed himself as a "Conservative;" John Beard, of Wayne, as a "Free Soiler;" and Mr. Burbank as an "Independent." The first two died long ago.

The people were divided in politics then pretty much as they are now, but as a rule each party took care to select first-class men as candidates for the convention, and there were many striking instances in the State where party was entirely ignored. In Marion County, for instance, two delegates to the convention were Democrats and two Whigs, and a like spirit prevailed in other parts of the State. The result was a convention of first-class representative men.

That they were such is not only shown by the wisdom of their work in the convention, but by the high place most of them continued to occupy in the confidence and esteem of the people. Most of them were quite successful in life, and many were elevated to places of high trust.

Of the members and officers of the convention three (Colfax, Hendricks and English) were chosen by their respective parties to which they belonged as candidates for Vice President of the United States, and the first two were elected to that high office.

Two were sent to represent the State in the United States Senate, and eleven to represent the people in the United States House of Representatives.

The Senators were John Pettit and Thomas A. Hendricks, and the Representatives Schuyler Colfax, Robert Dale Owen, David Kilgore, James Lockhart, Smith Miller, Thomas Smith, William S. Holman, Thomas A. Hendricks, William McKee Dunn, James B. Foley, William H. English. Mr. Colfax was speaker of the United States House of Representatives several sessions.

Senator Pettit is dead long since, and all of the representatives but the last six named. All of the living are present at this reunion but Mr. Graham, who is detained at his home at Red Wing, Minn., but who has written a letter to this meeting which will be published with the proceedings. Two were Governors of Indiana—David Wallace and Thomas A. Hendricks—and one Lieutenant Governor—Samuel Hall. Three were elected judges of the Supreme Court—Judge Horace P. Biddle and Gen. A. P. Hovey—both of whom, I believe resigned the position, and John Pettit. Two others—Judges Niles and Howe—were the chosen candidates of their party for that position, and both very superior and deserving men. I think at least twelve were elected judges of other State Courts.

Three were sent abroad as United States ministers—Judge Borden, Robert Dale Owen, both dead, and General Hovey, who survives.

Two were distinguished generals in the Union army in the great civil war. One of these, General Milroy, sends us from a distant land an interesting letter of brotherly greeting. The other, General Hovey, I hope you will have the pleasure of hearing from during the progress of this meeting, and also from Judge Biddle, his colleague, on the Supreme Bench.

Another member of the convention, General William McKee Dunn, for many years held the important position of Judge

Advocate General of the United States Army. He is present, and you will no doubt have the pleasure of hearing from him before our adjournment.

Mr. Dunn's colleague in the convention, Michael G. Bright, served in the important position of Agent of State, and died in this city after long sickness, universally lamented.

Horace E. Carter, who was elected Reporter of the Supreme Court, was the third member of the convention to die.

Two were elected Auditor of State—John P. Dunn and Joseph Ristine—both long since dead.

Several were elected Mayors of important cities—Grafton F. Cookerly, Mayor of Terre Haute, died recently, but John A. Graham, Mayor of Peru, I am glad to see, is present at this reunion.

There are many others equally worthy and deserving, no doubt, who were less fortunate in their aspirations, or who, perhaps wisely, chose the more peaceful and quiet walks of private life.

It is a source of gratification that after thirty-five years I cannot recall that any member of the convention (and it was a numerous body) was ever prosecuted for a violation of law, or even accused of a dishonorable act. In their day and generation they were important factors in molding the institutions of their county, and constructing its affairs. Their name and fame are the common property of the State, and when its annals are properly written, will not be forgotten. They deserve to be held in grateful and affectionate remembrance by all.

It was a noticeable fact that the body was composed of men in the prime and full vigor of life, there being, as far as I know, but one member under 25 years of age and but one over 66. They were, in the main, heads of families, there being less than a dozen unmarried men in the body, and most of these, I believe, made amends to the fair sex afterwards.

I have no information as to the age, at the time of the convention, of some half dozen of the members. I have already stated that one was under 25 and one over 66. As to the age of the others at the time, 16 should be classed at from twenty-five to thirty, fourteen from thirty to thirty-five, twenty-seven from thirty-five to forty, twenty-six from forty to forty-five, twenty-five from forty-five to fifty, fifteen from fifty to fifty-five, twelve from fifty-five to sixty, and four from sixty to sixty-six. It will then be seen that the convention was composed of men then in the meridian of life, the bulk of them being from thirty-five to fifty years of age.

Mr. Vanbenthusen, a delegate from Shelby County, was the first to die. This was in the order of nature, as he was seventy-two years of age and the oldest member of the convention. But death, to show he is no respecter of persons or of age, took, as his next victim Mr. Bascom, who was only twenty-six; and next Mr. Carter, who, I think, was the youngest member of the convention.

Where are now the 150 hale and vigorous men I met here thirty-five years ago, full of honorable ambition, and busy with all the joys and sorrows and anxieties of life?

Of the long roll I called so often then, as Secretary of the convention, how few are left to answer now, and how near the time when none will be left to respond! What a sad reflection is this to those of us who are still here! Who will be the next to go? Who the last to survive? It is perhaps well that we can not lift the veil of the future.

It is enough that it will be but a little while now until every member and officer of that great body which framed the present constitution of the State, will have gone to his eternal rest.

One hundred and seventeen have already been called away. A little band of only thirty-three remains. And when the summons comes to those of us who are still here "to join the innumerable caravan that moves to that mysterious realm, where each shall take his chamber in the silent halls of death," may be, with consciousness of duty faithfully performed, and "sustained and soothed by an unfaltering trust, approach the grave like one who wraps the drapery of his couch about him and lies down to pleasant dreams."

Enough material to cover about one page has been omitted because the account in the Journal *herein gives only a review of the remarks of Hon. Wm. McKee Dunn's address; whereas, his complete remarks may be found elsewhere in this appendix. The* Journal *states Dunn's "reference to the Democratic black laws of Indiana created considerable sensation among the number of prominent Democrats who occupied seats upon the state!" See Dunn's very interesting remarks published with other documents included in this appendix.*

Reverend O. P. Badger's Remarks.

Reverend Oliver P. Badger, a member of the convention from Putnam County, was the next speaker. He spoke as follows of the dead members:

And first I call to mind the genial and gentlemanly Colfax. He was a young man of great promise, nor did he disappoint the hopes of his friends. Judge Niles, the eloquent, the pure statesman, the able jurist. John Pettit was massive, bold, defiant, strong and earnest in defense of what he felt to be right. Next was the cool and calculating Dobson, of large inherent powers. He was a firm friend, a safe counselor, an honest man. Near by sat the brilliant young Carter, long since become the victim of strong drink. One of his colleagues was Davy Shannon, a man of deeds rather than of words.

We also miss the plain face and fervid eloquence of David Kelso. He was ready at offhand debate, and woe betide the man who became the subject of his withering sarcasm. The next on M. roll of honor was young Bascom, a man of blameless physique. Judge Rariden was a man of broad and varied experience as a law maker and jurist. Nor shall the name of my quondam friend, Robert Dale Owen, be omitted from this roll on account of neglect on my part; he was learned and logical, polite and courteous. Nor shall we forget the name of that man of great promise, Thomas Walpole; he filled an early grave. Our Ex-Governor Davy Wallace, bright and cheerful, though at the noon time of human life, soon followed. Next was the tall and manly Judge Borden. He was a man of great "suavity in modo," but less "Zoztiteriu Ru." The brother of our popular President Carr, tall and commanding in person, and ready to do a dare for the right. The name of Captain Gibson must have honorable mention, too. He who wanted gentleman to keep their dogs up if they didn't want them hurt, but soon learned that pigs at time need penning in order to their safety.

Judge Kilgore, who seemed not to have reached by a cycle of years the meridian of life, is among the absent. Judge Newman, calm and yet courageous, is not. George Moore, of Owen, has left a enviable name as a heritage to posterity. A. B. Cole was my friend and brother: he was of small stature, best in voting, weighty and powerful. Milton Gregg, of Jefferson, was logical and infusive. Thomas Smith, of Ripley, was bold and daring. Dr. Foster, of Monroe, a massive brain and close reasoner. Pepper and Prather, calm, sober and faithful to their trusts. But the scythe of grim seems to have had great respect for all our officers for according to the printed list, not one is gone: our beloved President Carr, our Chief Secretary English, his assistants, Evans, Barkwell and Silas, our Doorkeeper Johnson, our Sergeant-at-Arms McKinzie, our Reporter Fowler, our printer, Austin Brown, are still on graying grounds and pleading terms, and who can tell but that it may be for a wise and gracious purpose? A hint to the wise.

One of my especial friends was Grafton F. Cookerly, whose . . . rotundity made him the admired of all. In this recital there stands out prominently the man of ugly name, and Wolfish. He was not blessed with an good supply of hands and arms as other men, and yet his excuse for an arm was sufficient to enable him to quench a personal broil, as my two friends Brother Kent and General Hovey can experimentally depose. And what shall I say of Maguire, the silent man, of Chapman, the shrewd, of Morrison, the scholar, of McLean, the quiet, of Carr, the sagacious, of Ballingall, the aged, of Bowers, the witty, of Bright, the muscular, of Thornton, the accomplished, of Miller, the modest, and of May, the sarcastic? For the time would fail me to tell of Jones, of Johnson, of Howe and Hitt, of Hall, Hamilton, and Holliday, of Sims, of Smith, and of Smiley, and a number of other greater and lesser lights, who through the storms of debate, the deliberations of committees and the labors of sessions, conform faithfully to the trust reposed in them by their constituency, for the long period of four months and more, and who gave the youthful State of Indiana a Constitution, under the benign workings of which we have grown in material wealth, in intelligence, and in all the elements that go to make a prosperous and happy people.

Colonel Taylor, formerly of LaPorte county, now of Chicago, eighty-four years old, and still a man of wonderful activity and of good, full voice, gave a humorous speech of personal reminiscences, after which the meeting adjourned.

There will be a meeting of survivors of the Constitutional Convention, and of several of the early Legislatures, this afternoon at 2 o'clock. The meeting at night will be public, and every one who desires can attend. The speakers to-night will be Judge Niblack, Colonel R. W. Thompson, Hon. W. S. Holman, Hon. John Lyle Kinf, of Chicago; Hon. R. N. Hudson, and others.[3]

FIRST LEGISLATURE UNDER NEW CONSTITUTION[4]

It was the understanding in advance that it was going to be a Legislature of unusual importance. The new Constitution had just been adopted by an immense majority of the electors. Its adoption made a careful revision of the laws necessary, in order that they should conform to its provisions. The work devolved on the Legislature was, in fact, a continuation of the work begun and outlined by the convention. The new Constitution required that the forms and practice in the courts, which had before that time been very intricate and voluminous, should be revised and simplified, the pleading made more uniform, the then prevailing distinction between law and equity abolished, and that the general statute law of the State should be reduced into a plain and systematic code.

"The whole temple of State government, from spire to foundation stone, had to be taken down, remodeled and rebuilt so as to conform to the new Constitution and the progress and improvements of the age."

To do all this properly, and much more that was devolved on the first Legislature, required time, and consequently that Legislature was not restricted by the Constitution as to length of session. It was necessarily longer in session than any Legislature ever held in the State, having met on the first of December, 1851, and adjourned on the 15th of June, 1852.

The public wisely recognized the need of doing the work well of these great reforms, and, looking to that end, elected a strong Legislature. Many of the members had served in the convention which formed the Constitution and in previous Legislatures, and, as a whole, was a splendid body of representative men.

A glance over the list will show many names of high standing and recognized ability, most of whom were called to high and honorable positions. Great as was the number of members of the Constitutional Convention called to represent the people in the Congress of the United States, more were called from this Legislature, vis.:

The rest of this part of his address gives a list of these congressmen and other particulars concerning the men who composed this legislature.

"MEN OF 1851:" MATERIAL FROM INDIANAPOLIS NEWSPAPERS[5]

The Reunion[6]

Remember that the reunion of the surviving members of the Constitutional Convention of 1850, and of all Indiana Legislatures prior to 1853, will organize at English's Opera House at 2 o'clock this afternoon. It will be an interesting event, and the public are invited. No admission fee or tickets required. There will also be a meeting at night at the same place. Our local columns give the details of the expected reunion. There will be addresses by prominent gentlemen, music, etc.

VICE PRESIDENT'S RETURN[7]

Vice President Hendricks returned from Atlantic City on Saturday night, and will be one of the speakers at the reunion to-night. He was in Washington but a short time during his absence. He goes to St. Louis on Wednesday, where he will be given a reception in the Chamber of Commerce on Thursday.

TODAY'S REUNION[8]

Of the Surviving Members of the Constitutional Convention of 1850.

To Be Followed by Another Reunion of the Surviving Members of the First Legislatures Under the New Constitution—The Programme.

The reunion of the surviving members of the Constitutional Convention of 1850, and of the surviving members of the several Legislatures of Indiana up to 1853, will begin at 2 o'clock this afternoon at English's Opera House, and promises to be one of the most interesting historical events ever occurring in the State. The object of the proposed reunion is to bring together the survivors, that the acquaintances of past years may be renewed and that steps may be taken to collect the history of the bodies and the men connected with them. There will be addresses and papers by the members and arrangements are making to publish the proceedings in pamphlet form. A number of the participants are already in the city, including Colonel George Whitfield Carr, President of the Constitutional Convention; Colonel E. D. Taylor and Dr. James Richey, delegates respectively from the counties of LaPorte and Johnson; Hon. William McKee Dunn, member of the first Legislature, from Jefferson County.

The meeting in English's Opera House this afternoon will be called to order by General McKee Dunn and presided over by Hon. George Whitfield Carr, who was President of the Constitutional Convention, and Hon. William H. English, who was Principal Secretary, will act in that capacity this afternoon and call the roll of members. The prayer will be offered by Rev. Oliver Perry Badger, of Putnam County, who was also a member of the Convention. A paper entitled "Reminiscences of the Inside History and Action of the Committee on Education," by John I. Morrison, now deceased, will be read by some member yet to be selected. Letters will also be read from General Milroy, C. C. Graham and other surviving members. At night there will be short addresses interspersed with songs and music. Vice President Hendricks will speak on "The Constitution and Its Amendments;" Hon. William H. English, on "The Indiana Constitution Convention of 1850, and the Personnel of Its Members;" General William McKee Dunn, on "A Review of the Proceedings of the Convention."

Congressman Holman, General Hovey and other distinguished gentlemen are expected to speak, but not yet having arrived, the subject cannot be stated.

Tuesday afternoon the legislative survivors will hold an informal meeting, and at night Mr. English, who was Speaker of the first House under the new Constitution, will preside and addresses will be made. The programme for the evening will be made to-day, and announced in tomorrow's Sentinel.

THE FIRST REUNION[9]

Of the Surviving Members of Indiana's Last Constitutional Convention

But Eighteen of the Organic Law Makers Respond to Roll-Call—Proceedings of the Afternoon and Evening Sessions—The Speeches

There was but a small gathering of visitors at the opening session of the reunion of the members of the Constitutional Convention of 1850 at English's Opera House yesterday afternoon, the meeting being simply for the purpose of organization. The spectators occupied the main auditorium, the stage being reserved for the members and the press. Hon. William McKee Dunn, delegate to the Constitutional Convention from Jefferson County, called the meeting to order and introduced the following motion:

Consultation called upon Carr being made President; resolution given in full in the Sentinel.

Carr was ushered to the chair and made a brief speech, as copied elsewhere. English called the roll.

The Invocation

After the roll-call was finished, the president announced that Hon. Oliver P. Badger, delegate from Putnam in the Constitutional Convention, would invoke the Divine blessing. The members rose to their feet, and Mr. Badger prayed as follows:

Help, Lord, for the godly man consent, for the faithful fail from among the children of man. We meet to-day, Our Father, under surroundings at once sad and joyful. We can but feel sad to know that so many strong and generous men have been stricken down by the hand of death since we toiled here together. But we rejoice to meet the survivors, and to speak to each other words of good cheer and warm congratulations. We bless thee that under the benign workings of the Constitution, which was the result of our deliberations, our beloved State of Indiana had grown in material wealth, in intelligence and in all elements that go to make a prosperous and happy people. And now, we devoutly pray, that the last days of those of us who survive may be days of happiness and peace. And may we leave our children a rich heritage, of fidelity to God and humanity, that they may be proud to emulate. Bless us in all our deliberations while this reunion shall continue. And when it is ours to cross the cold river, may we so have lived, and loved, and labored, as to have an hour of peace in which to die, and leave with our survivors a lasting evidence that we have gone from the evil to come to where the wicked cease from trouble and the weary shall find an eternal rest. And to God Our Father, through Jesus Christ our redeemer, be present and everlasting praises. Amen.

REMARKS OF WILLIAM MCKEE DUNN, 1885.[10]

Mr. President and Gentlemen:

We, venerable looking men, are the few survivors of that body of one hundred and fifty delegates, mostly in the prime of life, who assembled in convention in this city thirty-five years ago, chosen by the people of the State of Indiana to revise, amend or alter the Constitution of the State. I was a delegate from the county of Jefferson. My colleagues were Hon. Milton J. Gregg and Hon. Michael G. Bright, both of whom are now deceased. Of that numerous body of delegates only thirty-three now survive. Another generation is now on the stage of action, in relation to that convention we survivors now stand in the midst of posterity. We are so far removed from the convention by time and the great events which have since transpired in our country that I look back to it, read its proceedings, and pass judgment on its action as if I had not been a member of that body, and as if the delegate therein, who answered to my name were not myself, but someone else with whom I used to be acquainted, but who had long since passed away. I had scarcely opened the volumes of the debates in the convention from their publication until within the last week or two. I take my place now with posterity to judge myself, as well as my associates in the convention. If posterity should take the trouble to read over the two volumes of the debates in the convention, it would find that those who were most conspicuous for their much speaking are not among the surviving members. Could this fact make the impression that much speaking is not conductive to longevity, that impression might have a very beneficial influence to restrain debate in legislative bodies. The reader might also discover that the members who started in to do all the work of the convention accomplished but very little. He would certainly be surprised at the many crude propositions that were presented, and the persistent efforts that were made to insert in the organic law of the State, matters which were properly within the province of the Legislature. He might discover that some members deserve as much credit for what they kept out of the Constitution as others do for what they put in it. Much of the debates the reader would do well to skip over, but some of them he would find very able and instructive. He might be surprised at the time wasted in the discussion of matters with which the convention had nothing to do, as, for instance, the compromise measures passed by Congress in 1850. If the reader is possessed of the liberty loving spirit of this generation he will be astonished to find what a different spirit sometimes manifested itself in the Convention, and will be pained to read the number of inhumane and cruel propositions that were introduced, advocated, and some of them passed in regard to the colored race.

I find my name among those who voted for the adoption of the Constitution as it was finally passed by the Convention, although it is recorded against several of the propositions contained in it and in favor of the insertion of other provisions which were not adopted. I am thankful my name is recorded against the Thirteenth Article of the constitution at any stage of its progress in the Convention, as it was also recorded against it at the polls, where this section was submitted to a separate vote of the people. I join posterity in its emphatic condemnation of that Article, although it was adopted by the people by a majority of over 80,000 votes. In our form of government the will of the majority must rule, but it by no means follows that the majority is always right. The Thirteenth Article of the Constitution referred to provided that no Negro or Mulatto should come into or settle in the State after the adoption of the Constitution, and all contracts made with such Negro or Mulatto should be void, and that all persons who should employ such Negro or Mulatto, or otherwise encourage him to remain in the State, should be fined in sum of not less than $10 or more than $500, and that the General Assembly should pass laws to carry out the provisions of that Article. I will give to the members who voted for that Article the benefit of a statement of the argument in its favor, much urged by them, which was that our neighboring State, Kentucky, had recently adopted a constitution containing a section requiring the General Assembly of that State to pass laws to provide that any free Negro or Mulatto immigrating to, and any slave thereafter emancipated in, and refusing to leave that State, or, having left, should return and settle herein, should be guilty of felony and punished by confinement in the penitentiary.

The advocates of the thirteenth section insisted that this section of the Kentucky Constitution would cause our state to be invaded by the free Negroes from that state, many of whom, old and infirm, we would have to support. What was the free Negro of Kentucky to do? If he remained in Kentucky he was to be confined in the penitentiary for the crime of being free. If he attempted to put his foot on Indiana soil he was to be driven back as a leper, and any one who should extend to him the ordinary acts of human kindness or give him employment, was to be fined as an offender against the laws of the State. Look at these Constitutional provisions through the lurid light of subsequent events.

"God moves in a mysterious way, His wonders to perform," but He moves. Posterity has struck Article Thirteen out of the Constitution of Indiana. The majority is on the other side now.

The State Bank of Indiana and the Common Schools.

I do not believe the obliterating power of thirty-five years can have wholly blotted from your memories a scene in the convention which occurred a few days before its final adjournment. Mr. Dobson, of Owen, offered a section to the constitution declaring that the Legislature might, in the passage of a general banking law, have power to extend the charter of the State Bank of Indiana for a period of five years, the profits derivable from the funds of the State invested therein to be devoted to common school purposes. On this proposition there arose one of the most exciting debates of the session. The question of the propriety of leaving the Legislature free to act on the subject of the re-charter of the State Bank had been before the convention in various forms and all such propositions met with fierce opposition from Hon. John Pettit, of Tippecanoe. The debate on Mr. Dobson's proposition became very earnest. It looked at one time as if the proposition would be adopted. This prospect threw Mr. Pettit into unwanted excitement even for him.

He attacked the section with an energy of assertion and emphasis of denunciation peculiarly his own. He said the siren song was repeated there by the Gentleman from Jefferson (Mr. Dunn), that the State made money by its connection with the State Bank. He pronounced the statement to be utterly visionary and fallacious. Warming up to his work he declared the naked truth to be that the State Bank of Indiana was broken, was rotten, was worthless; that it could never redeem its liabilities, and it wanted an extension of its charter for five years in order to hide its worthlessness; that the design was to cover up and conceal as long as possible the rottenness of the institution, while it continued to filch from the State every dollar that could be drained from it, and charged the bank with stealing from the citizens of the State their hard earnings and sucking their very life-blood. He declared if we adopted that section every one who voted for it would go home branded with the charge of having been bribed and bought up by this monster. He concluded with the following words uttered with great dramatic power:

"Sir, I feel as did the proud women mentioned in history, who, when about to be robbed of her honor, took a dagger and buried it in her breast, saying, 'Mine eyes shall not see my disgrace.' Sir, my eyes shall not look upon this outage." [Enthusiastic Applause.] And then the virtuously indignant delegate from Tippecanoe, throwing his cloak over his shoulders and seizing his hat, with ponderous tread strode out of the hall. As soon as Mr. Hamilton, of Allen, who was an officer of the State Bank could get the floor, he said he was exceedingly sorry the gentleman from Tippecanoe had left the house. (He had requested him to stay.) He pronounced his statements as false and without any foundation whatever. Evidently Mr. Hamilton's Irish blood was up. His indignation was creditable alike to his head and his heart. He declared he would not sit quietly by and hear those connected with the State Bank denounced as swindlers. When such a charge was made he would pronounce it to be false let it come from whatever source it might. Had Mr. Pettit been in the hall while Mr. Hamilton was speaking I doubt whether Mr.

Hamilton could have kept his language even within the widest limits of parliamentary debate. Other sympathizers with Mr. Pettit followed him in similar, though weaker strains. One of them dared the friends of Mr. Dobson's proposition to pass it and go home to their constituents. However, Mr. Pettit did not stab himself "like the proud woman mentioned in history." He lived to return to the hall and finally triumph over the friends of Mr. Johnson's proposition. The section was defeated by a majority of six. A change of four votes from the negative to the affirmative would have caused its adoption. You, Mr. President, voted with the minority. The statements which Mr. Pettit was pleased to call the "siren song of the gentleman from Jefferson" may be found in the following extract from a speech of that gentleman delivered that day:

"The State borrowed for banking purposes $1,390,000, and issued her bonds for that amount bearing five percent interest, payable as follows: $500,000 in September, 1864, $450,000 in August, 1865, and $440,000 in July, 1866. Of these bonds $84,000 have been redeemed by the bank, leaving outstanding $1,306,000. I think it a safe calculation that the bank can make ten percent interest on this money, five of which will pay the interest on the bonds, and five per cent will remain as a profit to be devoted to the use of common schools. Putting this profit at the sum of $55,000 per annum, it would amount in five years to the sum of $325,000. That is a large sum of money and ought not be inconsiderately thrown away. The bank bonds were negotiated on better terms than they could now be negotiated. The question before the convention is not one of borrowing money, but whether we should pay, before it is due, money borrowed on favorable terms. The charter of the bank expires in 1857, and none of the bonds mature before 1864. If the charter should be extended to 1862, it would then expire in ample time before the maturity of the bonds, to enable the bank to pay them promptly as they fall due.

"I do not hesitate to make this extension imperative upon the Legislature, but I do desire that the question may be left to be decided by the people through their representatives in such a manner as they, upon mature deliberation, may think best. (Debates, Vol. 2, page 1985.)"

In a previous speech "the gentleman from Jefferson" had stated that the investment of Indiana in the State Bank had already yielded a profit of over $870,000, which under its charter was devoted to common school purposes. Posterity can now judge between the assertions of the gentleman from Tippecanoe and the "siren song of the gentleman from Jefferson." On the expiration of the charter of the bank, every bill issued by the various branches thereof was, on presentation, promptly paid in gold or silver, every dollar due to the depositors and all obligations of every kind were also promptly paid. The stockholders in the bank including the State were paid in full the amount of their stock and a large premium thereon. The bonds issued by the State for the money borrowed to pay for her stock in the bank were duly paid. Moreover, the State received from the bank for her profits on the investment therein up to November 15, 1858, over $2,780,000, as by the message of Governor Willard delivered to the legislature the following January.

The State Bank of Indiana wound up its affairs with a record for ability, integrity, and usefulness, on the part of its managers, not surpassed in the history of the management of any other institution of the kind in the United States. I am happy today to have the opportunity of this vindicating the reputations of Samuel Merrill, James M. Ray, Calvin Fletcher, J. F. D. Lanier, and others prominently connected with, and responsible for the management of the affairs of, this bank from the foregoing groundless charges now shown to be such by the public records of the State. I must not fail to mention the name of Hon. Hugh McCulloch, who still lives to enjoy an exalted reputation for financial ability and integrity founded largely upon his long connection with the management of the affairs of the State Bank of Indiana. I had no purpose to prepare any remarks for this occasion until I read over the few days ago the debate on Mr. Dobson's proposition. The history of the State Bank of Indiana is a part of the history of the State and a most creditable part thereof, and I have felt that I owed it to that history and to the reputation of the men, who, for more than a quarter of a century so ably and honorably conducted its affairs to confront the unfounded assertions and unmerited denunciations recorded in the debates of the convention by the plain facts as posterity sees them. I would do gross injustice to the majority of those who voted against the extension of the charter of the State Bank were I to leave the impression that they sympathized with Mr. Pettit in this tirade against the Bank. They certainly did not. That majority was secured by a combination of those who were for chartering a new State Bank, those for free banks exclusively, and those who were opposed to all banks. I voted for the constitutional provision, which authorized the legislature to establish a free banking system, "based on ample collateral security readily convertible into specie for the redemption of the bills in gold or silver," but I was not for free banking exclusively. By subsequent legislation free banking was authorized in this State, but unfortunately "ample collateral security" for the redemption of the bills was not required, or if required was not obtained. Engravers suddenly came into great demand. Free bank bills were for a time as plentiful as blackberries in July. Soon the bubbles began to burst and the people of Indiana lost millions of dollars by the depreciation of the free bank money. In the meantime the old State Bank moved on towards the expiration of her charter furnishing the people with a good, safe currency, based on good management and gold or silver. Without going into further details I may say that from the earnings of that loan made by the State more than fifty years ago, of $1,390,000 on which to establish the State Bank of Indiana, there is now in the school funds of the State over four millions of dollars about forty percent of the whole fund of the State, the annual interest on which as I am informed by the Auditor of the State, amounts to over $234,000 and is devoted to the support of our common schools.

THE JUDICIARY.

The stumbling block in the way of my voting for the adoption of the Constitution was the provision for the election of judges of the Supreme and Circuit Courts by the people. Under the old Constitution the Judges of the Supreme Court were nominated by the Governor and confirmed by the Senate. The judges of the Circuit Courts were elected by joint ballot of the two houses of the legislature. I did not favor the change made in the manner of selection. As I have lived out of the State so many years since the adoption of the Constitution I am not able to say what is the judgment of posterity on that change. I hope posterity will some time cease to laugh at the convention for inserting in the Judicial Article of the organic law of the State this section, "Every person of good moral character being a voter, shall be entitled to practice law in all courts of justice." Notwithstanding the stumbling block I voted for the Constitution on account of its superiority to the Constitution of 1816. We had outgrown that. The great progress the State had made in population, wealth, commerce and manufactures made changes necessary in the organic law. Special and local legislation had become an unendurable evil, but one which could not be prevented except by a change of the State Constitution. Other amendments were made which posterity had fully approved. While our Constitution laid such restrictions as seemed to be necessary to restrain the hot blood of the young giant State in legislation, it left his limbs loose enough to enable him to freely use them in the great work that was before him.

EDUCATION.

Mr. President, no part of the Constitution which we prepared and the people then adopted affords me more satisfaction than Article Eight, on education, of which the following is the first section:

"Knowledge and learning, generally diffused throughout a community, being essential to the preservation of a free government; it shall be the duty of the General Assembly to encourage, by all suitable means, moral, intellectual, scientific and agricultural improvement;

and to provide, by law, for a general and uniform system of common schools, wherein tuition shall be without charge, and equally open to all." Then follows a careful enumeration of which the common school fund shall consist, and then section third, which declares that "the principal of the common school fund shall remain a perpetual fund, which may be increased, but shall never be diminished; and the income thereof shall be inviolably appropriated to the support of common schools, and to no other purpose whatever."

The sixth section of the act provides that the several counties shall be held liable for the preservation of so much of the school fund as may be entrusted to them, and for the payment of the annual interest thereon.

Hon. John I. Morrison, a delegate from Washington County, was chairman of the Committee on Education, and to his wisdom in preparing, and good sense in advocating the passage of this Article, posterity owes him a debt of gratitude. It should recognize though it may never be able to pay. He has erected in the Constitution a monument to his memory. School houses should be named for him all over the State.

More than a third of a century has passed away since the ancestors of the present generation so formally and emphatically declared that the general diffusion of knowledge and learning throughout a community was essential to the preservation of a free government. That necessity is even more apparent now than it was when the declaration was made. Ignorance is a soil congenial to vice, and the one in which demagoguism takes root and finds most vigorous growth. An ignorant man is an easy dupe. To hold the turbulent spirits of our large cities in check we must oppose to them the intelligent and law-abiding citizens of the country. Our common schools are training schools for our future voters and lawmakers.

You and I, Mr. President, had no such opportunities for education as have the children of this generation. We were born in the territory of Indiana when four-fifths of what is now embraced in the limits of the State was wilderness. Our early lives were among the pioneers, the State builders. We remember and bore some part in the hardships they endured as they blazed the way for advancing civilization.

We know the respect in which they should be held for their manly virtues. We have witnessed the growth of this State from the wilderness to its present greatness and rejoice in its prosperity. The few years most of us survivors may hope to live, we may count on the fingers of one hand. We are but thirty-three now. One hundred who served thirty-five years ago have crossed the floor and I might almost say we are crossing now. Long ago we said of the members of the Constitutional Convention of 1850, "They are all gone," but while life remains we may pray for the blessing of heaven to rest upon the people of this State and not only upon them, but upon the people of all the States of our Union.

[1] *Indianapolis Journal,* 4 October 1885. (Editorial; copied in full. Title given here is supplied.)

[2] *Indianapolis Journal,* 6 October 1885. The article had five headings as indicated. This paper has a much better account of the convention than that given in the daily *Sentinel.*

[3] This concludes the account given in the October 6, 1885 issue of the *Indianapolis Journal*; account has been copied verbatim except for the omission in regard to remarks on Dunn's address as explained in the text.

[4] *Indianapolis Journal,* 7 October 1885. From an address delivered by Honorable William H. English on the work of early legislatures. Only the portion dealing with the legislature of 1851-1852 is herein included. The legislators held a reunion at the same time the members of the constitutional convention met.

[5] The *Sentinel* has fairly complete reports but material used consists of that not discussed fully in the *Indianapolis Journal.* Both papers are very valuable as sources and have many interesting items about the reunions of the various groups.

[6] *Indianapolis Journal,* 5 October 1851. This item is an editorial comment.

[7] *Indianapolis Journal,* 5 October 1885.

[8] Ibid. This article indicates that one purpose of the meeting was to collect historical information; it may be that English had this purpose in view. Evidence points to that view. It was not possible to find a publication of the proceedings (in pamphlet form) for use in this thesis; none could be found.

[9] *Indianapolis Journal,* 6 October 1885. This article occupies the space of about seven columns, only a very small portion of which is copied here. For the most part the report is much like the report given to the *Journal* and copied in this appendix.

[10] *Remarks of General William McKee Dunn, Indianapolis, October, 5, 1885, at the Reunion of the Surviving Members of the Indiana Constitutional Convention of 1850.* Taken from a pamphlet in the stacks of the Indiana University library. This copy is added here because the accounts in the *Journal* and *Sentinel* did not give a complete account of Dunn's remarks.

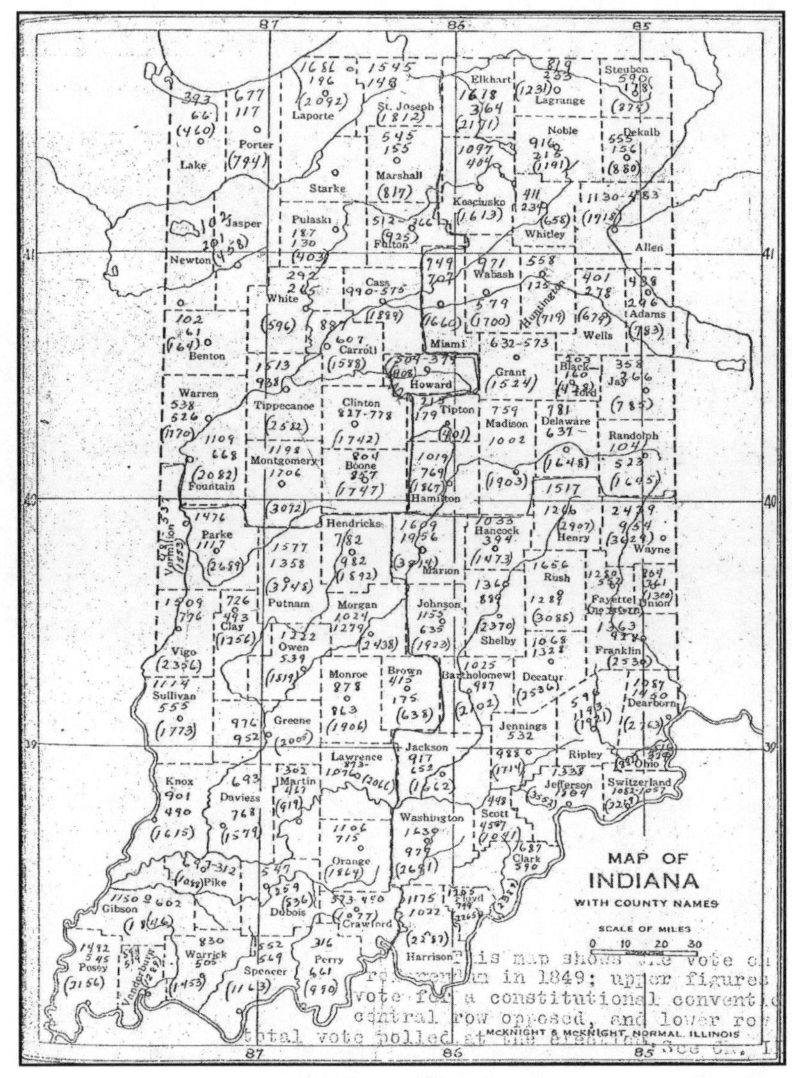

Photo Courtesy Donald F. Carmony and Edith Hagelskamp

This map, prepared by the author and Edith Hagelskamp, depicts votes for and against the Referendum of 1849 calling for a constitutional convention.

APPENDIX IV

CONVENTION REFERENDUMS
INTRODUCTION TO REFERENDUM OF 1823[1]

The referendum in 1823 was the first, of the five, which was held under the old constitution. December 12, 1822, the Senate had appointed a special committee of five "to inquire into the expediency of a law to authorize the qualified voters throughout the State, at the next August election, to vote for or against calling a convention for the revision of the State constitution. . . ."[2] December 23 this committee reported a bill which passed the Senate six days later. It passed the House January 1, 1823, and was approved by Governor William Hendricks January 6.

The chief changes urged by the advocates of constitutional reform, at this time, were: substitution of biennial or triennial sessions of the General Assembly for annual sessions; authorizing the governor to call special sessions of General Assembly in cases of emergency; abolition of the office of associate judge; abolition of the "legislative divorces" by conferring this power on the courts; reconstruction of the Supreme Court so as to bring it nearer to the people; and conferring on the General Assembly the power to fix the time of its own meeting to suit the general convenience.[3] Kettleborough adds: "But there is tolerably conclusive evidence that the real reason for calling a constitutional convention was to eliminate from the Constitution the provision excluding slavery and involuntary servitude from the State."[4]

The formal arguments of the anti-conventionists were: that the calling of a convention would entail a serious risk as no one knew what kind of a constitution a convention would frame; the expense would be at least $8,000 or $10,000 dollars; evils were not such as to call for such action; the General Assembly had just appointed Gov. Hendricks to revise and codify the laws and the convention would make all of this in vain; it would be unfair to those who had recently emigrated from other states thinking that the constitution would not be changed; a vote would be unconstitutional as 1823 was not at the end of a regular twelve-year period; and frequent changes would produce political instability.

The Indiana Gazette *opposed the movement for a convention. The* Western Sun *favored changing the constitution by a convention. "The question of calling a convention was probably more widely discussed in 1823 than at any time prior to 1849, and the defeat of the proposition assured from the start."*[5] *The referendum was voted upon at the general election on August 4, 1823. Returns were received from thirty-one counties. There were 2,601 votes cast for a convention, with 11,991 against a convention.*[6] *This ended the first formal attempt to modify the constitution of 1816.*

Constitutional Referendum in 1823[7]

AN ACT to authorize the qualified voters of this State to vote for or against a convention for the revision of the constitution of this state.

Section 1. *Be it enacted by the General Assembly of the State of Indiana,* That the qualified voters of the different townships throughout this state, be and they are hereby authorized, on the first Monday of August next, when they vote for senators and representatives, to express by vote, on the same ticket, at the bottom thereof, whether they are in favor, or against calling a convention, for the revision of the constitution of this state; which vote shall be expressed in one of the following words, to wit: "convention," or "no convention," as the case may be.

Sec. 2. It shall be the duty of the inspectors and judges, in different townships in each county, to receive, count, and make a true return, of all the votes given, as contemplated in the foregoing section, at the same time, and in the same manner, that they count and make returns of votes given for senators and representatives: and it shall be the duty of the clerk of the circuit court, in each and every county, throughout the state, to seal and forward to the secretary of state, on or before the first Monday of December next, a certificate under his hand and seal, of all the votes taken as aforesaid; and should any of the clerks of the circuit court, fail or neglect to perform the duty enjoined on him by this act, he shall forfeit and pay the sum of one hundred dollars for such neglect, recoverable by presentment or indictment, in any court having competent jurisdiction.

Sec. 3. It shall be the duty of the secretary of state, to lay before the next General Assembly, on the second Monday in December next, all the returns by him received, pursuant to the provisions of this act.

Sec. 4. It shall be the duty of the clerks of the circuit courts, when they make out the poll books, for the general election, to make out and rule two separate columns in the same, for the purpose of tallying the votes taken, as contemplated by this act.

Approved, January 6, 1823.

Introduction to Referendum of 1828

When the twelfth General Assembly met, it was possible for both the strict and loose constructionists to unite in submitting a referendum to the people as such procedure would be in perfect accord with the "twelve-year" clause. December 18, 1827, a bill to provide for a convention was introduced in the Senate. January 4 the bill passed the Senate and four days later was approved by the House. The act was very much like the act of 1823; it was definitely stated that the question was being submitted "in pursuance of the eighth article of the Constitution."

There was no doubt as to the constitutionality of the measure. Kettleborough explains that ". . . voters were too engrossed in national issues and the zealous magic of Jacksonian Democracy that the convention proposition aroused very little popular interest."[8] *Even the slavery question came in for comment again. The* Lawrenceburg Palladium, *July 19, expressed the conviction that the time was "inauspicious" because of the general agitation attending the presidential election.*[9] *July 3 the* Indianapolis Gazette *published the act and advocated approval at the polls.*[10] *July 10 the* Indiana Journal *printed the act without comment.*[11]

The poll was held at the general election on August 4, 1828. The returns of the secretary of state show 10,092 votes for to 18,638 votes against a convention.[12]

Constitutional Referendum in 1828[13]

AN ACT to authorize the qualified voters of this State to vote for or against a convention for a revision of the constitution of this state.

Section 1. *Be it enacted by the General Assembly of the State of Indiana,* That it shall be and is hereby made the duty of the inspectors and judges of elections, in the several townships within each county in this state, at the annual elections, on the first Monday in August next, to open a poll in pursuance of the eighth article of the constitution of this state, in which shall be entered all the votes given for and against a convention, and the clerks of the circuit courts are hereby required, when they make out poll books for the inspectors of elections, to extend two additional columns for that purpose.

Sec. 2. It is hereby made the duty of the inspectors and judges aforesaid, at the time they announce the name of the voter to their clerks, to put the questions in the following words, "are you in favor of calling a convention or not?" and the clerks of said election, shall enter the votes on the poll books, in the proper column accordingly; and the inspectors and judges shall certify the votes given for and against a convention to the clerks of the circuit courts respectively, in the same way and manner, and under the same restrictions and penalties that votes for state and county officers are required to be certified.

Sec. 3. It shall be the duty of the clerks of the circuit courts throughout the state, to certify and make returns of all the votes given for and against a convention, to the Secretary of State, in the same way and manner that votes given for Governor and Lieutenant Governor are required by law to be certified, and subject to the same penalties for a neglect of duty. It shall be the duty of the Secretary of State to lay before the next General Assembly, on the second Monday in December next, all the returns by him received, pursuant to the provisions of this act.

Approved, January 14, 1828.

INTRODUCTION TO REFERENDUM OF 1840

In 1840, at the end of the second twelve-year period, was held the third constitutional referendum. The bill, which led to the referendum, was introduced in the House on January 23, 1840. February 4 the bill passed the House and eight days later was acted upon favorably by the Senate. It was signed by the governor on January 23, 1840. The act is very similar to that of 1828. It is worthy of note that the act of 1840 stated that the referendum was being held "in obedience to the constitution of this State, and that the people of their respective counties will not have the right to vote for or against another convention for the space of twelve years."

W. W. Thornton, in an address before the Indiana State Bar Association, July 9, 1912, stated, "In the rollicking campaign of 1840 the question of constitutional revision was almost buried out of sight, because of the public excitement upon other questions." This view, that the Log Cabin and Hard Cider campaign attracted all the attention to national issues, has probably been held too freely. However, "the Tri-Weekly Journal *of Indianapolis, one of the most alert and enterprising papers in the State, did not refer to the convention question in a single issue of the year."*[14] *Apparently the voters were not interested in constitutional revision.*

Seventy counties gave a total of 75,380 votes on the proposition: 12,666 were for and 62,714 were opposed to a convention. Steuben County was the only one in the State to return a majority in favor of a convention.[15] *The total vote was larger than in 1828 but proportion of votes favorable was much less.*

Referendum in 1840[16]

AN ACT to authorize the qualified voters of this State to vote for or against a convention for a revision of the constitution of this State.

Section 1. *Be it enacted by the General Assembly of the State of Indiana,* That it shall be, and is hereby made the duty of the inspectors and judges of elections, in the several townships within each county in this State, in the annual election on the first Monday in August next, to open a poll, in pursuance of the eighth article of the constitution of this State, in which shall be entered all the votes given for and against a convention; and the clerks of the circuit courts are hereby required, when they make out poll books for the inspectors of elections, to extend two additional columns for that purpose. And for the purpose of more expressly calling the attention of the people of the State, to the propriety of voting for or against said proposed convention, it is hereby made the duty of the several sheriffs in this State, to give six-weeks public notice, in a newspaper, if one is published in his county; if not by written notices, in all the townships in said county, in writing, calling on the people to vote for or against a convention and that, in the language of the present constitution, there will not be a convention called unless a majority of all the votes given at such election, shall be in favor of a convention; and setting forth in said notice, that said voting for or against said convention, is in obedience to the constitution of this State, and that the people of their respective counties will not have the right to vote for or against another convention for the space of twelve years.

Sec. 2. It is hereby made the duty of inspectors and judges aforesaid, at the time they announce the name of the voter to their clerks, to put the question in the following words: "Are you in favor of calling a convention, or not?" And the clerks of said election shall enter the votes on the poll-books in the proper column, accordingly;

and the inspectors and judges shall certify the votes given for and against a convention, to the clerks of the circuit courts respectively, in the same way and manner, and under the same restrictions and penalties that votes for State and county officers are required to be certified.

Sec. 3. It shall be the duty of the clerks of the circuit courts throughout this State, to certify and make returns of all the votes given for or against a convention, to the Secretary of State, in the same way and manner that votes given for governor and lieutenant governor are required by law to be certified, and subject to the same penalties for a neglect of duty. It shall be the duty of the Secretary of State to lay before the next General Assembly, on the second Monday in December next, all the returns by him received, pursuant to the provisions of this act.

Approved, February 22, 1840.

Official Election Notice, 1840.[17]

Pursuant to the provisions of an act of the last General Assembly of the State of Indiana entitled "An act to authorize the qualified voters of this State to vote for or against a Convention for a revision of the Constitution of this State," approved February 22, 1840, the qualified voters of Knox County are hereby notified that a poll will be opened in the several townships, by the inspectors and judges of elections, on the first Monday in August next, for the purpose of receiving their votes for or against a convention to revise the constitution of Indiana; and it is made the duty of said inspectors and judges, at the time they announce the name of the voter, to put to said voter this question- "Are you in favor of calling a Convention, or not?"-And in pursuance also of said law, the people of said county are hereby urged to vote for or against said convention; and they will not have the right to vote for or against another convention for the space of twelve years.

Given under my hand at Vincennes, in said county,
this eleventh day of July, 1840. Z. Pulliam, Sheriff.

INTRODUCTION TO REFERENDUM OF 1846.

The fourth constitutional referendum was held in 1846. The movement for a convention came more nearly succeeding at this time than at any other time before 1849. December 10, 1845, the House adopted a resolution instructing the Judiciary Committee to report a bill providing for a constitutional referendum. Accordingly, a bill was reported on December 15 and was passed by the House three days later. January 17, 1846 it was passed by the Senate; nineteen Democrats and twelve Whigs voting favorably, four Democrats and ten Whigs opposed.[18] *The bill was approved by Governor Whitcomb January 19. Several states held constitutional referendums during this period.*

The Indiana State Sentinel, *the leading Democratic paper, advocated the call of a convention. They were joined in this campaign by the* Lafayette Courier, Vincennes Gazette, Goshen Democrat, St. Joseph Register, *and* Ft. Wayne Times. *Mass meetings calling for convention were held in Marion and Washington Counties. There were many changes demanded by the electors.*[19]

The election was held August 3 and returns were received from seventy-six counties. 32,468 electors voted for a convention, with 27,123 voting against a convention; the official poll totaled 126,969. Less than half of the electors had expressed their opinion at the poll. In order to be constitutional, a majority vote was required.

Several questions arose as a result of the contest. Did a majority mean half of the total poll or a mere majority of those who voted on the referendum? Was the twelve-year clause restrictive so that a convention would be unconstitutional? The Indiana State Sentinel *contended that the General Assembly could not prohibit the holding of a convention and that in case they do not enact the necessary legislation the people may proceed to hold the convention anyway.*[20]

Kettleborough supports the view that the General Assembly of 1846-1847 acted upon the matter in a partisan manner.[21] *The General Assembly which had submitted the referendum was controlled by the Democrats; the new Assembly was slightly Whig in both branches. After prolonged debate and committee reports, the matter was at last permitted to lie dormant. It was the most discussed contest thus far.*

Referendum of 1846[22]

An Act to provide for taking the sense of the qualified voters of the State on the calling a Convention, to alter, revise, or amend the Constitution of this State.

Section 1. *Be it enacted by the General Assembly of the State of Indiana*, That it shall be the duty of inspectors and judges of elections, in the several townships within each county in this State, at the annual election in August next, to open a poll in which shall be entered all the votes given for or against a convention to alter, revise, or amend the Constitution of this State.

Sec. 2. Every qualified voter of this State may, if he choose, at the annual election in August next, vote for or against the calling of a convention for the purpose mentioned in the first section of this act.

Sec. 3. If such voter shall be in favor of a convention, he shall write or print, or partly write and partly print on the same ballot with which he votes for state or county officers, the words, "for a convention;" if against a convention, he shall in the same manner have the words "against a convention," on his ballot as aforesaid.

Sec. 4. It is hereby made the duty of inspectors and judges of elections, to certify the votes given for and against a convention, to the clerks of the circuit courts, respectively, in the same way and manner, and under the same restrictions and penalties, that votes for State and county officers are certified.

Sec. 5. It shall be the duty of the clerks of the circuit courts throughout this State, to certify and make returns, of all the votes given for and against a convention, to the Secretary of State, in the same way and manner that votes given for governor and lieutenant governor are required by law to be certified: and they shall be subject to the same penalties for a neglect of duty. It shall be the duty of the Secretary of State to lay before the next General Assembly, on the second Monday of December next, all the returns by him received pursuant to the provisions of this act.

Sec. 6. It shall be the duty of the several sheriffs of this State, to give six weeks' public notice, in a newspaper, if one be published in his county; if not, by written notices in each township of his county, that there will be a poll opened for the purposes specified in this act.

Approved, January 19, 1846.

Official Election Notice (1846)[23]

CONVENTION NOTICE

The qualified voters of Cass County, Indiana, are notified that at "the annual election in August next" (1846), a poll will be opened in the several townships in said county, to receive votes *for* or *against* a convention to alter, revise, or amend the Constitution of this State, at which every voter, if he choose, may vote for or against the calling of a convention, and if such voter shall be in favor of a convention, he shall write or print on the same ballot with which he votes for State or County officers, the words, "*For a Convention*;" but if against a convention, he shall in the same manner have the words "*Against a Convention*," on his ballot as aforesaid. It is made the duty of the inspectors and judges of elections to certify the votes given for and against a convention to the clerk of the circuit court in the same way and manner, and under the same restrictions and penalties that votes for State and county officers are certified.

June 22, 1846.
A. Vanness, Sh'ff. C.C.

Whitcomb's (Governor) Reference to Election (1846)[24]

In conformity with the act providing for taking the sense of the qualified voters as to the propriety of calling a convention to alter, revise, or amend the constitution of this State, approved January 19, 1846, a poll was opened at the annual election held in August last, for receiving votes upon that question. The returns, so far as made to the Secretary of State, as required by that act, show that 32,521 votes were cast for, and 27,485 votes were cast against calling a convention. They also show that the aggregate number of votes returned as having been cast upon that question, is less than one-half of the number of voters who attended the polls and voted upon other questions, and that from thirteen counties no returns whatever upon that question have been received.

Referendum Act of 1849.[25]

AN ACT to provide for taking the sense of the qualified voters of the State on the calling of a Convention to alter, amend, or revise the constitution of this State.

Section 1. *Be it enacted by the General Assembly of the State of Indiana*, That it shall be the duty of Inspectors and Judges of elections in the several townships within each county in this State at the annual election in August next, to open a poll in which shall be entered all the votes given for or against the calling of a convention to alter, revise, or amend the constitution of this State.

Sec. 2. Every qualified voter in this State, may, if he choose, at the annual election in August next, vote for or against the calling of a convention, for the purpose mentioned in the first section of this act.

Sec. 3. The Inspectors of elections at the several places of voting, shall propose to each voter presenting a ballot the question "are you in favor of a convention to amend the Constitution" and those who are in favor of such convention shall answer in the affirmative, and those who are against such convention shall answer in the negative, which answers shall be duly recorded by the Clerks of such election, and the Clerks of the Boards doing the county business shall furnish a poll-book with proper columns for that purpose.

Sec. 4. It is hereby made the duty of the Inspectors and Judges of elections to certify the number of votes given for or against a convention to the Clerks of the circuit courts respectively, in the same way and manner, and under the same restrictions and penalties that votes for State and county officers are given and certified.

Sec. 5. It shall be the duty of the Clerks of the circuit courts throughout the State to certify and make returns of all the votes given for and against a convention, and also all the votes that were given at such election, to the Secretary of State in the same way and manner that votes for Governor and Lieutenant Governor are required by law to be certified, and they shall be subject to the same penalties for neglect of duty. It shall be the duty of the Secretary of State to lay before the next General Assembly on the second Monday of December next all the returns by him received, pursuant to the provisions of this act.

Sec. 6. It shall be the duty of the several Sheriffs of this State to give six weeks' notice in the newspaper, if one is published in his county; if not, by written notices in each township of his county, that there will be a poll opened for the purposes specified in this act.

Approved, January 15, 1849.

Official Election Notice, 1849.[26]

Notice is hereby given to the qualified voters of Jefferson County, Indiana, that there will be an election held at the usual place of holding elections in said county—also at North Madison, in Madison Township—on Monday, the sixth day of August next, it being the first Monday in August, according to the law, for the purpose of electing one Governor and one Lieutenant-Governor for the State of Indiana; and a Congressman for the Second Congressional District of Indiana; three Representatives to the State Legislature for said county; one Sheriff; one Treasurer; one Auditor; one Recorder; one Assessor; and one County Commissioner for the Third district, to fill the vacancy occasioned by the expiration of the term of John E. Gale, Esq.; also for or against the calling of a Convention to clear, amend, and revise the Constitution of Indiana; also for or against the act of the Legislature of Indiana, 1848-49, to increase and extend the benefits of the common schools.

Henry Deputy, Sheriff Jeff. Co.

[1] Charles Kettleborough, *Constitution Making in Indiana: A Source Book of Constitutional Documents with Historical Introduction and Critical Notes* (Indianapolis: Indiana Historical Commission, 1916), 1: Introduction. This is a very excellent source for the student of Indiana constitutional history and the source most widely used here.

[2] Ibid., 1: xli.

[3] Ibid., 1: xlii.

[4] Ibid., 1: xliii.

[5] Ibid., 1: li.

[6] Ibid., 1: lii. Quoted from *Journal of the House of Representatives Being the Eighth Session of the General Assembly* (Indianapolis: State Printer, 1824),52.

[7] *Laws of the State of Indiana, Passed at the Seventh Session of the General Assembly* (Indianapolis: J.P. Chapman, 1859), 121. G.W. Johnson was speaker of the House of Representatives, Ratliff Boon was president of the Senate, and William Hendricks was governor.

[8] Kettleborough, *Constitution Making*, lv.

[9] Ibid., 1: lvi.

[10] Ibid.

[11] Ibid.

[12] Ibid., 1: lvii.

[13] *Laws of the State of Indiana, Passed at the Twelfth Session of the General Assembly* (Indianapolis: J.P. Chapman, 1864), 22. James B. Ray was governor. The act had been introduced in the Senate December 18, 1827 by John S. Simonson. Section two is a good example of *viva voce* voting.

[14] Kettleborough, *Constitution Making*, 1: lxi.

[15] Ibid., quoting from documents.

[16] *Laws of the State of Indiana, Passed at the Twenty-fourth Session of the General Assembly* (Indianapolis: J.P. Chapman, 1876). David Wallace, a Whig, was governor. The bill was introduced in the House by Jesse Morgan.

[17] Kettleborough, *Constitution Making*, 1: 162-163. Quoted from *Western Sun* and *General Advertiser*, 8 August 1840. This is an election notice as spoken of in section one of the act calling for a referendum.

[18] Kettleborough, *Constitution Making*, 1: lxiii.

[19] Ibid., 1: lxiv-lxvi, gives a list of thirty proposed changes.

[20] Ibid., 1: lxviii.

[21] Ibid., 1: lxix.

[22] *Laws of the State of Indiana, Passed at the Thirtieth Session of the General Assembly* (Indianapolis: J.P. Chapman, 1882), 97-98. James Whitcomb, Democrat, was governor. Kettleborough quotes from the *Indiana State Journal*, 27 August 1845 indicated that Senate had twenty-five Whigs and twenty-five Democrats. The House had forty-five Whigs and fifty-five Democrats.

[23] Kettleborough, *Constitution Making*, 1: 167. Quoted from *Logansport Telegraph*, 27 June 1846.

[24] Ibid., 170. Quoted from *Journal of the House of Representatives Being the Thirty-first Session of the General Assembly* (Indianapolis: State Printer, 1847), 22.

[25] *Laws of the State of Indiana, Passed at the Thirty-third Session of the General Assembly* (Indianapolis: J.P. Chapman, 1885), 36. No introduction to this referendum is given here because it has been fully discussed in the body of the thesis. This was the fifth and last referendum.

[26] Kettleborough, *Constitution Making*, 1: 193. Quoted from *Madison Weekly Courier*, 30 June 1849. Kettleborough states that this proclamation was issued on June 27, 1849.

On Behalf of the Women of Indiana.

Deprecating the efforts of those of our sex who desire to enter the political arena—to contend with men at the ballot box, or sit in our public councils, and demanding only protection for the property that Providence may enable us to give our daughters—protection for our sex against the improvidence of the vices of weak or bad men; we tender our sincere acknowledgements to the high-minded gentlemen, Delegates in the Constitutional Convention, who favored the adoption of the securing to the married women of Indiana, independent rights of property; and we have determined to present to the Hon. ROBERT DALE OWEN as the original mover, a testimonial in the form of a piece of plate, with suitable inscriptions, as a slight token of our lasting gratitude.

That the women of Indiana, generally, may have an opportunity to contribute to this most laudable object, we have limited the contribution to one dollar from each.

ALICE READ, Bloomington, Indiana.
JANE H. PEPPER, Rising Sun, do
LOUISA F. KENT, New Albany, do
ANN E. SMITH, do do
P. HOLMES DRAKE. Indianapolis. do
PAULINE CHAPMAN, do do
ANN O. MORRISON, do do
MARY E. ELLSWORTH, Lafayette do
MARY B. WEST, Indianapolis, do
S. M. HUNTINGTON, Cannelton, do
MARY ST.C. BUEL, Lawrenceburgh do
MARY HAMMOND, Indianapolis, do
MARY F. LANE, Lawrenceburgh, do
SOPHIA A. HALL, Princeton, do
SARAH T. BOLTON, Indianapolis, do

It will be estemed a favor if the press throughout the State will insert and notice this Circular. Communications or subscriptions to the testimonial, accompanied with the names and address of contributors, may be addressed to Gen. James P. Drake, Treasurer of State, Indianapolis.

Courtesy Indiana Division, Indiana State Library

Proponents of women's property rights raised money to present Robert Dale Owen with a testimonial, acknowledging his attempts to include rights for women in the Constitution. This article, raising money for the gift, appeard in newspapers around the state, including *The Indiana True Democrat* (December 1850).

APPENDIX V

MISCELLANEOUS MATERIAL

Act Calling For the Convention, 1850.[1]

AN ACT to provide for the call of a Convention of the people of the State of Indiana, to revise, amend, or alter the Constitution of said State.

WHEREAS, An act was passed by the General Assembly of this State at its last session, to provide for taking the sense of the qualified voters of the State, on the propriety of calling a convention to alter, amend, or revise the Constitution of this State, approved January 15, 1849; AND WHEREAS, A large majority of all the votes given at said election was in favor of holding said convention; AND WHEREAS, It is the duty of the Representatives of the people, promptly, and without delay, to provide for carrying the public will thus expressed into immediate effect: Therefore,

Sec. 1. *Be it enacted by the General Assembly of the State of Indiana*, That the citizens of this State qualified by law, to vote for members of the General Assembly, shall meet at the respective places of holding elections in the several counties of this State, on the first Monday in August next, and proceed to elect delegates to constitute a convention, for the purpose of considering the Constitution of this State, and making such amendments to, alterations of, and changes in the same, as they may deem proper, which amendments shall afterwards be submitted to a vote of the people of this State to be by them ratified or rejected.

Sec. 2. The said convention shall consist of a number of delegates equal to the whole number of the members composing the Senate and the House of Representatives of this State who shall be apportioned in the same manner that members of the General Assembly shall then by law be apportioned, and they shall be chosen in the same method, at the same places, and by the same electors that choose the General Assembly, and all persons entitled to vote by this act for delegates shall be eligible to be elected to a seat in said convention: *Provided, however*, That the legal voters of Hamilton county alone shall elect the Senatorial delegate in the Senatorial district composed of the counties of Hamilton, Boone and Tipton: *And provided further*, That the counties of Daviess and Martin shall elect one delegate each separately, instead of two delegates jointly as above contemplated in this section.

Sec. 3. That said election, when not otherwise provided for by this act, shall in all respects be conducted, and the poll books kept, in the manner prescribed by law for the election of members of the General Assembly of this State; and the several provisions of the fifth chapter of the first part of the Revised Statutes, and the acts amendatory thereof, regulating the hours and places of holding elections, the qualifications and disabilities of voters, the duties of inspectors, judges, and clerks of elections, the keeping of the ballot boxes, the opening of the elections, voting, and challenges, the closing of the polls, the counting the votes, returning and canvassing the same, declaring and certifying who are elected, or who have received the highest number of votes, and all other laws regulating general elections in this State as far as the same are applicable, shall be in force and govern in the said election of delegates, and all inspectors, judges, clerks, sheriffs and other officers, shall perform the same duties at said election, and shall receive the same compensation therefor, and be paid in like manner as they are now directed to be paid by law for similar services at elections for members of the General Assembly of this State.

Sec. 4. The board of county canvassers in each county shall meet on the Wednesday succeeding the said first Monday in August next, and proceed to canvass the votes received in each township for delegates to said convention in the same method that is now required of them by the laws regulating the election of members of the General Assembly of this State, and when any county shall alone constitute a senatorial or representative district said board of canvassers shall in the same manner as now provided by law in regard to the election of Senator or Representative for said county, declare who are duly elected senatorial and representative delegates to said convention, from said county, and the clerk of the circuit court of said county shall, on the same or succeeding day, make out under his hand and official seal, certifications of election for each of the said delegates so declared elected as aforesaid, and hand them to the sheriff of said county who shall without delay deliver or cause to be delivered to said delegates elect, and said clerk shall also forthwith transmit to the Secretary of State by mail the names of the persons so declared elected, duly certified under his seal of office.

Sec. 5. When two or more counties shall compose a district for the purpose of electing a Senator or Representative the clerk of the circuit courts in the respective counties constituting said district shall on the next day succeeding the return of said election, make out a certificate of all the votes received by each individual for Senatorial or Representative delegates to said convention in said county and deliver the same to the sheriff of his county.

Sec. 6. The sheriffs (or their deputies duly appointed) of the several counties constituting said Senatorial or Representative district, shall meet on the Wednesday next following the return day of such election, at the same hour and place, and in the same county now required by law for them to meet to canvass the vote for Senators or Representatives (as the case may be in said district) and proceed to compare the several certificates so delivered to them by said clerks of their respective counties as aforesaid, and after having ascertained who are duly elected Senatorial or Representative delegates to said convention in said district, they shall jointly make out and forward by the hand of one or more of their number to the person or persons by them so declared elected as delegates to said convention, certificates of their election; and said sheriffs shall also deliver to the clerk of the circuit court in the county where said certificates are compared, a statement in writing of the names of the person or persons by them declared duly elected delegates as aforesaid, who shall file the same in his office and immediately transmit by mail a certified copy thereof, attested under his seal of office to the Secretary of State.

Sec. 7. That all willfully, corrupt, and false swearing in taking any of the oaths or affirmations rendered necessary by virtue of this act, at or in relation to said election of delegates, shall be deemed perjury, and shall be punished in the same manner now prescribed by law for the punishment of perjury; and all laws prohibiting and providing penalties for illegal voting at the general elections in this state, and also providing penalties for betting on, and misconduct at elections, and all laws requiring the performance of any duty from any officer in regard to the election of members of the General Assembly of this State, shall be, and is hereby declared in full force; and said officers shall be liable for any neglect of duty to the same penalties now prescribed by law for the neglect of similar duties in respect to the election of members of the General Assembly of this State.

Sec. 8. In case of a contested or disputed election of delegates to said convention, the contesting candidate, or other person contesting said election, shall pursue the same course, and be governed in all things by the same rules and regulations as are now provided by law in cases of contested or disputed elections of Senators or Representatives of the General Assembly of this State.

Sec. 9. The delegates who shall be elected as aforesaid, shall assemble in convention at the capitol, in the city of Indianapolis, on the first Monday in October next, and organize by electing a president and all other officers necessary. It shall be the duty of the

Secretary of State to attend the said convention on the opening thereof, to call over the lists of districts and counties, receive the credentials of the delegates, and generally to perform the like duties in the organization of the same, that are usually discharged by the officer whose duty it is by law to attend to the organization of the House of Representatives of this State at the commencement of its session; and should the Secretary of State fail to attend in person or by deputy, by 10 o'clock, A.M., on said day, then it shall be the duty of the Auditor of this State to attend for such purpose; and it shall be the duty of the State Librarian immediately after the General Assembly shall adjourn, to prepare the Hall of the House of Representatives for the reception of, and the sittings of said convention.

Sec. 10. The said delegates, before entering upon the discharge of their duties, shall be duly sworn or affirmed to support the constitution of the United States, and also faithfully, and to the best of their respective abilities, perform the duties of their office; which oath or affirmation may be administered to them by any judge of the supreme, or presiding judge of the circuit courts of this State; and should no such judge be in attendance at the opening of the sitting of said convention, then by any officer of the county of Marion duly authorized by the laws of this State to administer oaths and affirmations.

Sec. 11. The members of said convention shall enjoy the same privileges in going to, attending upon, and returning from said convention, that members elected to and attending on the General Assembly are entitled, by law. Said convention shall be the judge of the elections, returns, and qualifications of its own members; it shall possess the same power to adopt rules, expel a member for disorderly conduct, and punish contempt, that are now exercised by either House of the General Assembly in similar cases. A majority of the members shall constitute a quorum to do business, but a smaller number may adjourn from day to day, and take measures to compel attendance of absent members. And the president, members, and secretaries of the convention shall be allowed the use of the books in the State Library, in the same manner and upon the same condition that the members of the General Assembly are allowed the use thereof.

Sec. 12. In case of the death or resignation of any member of said convention, the Governor of this State shall issue a writ of election, directed to the sheriff or sheriffs of the proper counties, directing a special election to be held to fill such vacancy, in the same manner now prescribed by law for supplying vacancies in the General Assembly of this State. The members of said convention shall receive three dollars per day while actually attending upon the sittings of said convention, and shall be allowed the like compensation for their travel as members of the General Assembly are allowed by law; and their secretaries, officers, and attendants shall be paid the same compensation as the officers of the General Assembly of this State are paid for similar services; which pay, together with the pay of a competent stenographer to report their debates, which stenographer shall be appointed by the Governor for that purpose, with the other expenses of the convention, shall be certified by the president of the convention, and shall be paid by the treasurer of this State on the warrant of the auditor of public accounts.

Sec. 13. The Secretary of State, and all other officers in this State shall furnish said convention with all such papers, statements, statistical information, copies of records or public documents in their possession as the said convention may order or require; and it shall be the duty of the proper officer or officers to furnish the members with all such stationery as is usual for the General Assembly while in session, which shall be paid for on the certificate of the president, in like manner as the contingent expenses of the House of Representatives are now paid by law.

Sec. 14. The roll containing the draught of the amended constitution adopted by said convention, and the proceedings of said convention, shall be deposited by the president and secretary thereof in the office of the Secretary of State, who shall file the same, and cause said constitution to be entered of record in his office; and said convention may submit one or more of the amendments which they may propose to the constitution as distinct propositions, to be voted upon by the people separately or together, as to them may seem expedient.

Sec. 15. It shall be the duty of the Secretary of State, so soon as the same is recorded in his office, to deliver to the Governor of this State a certified copy of said amended Constitution, who shall, on the meeting of the General Assembly of this State at its next session, lay the same before them; and it shall be the duty of the said General Assembly to pass all laws necessary and proper for submitting the same to the qualified voters for their approval and rejection; and also for organizing the government under the amended constitution, in case it should be adopted and ratified by such voters.

Sec. 16. It shall be the duty of the Secretary of State to immediately cause three thousand copies of this act, and the appendix hereinafter provided for, to be printed and forthwith forwarded by mail, not less than twenty nor more than thirty thereof to the clerk of each of the counties in this State, who shall cause the sheriff of the county to deliver one or more of the said copies to each inspector of elections in said county, and said clerk shall certify to the sheriff that the delegates are to be elected, and the said sheriff shall give notice of the said election in the same manner now provided by law in regard to the election of members of the General Assembly of this State.

Sec. 17. It shall be the duty of the Secretary of State to prepare and have printed blank forms of the caption of the poll books, and the returns required of the inspectors and judges of elections; the certificates required of the county canvassers, clerks, and sheriffs, and all other reforms required by this act, and which may be necessary and proper to carry the same into full effect which shall be added by way of appendix to this cause a suitable number of blank forms of poll books with proper captions, and forms of the returns required to made by the inspectors and judges of the election, to be made out, conforming them to those prescribed by the secretary of State, and deliver them to the sheriff of said county;

and said sheriff shall, at least twenty days previous to the election, deliver one or more copies thereof to each inspector of elections in the several townships in the county.

This act to take effect and be in force from and after its passage.

Approved, January 18, 1850.

Democratic Campaign Circular, 1850[2]

The Whig members in the Indiana legislature, at the recent session ere they left the capital held a secret session, together with some others of the party, in which were no doubt fully and freely discussed the means of gaining a party triumph, either in the next legislature or State convention, to assemble in October, to alter and amend the Constitution of our State, if not in both. This meeting resulted in the adoption of an unusually long string of resolutions, which has been thrown out as Whig principles for the coming canvass.

In relation to the great subject of constitutional reform, there appears to be a studied effort to deceive. It is well known that nearly all the new constitutions that have been lately adopted, have been the work of Democratic conventions. In the acts of these conventions the capacity of the people to elect all their officers, judicial as well as legislative, has been fully vindicated. The power of legislative bodies to contract debts, by a combination of local interests, so disastrous to our own State, has been curtailed in these Democratic Constitutions, and this feature of reform is very popular in Indiana. Many other questions, under the controlling influence of the spirit of the age, have become self-evident propositions. A number of these have been seized upon by the secret caucus above alluded to, and appropriated as the exclusive property of the Whig party of Indiana. We are glad to see our opponents coming over to these measures, but we demur to the claim they set up. But the question here arises, are these self-evident propositions the only reforms to be made in our State constitution? If so, why all this expense of one hundred and fifty delegates to attend the convention? Why so much interest manifested, that every portion of the State should be represented? No, fellow-citizens, the object in the adoption of these resolutions was to deceive. It is said, that Satan himself sometimes assumes the appearance of an angel of light, and we know that our first parents were thus deceived. We should profit by the lesson. The whole constitution of our State will be thrown open for alteration and amendment. Democratic conventions have made constitutions in accordance with the spirit of the age and are therefore to be trusted, and we believe there are very many persons, still acting with the Whig party, that would much rather trust our constitution in the hands of a Democratic convention than with their own party friends. . . .

As we believe the time has now come for action, and as we believe that the people of the townships and counties throughout the State, should act on the great questions at issue for themselves, we would respectfully suggest a plan of bringing this desired object about, as follows:

1. We recommend that the Democrats of every township on the State meet at the place of holding the township elections, in each county, on the first Monday in April, and select delegates to a county convention, to nominate candidates for the August election.

2. That the county conventions, for the nomination of candidates, be held in each county, on Saturday, the 13th of April, if some other day shall not be fixed upon.

3. We would also respectfully recommend that at the county conventions, the Democrats in the county generally, nominate a full ticket, embracing delegates to the convention to amend the Constitution, as well as all other officers.

Delegates To The Convention.[3]

MR. PRESIDENT:

The committee of elections, to whom was referred the credentials of Delegates to this Convention, have carefully examined the same, and now report, that as shown by said credentials (which are properly and legally certified) that the following delegates are duly elected as Senatorial Delegates, to wit:

From the counties of Allen, Adams, and Wells—James W. Borden.

From the counties of Bartholomew and Jennings—Hiram Prather.

From the counties of Carroll and Clinton—Hiram Allen.

From the counties of Cass, Howard, and Pulaski—Horace P. Biddle.

From the county of Clark—James G. Read.

From the county of Daviess—Elias S. Terry.[4]

From the counties of Dubois and Gibson—Smith Miller.

From the county of Dearborn—William S. Holman.

From the county of Decatur—James B. Foley.

From the counties of Dekalb, Steuben, and Noble—Robt. Work.

From the counties of Elkhart and LaGrange—Joseph H. Mather.

From the counties of Fayette and Union—Daniel Trembly.

From the county of Fountain—Joseph Coats.

From the county of Franklin—George Berry.

From the county of Floyd—Phineas M. Kent.

From the counties of Grant and Delaware—Walter March.

From the county of Hamilton—Albert B. Cole.

From the county of Harrison—John Zenor.

From the county of Hendricks—Henry G. Todd.

From the counties of Huntington, Whitley, and Kosciusko—Elias Murray.

From the county of Henry—Isaac Kinley.

From the counties of Jackson and Scott—John F. Carr.

From the county of Jefferson—Milton Gregg.

From the county of Johnson—James Ritchey.

From the county of Knox—James Dick.

From the county of Lawrence—George W. Carr.

From the counties of LaPorte, Porter, and Lake—Samuel J. Anthony.

From the counties of Madison and Hancock—Thomas D. Walpole.

From the county of Marion—Alexander F. Morrison.

From the counties of Monroe and Brown—Daniel Read.

From the county of Montgomery—Henry T. Snook.

From the county of Morgan—James Crawford.

From the counties of Miami and Wabash—Harrison Kendall.

From the counties of Switzerland and Ohio—Abel C. Pepper.

From the counties of Orange and Crawford—William F. Sherrod.

From the counties of Owen and Greene—David M. Dobson.

From the counties of Parke and Vermillion—Oliver P. Davis.

From the counties of Perry and Spencer—John P. Dunn.

From the county of Putman—Alexander C. Stevenson.

From the counties of Posey and Vanderburgh—James Lockhart.

From the counties of Randolph, Jay, and Blackford—Nathan B. Hawkins.

From the county of Ripley—Thomas Smith.

From the county of Rush—Jesse Morgan.

From the county of Shelby—Thomas A. Hendricks.

From the counties of St. Joseph, &c.—Hugh Miller.

From the county of Tippecanoe—Joel B. McFarland.

From the counties of Vigo, Clay, and Sullivan—William R. Haddon.

From the counties of Warren, White, and Jasper—Robert C. Kendall.

From the county of Wayne—John S. Newman.

From the county of Washington—John I. Morrison.

Your committee also find and report the following gentleman duly elected Representative Delegates to this convention, viz:

From the counties of Adams and Wells—Erastus K. Bascom.

From the county of Allen—Allen Hamilton.

From the counties of Blackford and Jay—Dixon Milligan.

From the county of Bartholomew—Zachariah Tannehill and Smith Jones.

From the county of Boone—William McLean and Mark Duzan.

From the counties of Benton, White, &c.—Jonathan Harbolt.

From the county of Brown—Shadrach Chandler.

From the county of Carroll—Robert H. Milroy.

From the counties of Cass and Howard—George A. Gordon.

From the county of Clark—Thomas W. Gibson and Jacob Fisher.

From the county of Clay—Francis B. Yocum.

From the county of Crawford—Samuel Pepper.

From the counties of Clinton and Tipton—Stephen Sims and Cornelius J. Miller.

From the county of Dearborn—Johnson Watts and John D. Johnson.

From the counties of DeKalb and Steuben—Edward R. May.

From the county of Decatur—Joseph Robinson.

From the county of Delaware—David Kilgore.

From the county of Dubois—Benjamin R. Edmonston.

From the county of Elkhart—Walter E. Beach.

From the counties of Fayette—Ross Smiley and William W. Thomas.

From the county of Floyd—Henry P. Thornton.

From the county of Fountain—Joseph Ristine.

From the county of Franklin—Spencer Wiley and George G. Shoup.

From the county of Greene—Thomas Butler.

From the county of Grant—Benoni C. Hogin.

From the county of Gibson—Samuel Hall.

From the county of Hamilton—Haymond W. Clark.

From the county of Hancock—George Tague.

From the county of Harrison—John Mathes.

From the county of Hendricks—Christian C. Nave.

From the county of Henry—George H. Ballingall and Daniel D. Mowrer.

From the counties of Huntington and Whitley—Jacob Wunderlich.

From the county of Jackson—Samuel P. Mooney.

From the county of Jefferson—Michael G. Bright and William McKee Dunn.

From the county of Jennings—John L. Spann.

From the county of Johnson—Franklin Hardin.

From the county of Kosciusko—James Garvin.

From the county of Knox—Willis W. Hitt.

From the county of LaGrange—John B. Howe.

From the county of LaPorte—John B. Niles and Edmund D. Taylor.

From the county of Lawrence—Melchert Helmer.

From the counties of Lake and Porter—Daniel Crumbacker.

From the county of Madison—John Davis.

From the county of Marion—Jacob P. Chapman, David Wallace, and Douglass Maguire.

From the counties of Marshall and Fulton—Amzi L. Wheeler.

From the county of Miami—John A. Graham.

From the county of Monroe—William C. Foster.

From the county of Montgomery—David A. Shannon and Horace E. Carter.

From the county of Morgan—Alexander B. Conduit.

From the county of Martin—Thomas Gootee.

From the county of Noble—Thompson P. Bicknell.

From the counties of Ohio and Switzerland—Daniel Kelso.

From the county of Owen—George W. Moore.

From the county of Orange—William Holliday.[5]

From the county of Perry—Samuel Frisbie.

From the county of Pike—Charles Alexander.

From the county of Parke—William R. Nofsinger and Samuel Davis.

From the county of Putnam—Alexander S. Farrow and Oliver P. Badger.

From the county of Posey—Robert Dale Owen and Alvin P. Hovey.

From the county of Randolph—Beat[t]ie McClelland.

From the county of Ripley—Henry J. Bowers.

From the county of Rush—William Bracken and Jefferson Helm.

From the county of St. Joseph—Schuyler Colfax.

From the county of Scott—Hezekiah S. Smith.

From the county of Shelby—James Vanbenthusen.[6]

From the county of Sullivan—Benjamin Wolfe.

From the county of Spencer—Wilson Huff.

From the county of Tippecanoe—John Pettit and Othniel L. Clark.

From the county of Union—Benjamin F. Brookbank.

From the county of Vigo—Thomas I. Bourne, Cromwell W. Barbour, and Grafton F. Cookerly.

From the county of Vermillion—Thomas Chenowith.

From the county of Vanderburgh—James E. Blythe.

From the county of Wabash—William Steele.

From the county of Warrick—Christopher C. Graham.

From the county of Warren—James R. M. Bryant.

From the county of Wayne—John Beard, James Rariden, and Othniel Beeson.

From the county of Washington—Ezekiel D. Logan and Rodolophus Schoonover.

Your committee report that from the county of Shelby James Elliott has been duly elected to supply the vacancy occasioned by the death of the Hon. James Vanbenthusen.

All of which is respectfully submitted.

DANIEL KELSO, Chairman.[7]

Speech Of Carr On Being Elected President[8]

GENTLEMEN: I rise to tender you my sincere and grateful acknowledgements for the distinguished honor you have conferred upon me in electing me to preside over this Convention. The memory of your partiality and this evidence of your confidence will be carefully cherished by me to the latest period of my life.

GENTLEMAN, you are assembled here for the discharge of high and important duties; and the fact that you have been selected by the people for the performance of those duties, is a sufficient guarantee to me, that your intercourse with each other will be constantly marked by that high-minded and liberal bearing which everywhere distinguishes a free people.

In entering upon the discharge of the duties of this place, I cannot but trust my ability to meet your expectations; but I shall throw myself upon your indulgence, and shall rely much upon the hope that I shall be constantly aided by your own wise counsel and experience.

With these assurances I accept the office to which you have called me, and promise, as far as my ability will permit, a faithful and fair discharge of its duties.

Farewell Speech of President Carr, February 10, 1851[9]

The object for which this body was called together being completed, and the time fixed for a final adjournment having arrived, we are now about to separate, and again return the power with which for a time we have been entrusted, to those to whom it legitimately belongs, and render an account of our stewardship, and submit, as a result of our deliberations, a new Constitution of organic law of the State, to the sovereign people for their approval or rejection. I think I may say for it, without disparagement to others, or egotism to ourselves, that, taken as a whole, it may justly be regarded as one of the very best Constitutions that has yet been framed for any State in this Union; by it, the rights of the individual citizen, in his person and property, are well secured; the freedom of speech, and of the press; the liberty of conscience is guaranteed to all the people of the State; in it will be found some very necessary and wholesome checks against hasty, inconsiderate, or reckless legislative enactments, and an effectual remedy for that most injurious enactments, and an effectual remedy for that most injurious evil in our legislation for many years past, know as local and special enactments. We hold it to be a correct principle in government, that every community united together by the same organic law, should have upon all general subjects the same statutory provisions; and I may here remark, that of the three departments into which governments are usually divided, that of the legislative or law making department or power, is the one above all others the most likely to encroach upon the rights of the citizen, and to subvert the liberties of the mass of the people; hence the necessity to restrain, (within proper and safe limits,) not the people themselves, but those to whom their power for a time may be delegated for the purpose of making laws for their government. I think it may justly be inferred, from the fact that as no particular sect or party in politics has given shape to the general provisions of this instrument, they therefore have been settled and agreed upon within a proper medium, to advance generally the interests of this growing State, and promote the prosperity and general welfare of the whole people.

This session, although regarded by many as a long one, will be found, by a comparison with the sessions of other Conventions in other States, to be positively a short session: and I here remark, without intending any disparagement to others, that this Convention; from its commencement to the close, has been the most assiduously industrious deliberative body I have ever seen, and therefore really merit praise for having accomplished their labors in the time they have, rather than censure for having wantonly protracted its sitting beyond its proper limit. It is alike gratifying to all and creditable to yourselves that your consultations and deliberations have been uniformly entirely free from those party feuds and animosities which but too frequently divide and distract the counsels of deliberative bodies to the great injury of the public; and notwithstanding feelings may occasionally have been produced in the excitement of debate, I have never seen a deliberative body close its labors with a more general good feeling than has marked the close of this Convention.

For myself, permit me to return to you my grateful acknowledgments for the general kind and courteous treatment I have received from you, and for the generous aid and support uniformly afforded by you, which has materially assisted me into the discharge of those duties devolving on the Chair. The high compliment you were pleased to award me by the adoption of the resolution referring to the manner in which I have discharged the duties of the position you assigned me, will ever be gratefully remembered by me. I, however, have not the vanity to suppose that in the discharge of my official duty I have been free from errors, but on the contrary feel assured I have committed many. But I trust you will believe me sincere when I say, I have intentionally committed none.

I now wish each member and officer of this body a safe journey to their respective places of abode; and I desire, whenever it may be my fortune hereafter to meet with any member or officer of this convention, personally to hail him as a friend.

I now discharge the last official duty incumbent upon me, by declaring this Convention adjourned *sine die*.

Owen's Compromise Resolutions[10]

WHEREAS, The Congress of the United States passed, at its last session, a series of Acts, commonly called the compromise measures; and

WHEREAS, certain misguided individuals, in various States of the Union, have expressed their determination to resist a portion of its laws; therefore, be it

Resolved, That, in the opinion of this Convention, the common sentiment of the people of Indiana sustains and endorses, in their general features and intentions, the said series of compromise measures as passed by Congress; and recognizes, in the success of these measures, an earnest of security and perpetuity to our glorious Union.

Resolved, That whatever may be the opinion of individuals, as to the wisdom or policy of the details of one or any acts of Congress above referred to, it is the duty of all the good citizens to conform to their requisitions; and to carry out, in good faith, the conditions of that compromise on the subject of domestic slavery, which is coeval with the Federal Constitution.

Resolved, That a copy of this preamble and resolutions be transferred to the Governors of each State and Territory of the United States, and to each of our Senators and Representatives in Congress.

Rariden's Compromise Resolutions[11]

WHEREAS, The Congress of the United States, at its last session, on account of the controversies which had grown out of the question of domestic slavery, connected with recent territorial acquisitions, in order to allay all irritation and reconcile all sections, passed a series of acts intending to accomplish this object: AND WHEREAS, Certain misguided persons, in some of the States, have manifested a purpose to set at defiance one of these measures, namely, the one in regard to the reclamation of fugitive slaves, and have given out from public meetings, and in published resolutions, that they will not obey its injunctions, that it is unconstitutional and void, and that those who have had any agency in its passage, or shall assist in its execution, or counsel obedience to its mandates, are traitors to God and humanity, and recommend forcible measures to its administration;

AND WHEREAS, We, the Delegates, of the people of Indiana, in Convention assembled, coming from every county, and feeling that we know the public sentiment of the State on this subject, and fearing that such proceedings and public outgivings, if unrebuked, may tend to discredit the allegiance of the State of the Union, and the fidelity of our people to the Constitution and laws, and thereby bring us into disrepute with our sister States: Therefore,

Resolved, That it is the opinion of the members of this Convention, that the common sentiment of the people of Indiana is, that the whole series of Compromise measures passed at the recent Congress of the United States, were adopted with a view to reconcile discordant opinions, and to restore the peace, harmony, and integrity of the Union; that they are founded upon generous and patriotic concessions from all sections, and, if faithfully carried out, will realize the hopes of their projectors, in the restoration of confidence and kind feeling among the great sisterhood of States.

Resolved, That the obstacles often interposed to the reclamation of fugitives from labor, by open resistance and subtle practices of the misguided, under pretence of humanity, obedience to higher laws than the Constitution, made the passage of more stringent laws than the act of 1793 imperative, and was the true cause which led to the passage of the act of 1850, and that those laws ought to be observed and executed, in good faith, every where.

Resolved, That whilst the people of Indiana stand ready, at all times to uphold the laws enacted for the benefit of those who live in the slave States, they will be found equally firm in resisting all lawless designs, from whatsoever quarter, intended to break up the great confederacy of States; they are friends of law and order, and devoted to the Union which our ancestors handed down to us, and are the enemies of all, whether in the North or at the South, who, upon any pretext, shall seek to overthrow it.

Resolved, That a copy of this preamble and these resolutions be transmitted to the Governor of each State and Territory of the United States, and to each of our Senators and members of Congress.

WOMAN'S RIGHTS[12]

It is her right to watch beside
The bed of sickness and of pain,
And when the heart almost despairs,
To whisper hopes of health again.

Her right, to make the hearth-stone glad,
With gentle words and cheerful smile;
And when man is with care oppress'd,
His wearied spirit to beguile.

It is her right to train her sons
So they may Senate chambers grace–
Thus, is she with more honor crown'd
Than if herself had filled the place.

It is her right to be admir'd
By ev'ry generous, manly heart,
When, with true dignity and grace,
She acteth well a woman's part.

She hath a dearer right than this;
To be in one true heart enshrined–
Who, though the world may all forsake,
Will cherish still, and still be kind.

And there is yet a higher right,
Which, also, is to woman given:
'T is hers, to teach the infant mind
Those truths divine, which came from heaven.

What would she more, than to perform,
On earth, life's holiest, sweetest tasks?
When you a perfect woman find,
No other rights than these she asks.

Disposition of Original Copies of Journals

Mr. Gordon submitted the following resolutions:

1. *Resolved*, That the Secretary of this convention do cause the manuscript Journal of the proceedings of this Convention to be well bound, and after the same is attested by him that he deposit it with the Secretary of State; and that the original documents in possession of the Convention, and connected with its proceedings, be deposited with the State Librarian.

2. *Resolved*, That each of the ROLLS containing drafts of the amended Constitution adopted by this Convention be enclosed by the Secretary of this Convention in a separate case, proper for its preservation; and one copy thereof be deposited as directed by the fourteenth section of the article calling for this Convention, with the Secretary of State, and the other shall be deposited with the State Librarian.

Which were adopted.[13]

Secretary to Prepare Constitution for Signing

On motion of Mr. Shoup.

The rules were suspended to enable him to introduce the following resolution:

Resolved, That the Secretary be directed to prepare suitable sheets of parchment, and call the roll of members of the Constitution, and that each member sign the Constitution as his name is called.

Mr. Kelso moved to amend by inserting after the word "Constitution," the words "by way of attestation."

Which was decided in the negative.[14]

Journals of the Convention

On Motion of Mr. Kelso,

The order of business was suspended to enable him to submit the following resolution:

Resolved, That a record of the proceedings of this Convention shall be kept in the following manner, to-wit: All that class of legislative matter usually contained in the Journals of the Legislature shall be journalized under the direction of the Principal Secretary. He shall prepare, or cause to be prepared, an index to said Journal; and, if printing of said Journal be ordered, he shall super-intend the same. He shall also prepare, or cause to be prepared, a manuscript copy, to be deposited by the President and Secretary, in the office of the Secretary of State, in pursuance of the 14th section of the act, entitled "An act to provide for the call of a Convention of the people of the State of Indiana to revise, amend, or alter the Constitution of said State." There shall also be kept a "Journal of Debates," under the direction of the Stenographer; but said Journal of Debates shall not contain that class of matter usually embraced in legislative journals further than may be actually necessary to identify and give a correct understanding of the subject matter under discussion.

The question being put upon the adoption of the said resolution. It was decided in the affirmative.[15]

Binding Of The Journals.

The chair laid before the convention the following communication:

Mr. President:

In compliance with the order of the Convention, I have made some further inquires in relation to the binding of the journals, and find that they can be bound in leather, in the same style as the book herewith exhibited, for the sum of fifty cents per volume, and in paper backs in the style that the journals of the legislature are usually distributed, at ten cents per volume.

There will be two volumes of the Journal of Debates and probably two of the Legislative Journal.[16] The resolution directs the binding of 750 copies, which will probably make in all 3,000 volumes. If bound in leather the cost of binding will therefore be $1,500; if bound in paper covers say $300.

I should like to know the pleasure of the Convention as to this subject.

I will add, that the first volume of the Journal of Debates bound in leather can be furnished each member before the adjournment at the price above mentioned. I take the liberty of suggesting, that after furnishing each member and office, and the clergy with one copy each, and each clerk's office in the State with three copies, there will still be from 250 to 300 copies undisposed of.

Very respectfully,

William H. English, Secretary.[17]

The question being on the adoption thereof, it was decided in the affirmative.[18]

Journals to Members of First Constitutional Convention

On motion of Mr. Watts,

The rules were suspended,

When,

He moved the adoption of the following resolution:

Resolved, That each surviving member of the Convention of 1816, of this State, be presented with a copy of the Debates and Journal of this Convention.

Which was decided in the affirmative.[19]

Journals to Be Sent to County Libraries.

On motion of Mr. Hitt,

The rules were suspended,

When,

He moved the adoption of the following resolution:

Resolved, That one of the three copies of the Journals of the Convention ordered to be sent to the Clerk's office of each county, be sent to the Public or County Library of said county.

Which was decided in the affirmative.[20]

Journals to Officers of General Assembly.

The rules were suspended, and Mr. Kelso submitted the following resolution:

WHEREAS, This convention on yesterday, the 6th instant,

passed a resolution allowing to each member of the present General Assembly, a copy of the Journal of Debates and Legislative Journal of this Convention, without including the officers of said General Assembly; therefore,

Resolved, That each of the officers of the present General Assembly shall be entitled to a copy of said Journals. *And be it further resolved*, That, as to this Convention, the term officers shall include all regular assistants for the entire term, and where the same cannot be otherwise satisfactorily ascertained, the Principal shall certify who were regularly employed as assistants.

Mr. Morrison of Washington moved to amend as follows:

Add "one copy of the Debates and one of the Journal of this Convention, be presented, through the Secretary of State, upon the requisition of their respective presidents, to each of the incorporated colleges and universities in the State."[21]

Copy of Journals to Higher Officials.

Mr. Dunn of Jefferson submitted the following resolution:

Resolved, That the Secretary of this Convention be directed to furnish a copy of the Debates of this Convention, and of the Journal, to the Governor, Lieutenant Governor, Treasurer, Auditor, and Secretary of State, the Judge and Marshall of the U.S. Court of this district, and the Judges of the Supreme Court.

Which was adopted.[22]

Proclamation (Governor) Making Constitution in Effect[23]

JOSEPH A. WRIGHT, Governor of the State of Indiana, to the several Judges, Inspectors, and Clerks and other officers of the several counties of this State, authorized by law to hold elections for the various offices of the State, and all others whom it may concern, Greeting:

KNOW YE, That the Convention which assembled on the first Monday of October, 1850, at Indianapolis, for the purpose of revising, amending, or altering the Constitution of this State, have, in pursuance of the law of the land, deposited said Constitution so made in the office of the Secretary of State, due notice of which has been given to me, and a copy of said Constitution is herewith published; and that by virtue of an act of the Legislature, approved on the 14th day of February, 1851, it is directed that said instrument shall be submitted to the people of this State for their adoption or rejection, at the next annual August election, and to say whether said instrument shall or shall not be the Constitution of the State, and among other things provided as follows, to-wit:

Section 2. There shall be a vote taken on the first Monday of August next, on the adoption or rejection of said Constitution, and on the adoption or rejection of the separate articles thereof, relating to the exclusion of negroes and mulattoes from this State; and for this purpose it shall be the duty of the inspectors and judges of elections in the several townships in this State, on said first Monday in August next, to open a poll, in which shall be entered all the votes given for or against the adoption of said Constitution, and of said separate article: Said election shall be by ballot, and shall be governed in all respects by the laws now in force in relation to general elections, so far as applicable.

Sec. 3. Those voting against the adoption of said Constitution, shall vote written or printed tickets in this form: "Against the Constitution," and those voting for its adoption shall vote written or printed tickets in this form: "For the Constitution;" In like manner those voting against the second article in relation to the exclusion of negroes and mulattoes, and their colonization, shall have written or printed on his ticket these words, "No exclusion and colonization of Negroes;" and every voter who is in favor of adopting said article shall have written or printed in his ticket these words; "Exclusion and colonization of Negroes and Mulattoes."

Sec. 4. Poll books shall be kept, votes counted and certified to the clerks of the different counties as in other elections, and the returns of the votes for and against the adoption of said Constitution, and for and against said separate article, shall be made by said clerks to the Secretary of State, within ten days after said election, and said returns shall, within twenty days thereafter, be examined and canvassed by the Auditor, Treasurer, and Secretary of State, or any two of them, in the presence of the Governor, and such other persons as may choose to attend; and proclamation shall be made forthwith, by the Governor, of the result of the election. If it shall appear that a majority of all the votes polled at such election were given in favor of the adoption of said Constitution, it shall then become the Constitution of the State of Indiana, from the first day of November, 1851; but if it shall appear that a majority of all the votes polled for or against the adoption of said Constitution, and said separate article, were given against the adoption of said Constitution, and said separate article, were given against the adoption of said Constitution, then the same shall be, and remain, inoperative and void. If it shall further appear that a majority of all the votes polled for or against the adoption of said Constitution and said separate article, were given in favor of the article in relation to the exclusion of negroes and mulattoes and their colonization, then said article shall be, and form a part of said Constitution; otherwise said article shall be void.

THEREFORE, In compliance with the provisions of said Constitution, and of the act aforesaid, I do hereby direct and enjoin upon all the officers of this State, authorized by law to hold the next annual August election, and all others whom it may concern, to observe and obey, and in all things conform to each and all the requirements and provisions of said law.

IN TESTIMONY WHEREOF, I have signed this Proclamation, and caused the Seal of this State hereunto affixed at Indianapolis, on this, the 25th day of

February, A.D. 1851, and in the thirty-fifth year of the State, and the seventh-fifth of the Nation.

Joseph A. Wright.

By the Governor:

Charles H. Test, Sec'y of State.

Proclaiming Constitution in Effect, 1851.[24]

I, Joseph A. Wright, Governor of the State of Indiana, do certify that on the third day of September, A.D. 1851, E. W. H. Ellis, Auditor, James P. Drake, Treasurer, and Charles H. Test, Secretary of State, at the office of said Secretary of State, in the city of Indianapolis, in my presence, and that of divers other citizens there in attendance, examined and canvassed all the returns made from the several counties of this State, of the votes polled for and against the New Constitution, by the electors of this State, on the first Monday of August, being the fourth day of said month, A.D. 1851; and that the whole number of votes polled "for the Constitution," in the counties making returns, is 109,319. And that the whole number of votes polled "against the Constitution," is 26,755, being a majority of 82,564 in favor of the Constitution.

I further certify, that at the same time and place, first aforesaid, the said Auditor, Treasurer, and Secretary of State, in my presence and of the persons aforesaid, examined and canvassed all the returns made from the several counties aforesaid, of the votes polled for and against the Thirteenth article of said Constitution, known as the article entitled "Negroes and Mulattoes" is 109,976; and that the whole number of votes polled against "exclusion and colonization of Negroes and Mulattoes," is 21,066, being a majority of 88,910 in favor of "*exclusion and colonization of Negroes and Mulattoes.*"

I do further certify, that no returns of the votes for and against the said Constitution, and for and against the said thirteenth article, have been received from the counties of Delaware, Noble, Porter, and Warrick.

I do, therefore, by virtue of the authority vested in me, declare and make known that the New Constitution is adopted by the good people of this State, as the Constitution of the State of Indiana; and that said thirteenth article is declared to be a part of said New Constitution, the whole to take effect and be in force on and after the first day of November, A.D. 1851.

And I do enjoin on all whom it may concern the observance of the eleventh section of the schedule of said Constitution, which provides that, "on the taking effect of this Constitution, all the officers thereby continued in office shall, before proceeding in the further discharges of their duties, take an oath or affirmation to support the Constitution."

In testimony whereof, I have hereunto set my hand, and cause the great seal of the State of Indiana to be affixed, at Indianapolis, this third day of September, A.D. 1851; the thirty-sixth year of the State, and of the Independence of the United States the seventy-sixth.

Joseph A. Wright.
BY THE GOVERNOR
Charles H. Test,
Secretary of State.

[1] *Laws of the State of Indiana, Passed at the Thirty-fourth Session of the General Assembly* (Indianapolis: J.P. Chapman,1886), 29. A discussion of this act may be found in the thesis; the thesis suggests the chief characteristics of this act.

[2] Charles Kettleborough, *Constitution Making in Indiana: A Source Book of Constitutional Documents with Historical Introduction and Critical Notes* (Indianapolis: Indiana Historical Commission, 1916), 1:212-213, quoting from *Daily Lafayette Courier*, 1 March 1850. Kettleborough says that this circular was issued on or about March 1, 1850 by the Democratic State Central Committee as an answer to the Whig Resolutions of January 16, 1850. Kettleborough quoted only those portions (he suggests) that deal with the question of constitutional reform as the circular had other material in it.

[3] *Journal of the Convention of the People of the State of Indiana to Amend the Constitution* (Indianapolis: H. Fowler, A. H. Brown 1851), 380-384. Compare with the map prepared by Baker & McFarland given elsewhere in appendix.

[4] December 21, 1850, Richard Clements of Daviess was sworn in to succeed Terry who had resigned.

[5] January 18, 1851, William Johnson of Orange appeared and was sworn in as a delegate by Biddle; he succeeded William Holliday who had resigned because of ill health; see *Journal*, 715.

[6] December 6, 1850, James Elliot of Shelby appeared and was sworn in as a delegate by Horace P. Biddle; he succeeded James Vanbenthusen who had died November 1. See *Journal*, 361.

[7] *Journal*, 56. The other members of this committee were: Shannon, Robinson, Fisher, and Cole. This committee was appointed along with the other standing committees.

[8] *Debates*, 6. This address was delivered on the morning of October 7, 1851 in the hall of the House of Representatives, where the convention had assembled. Carr was elected president by a vote of 154 to six blank votes; there was no opposition candidate. George W. Carr was a delegate from Lawrence County.

[9] *Debates*, 2077. This speech is also contained in the *Convention Journal*, 996-998. These were the concluding remarks of the president in adjourning the convention and the last words recorded in the *Journal* and *Debates*.

[10] *Journal*, 331-332. Also see *Debates*, 914. The resolutions were adopted by a vote of ninety to twenty-five, Rariden voted for them. A reading of the debate over these resolutions gives a very good understanding of the extent to which the people had become agitated over the subject.

[11] *Journal*, 323; also see *Debates*, 744. Rariden of Wayne was a leader of the Whigs and was accused of trying to make political capital out of the resolutions. By a vote of ninety-nine to twenty-three these resolutions were stricken out and resolutions of Owen substituted. This whole controversy, over the resolutions, was prolonged and very partisan.

[12] *Debates*, 819. Written by Mrs. N. P. Lasselle and quoted by Badger stating that these "are my sentiments." This poem was quoted in many of the papers of the period. A careful reading of the poem shows the conservatism of its tone and yet no one would dare say that its tone was anything other than friendly to the best interests of women as viewed by the author and those who quoted it.

[13] *Journal*, 906.

[14] Ibid., 906.

[15] Ibid., 107. Adopted October 21, 1850.

[16] The *Journal* was bound in two volumes: however, the *Legislative Journal* was all bound in one large journal.

[17] *Journal*, 922.

[18] Ibid., 922-923.

[19] Ibid., 924.

[20] Ibid., 924-925.

[21] *Journal*, 946.

[22] Ibid., 995.

[23] Kettleborough, *Constitution Making*, 1: 416-418, quoted from *Weekly State Journal*, 1 March 1851. The leading contemporary newspapers of the state published this proclamation; some in several issues. The original is kept in archives of the Secretary of State.

[24] Ibid., 421-422, quoted from *Weekly State Journal*, 26 September 1851. This was issued in several papers of the State and often in several issues.

BIBLIOGRAPHY

Newspaper Sources

Independent Press. 18 October 1850 to 22 August 1851.

Published at Lawrenceburg, Indiana, by Henry L. Brown and James E. Goble. Professed to be non-partisan in politics. Was friendly to the convention and the new constitution; a very desirable source.

Indiana Law Journal. February 1930.

Articles by Hugh Willis, James W. Noel, and Albert Stump, which discussed the present-day controversy over the calling of a convention.

Indiana State Journal. January 1848 to December 1851.

Published by John D. Defrees; the Whig organ of the state. The *Journal*, *Indiana Statesman*, and *Indiana State Sentinel* were most used in preparing this thesis.

Indiana State Sentinel. January 1849 to September 1851.

Published by Austin Brown and edited by W. J. Brown. The organ of "regular orthodox Democracy" in the state and a friend and defender of the convention.

Indiana Statesman. September 1850 to August 1852.
Published by B. W. H. Ellis and J. S. Spann. Was a revolt from the "Dunkerism" of the *Sentinel* and represented the "liberal Democracy" of the state. Accused of "Free Soilism" by the *Sentinel.*

Madison Weekly Courier. January 1850 to September 1851.
Published by S. P. and J. B. Covington; Democratic in politics.

Madison Weekly Tribune. 12 April 1851 to 5 November 1851.
Published by Milton Gregg, who was a member of the convention. Gregg, in the first issue, terms himself a "Union Whig." Predicted ratification of constitution.

New Albany Weekly Ledger. January 1850 to December 1851.
Published by Kent and Norman; Democratic in politics.

Prairie Chieftain. 17 September 1850 to November and December 1851.
Published by Lovejoy and Reed. Professed "strict neutrality" in politics.

Other Primary Sources

Documentary Journal of the General Assembly of the State of Indiana. Indianapolis: State Printer, 1869- .
Various editions.

English Collection. Chicago University Library, Chicago.
This was not used in writing this thesis but there is evidence to make one believe that it would be a most valuable source for further research; especially biographical material.

Indiana Constitution.

Indiana Constitution (1816).

Journal of the Convention of the People of the State of Indiana to Amend the Constitution. Indianapolis: A. H. Brown, 1851.
A large volume containing a bare outline of the work of the convention and committees. Very little duplication between the *Journal* and *Debates.*

Journal of the House of Representatives of the State of Indiana, Being the . . . Session of the General Assembly. Indianapolis: State Printer, 1825-1853.
Various editions.

Journal of the Indiana State Senate During the . . . Session of the General Assembly. Indianapolis: State Printer, 1858-1885.
Various editions.

Kentucky Constitution (1850).

Laws of the State of Indiana, Passed at the . . . Session of the General Assembly. Indianapolis: J. P. Chapman, 1853-1885.
Various editions.

Northwest Ordinance (1787).

Ohio Constitution (1851).

Report of the Debates and Proceedings of the Convention for the Revision of the Constitution of the State of Indiana, 1850. Indianapolis: A. H. Brown, 1850.
Published by the convention. Very complete and several copies are still available in both the State and Indiana University Libraries.

Report of the Debates and Proceedings of the Convention for the Revision of the Constitution of the State of Kentucky. Frankfort: A.G. Hodges & Co., 1849.

Secondary Sources: Non-Biographical

Brayton, Ruth. "The Constitution of 1816." M.A. thesis, Indiana University, 1929.

Bryce, James. *The American Commonwealth*. New York: MacMillan Company, 1921.

Dillon, J. B. *History of Indiana from Its Earliest Exploration by Europeans to the Close of Territorial Government in 1816.* Indianapolis: Bingham & Doughty, 1859.

Dodd, W. F. *The Revision and Amendment of State Constitutions.* Baltimore: John Hopkins Press, 1910.

Dunn, J. P. *Indiana, A Redemption from Slavery*. Boston: Houghton, Mifflin and Co., 1896.

Dunn, J. P. *Indiana and Indianans: A History of Aboriginal and Territorial Indiana and the Century of Statehood.* Chicago: American Historical Society, 1919.

Esarey, Logan. *History of Indiana from Its Exploration to 1922.* Dayton, Ohio: Dayton Historical Pub. Co., 1924.

Indiana Magazine of History. 1913-
Various volumes and issues.

Kettleborough, Charles. *Constitution Making in Indiana: A Source Book of Constitutional Documents with Historical Introduction and Critical Notes*. Vols. 1-3. Indianapolis: Indiana Historical Commission, 1916.
A most valuable collection of sources and interpretation for the student of Indiana Constitutional History.

Ogg, Frederic Austin, and P. Orman Ray. *Introduction to American Government*. New York: Century Co, 1922.

Smith, W. H. *The Voice of the People on the Only Complete History of the State of Indiana*. Indianapolis: B.L. Blair & Co., 1898.

Thornton, W. W. *Indiana Constitutional Convention of 1850*. Indianapolis, 1902.

Turner, F. J. *The Frontier in American History*. New York: H. Holt and Company, 1920.
Very good to get frontier spirit; essential in writing thesis.

Woodburn, James A. *Constitution of Indiana with Questions and Notes for Its Study in Indiana Schools*. New York: Longmans, Green and Co., 1926.

Secondary Sources: Biographical

This is not an attempt to list all possible sources.

A Biographical History of Eminent and Self-Made Men of the State of Indiana. Cincinnati: Western Biographical Pub. Co., 1880.

Cumback, W. *Men of Progress, Indiana: A Selected List of Biographical Sketches and Portraits of the Leaders in Business, Professional and Official Life, Together with Brief Notes of the History and Character of Indiana*. Indianapolis: Indianapolis Sentinel Company, 1899.

Dunn, J. P. *Memorial and Genealogical Record of Representative Citizens of Indiana*. Indianapolis: B.F . Brown, 1912.

Dye, Charity. *Some Torch Bearers in Indiana*. Indianapolis: Hollenbeck Press, 1917.

Reed, George Irving. *Encyclopedia of Biography of Indiana*. Vols. 1-2. Chicago: Century Pub. and Engraving Co., 1895.

Woollen, W. W. *Biographical and Historical Sketches of Early Indiana*. Indianapolis: Hammond and Co., 1883.

Special Mention of Primary Original Sources

Constitution of 1851. One copy kept in the private office of the secretary of state; another is being preserved in the vaults of the State Library by the Indiana history attendants. Both are original pen-written copies and show the signatures of all but four delegates.

Constitution of 1816. The original is preserved in the private office of the Secretary of State.

Table by Baker and McFarland. This table, Photostat copies of which have been given in each appendix of the thesis copies, was found in the vault in the Indiana Section of the State Library and is being very carefully preserved.

Miscellaneous Records of State 1845-1866. Preserved and in very good condition. Written in handwriting. Has the following contents in relation to the Convention and Constitution: 1. Vote for and against the ratification of the Constitution; Vote for and against Negro Exclusion, Article 13. Vote is complete for every county on both issues. Found on pages 333-338. 2. Report of the official statement of the vote in the August election in 1851. Shows a total of 109,319 for the Constitution to 26,755 against; with 109,976 for to 21,066 against Negro Exclusion. Found on page 338. 3. Proclamation of Governor Wright giving the official statement and account of the election returns of August 1851. Found of the page and one half following page 342. This material is kept in the archives of the Indiana secretary of state; now located in the basement of the Capitol Building.

Journal of the Convention. In the archives of secretary of state. In handwriting and bound in two volumes. In good condition. Note copies from last page of Volume I says: "Deposited in the Office of the Secretary of State, by the officers of the Convention on the twenty fifth day of February 1851." The Journal as printed has but one volume.

Documentary Journal of Indiana, 1849. Kept in the Indiana section of the State Library; locked in safe. Shows the returns of the August 6, 1849 vote on the referendum which led to the Convention. There were ninety-one counties in the State at that time and reports are complete for all but Starke. This vote is found on pages 81-82 as a part of the report of the Secretary of State to the General Assembly. It is in printed form.

Acts and Joint Resolutions, 1852. Original hand written copy of the acts and resolutions of the General Assembly (Upper House Only). Volume is in good condition.

The references given in the preceding pages are representative and, it is hoped, fairly complete. There are men now living who could tell much of the lives of some of these men (the delegates and officers of the Convention) and grandchildren of many others could tell many items of interest. This later source was unexplored as far as the work of this thesis is concerned.

FOR FURTHER READING*

Also by Donald F. Carmony

A Brief History of Indiana. Indianapolis: Indiana Historical Bureau, 1966.

Family and Personal History. New York: Lewis Historical Publishing Company, 1954. With John D. Barnhart.

Handbook on Indiana History. Indianapolis: Indiana Sesquicentennial Commission, 1963.

Indiana. New York: Harcourt, Brace and Company, 1941. With Mabel B. Casner.

Indiana, 1816-1850: The Pioneer Era. Volume II, *The History of Indiana*. Indianapolis: Indiana Historical Bureau & Indiana Historical Society, 1998.

Indiana: A Self-Appraisal. Bloomington: Indiana University Press, 1966.

Indiana's Century Old Constitution. Indianapolis: State Constitution Centennial Commission, 1951. With John D. Barnhart.

* This reading list and the index following it were added by the editors.

Indiana from Frontier to Industrial Commonwealth. New York: Lewis Historical Pub. Co., 1954. With John D. Barnhart.

Indiana's Newspaper Heritage. Bloomington: Indiana University Library, 1945.

Indiana University: From Seminary Square to Dunn's Woods, 1820-1885. Bloomington: Indiana University Publications, 1987.

Books and Journal Articles

Adams, W. P. *The First American Constitutions.* New York: Rowman and Littlefield Publishers, 1973 (2003 ed.).

Baker, Jean H. *Affairs of Party: The Political Culture of Northern Democrats in the Mid-Nineteenth Century.* Ithaca: Cornell University Press, 1983.

Barnhart, John D. "Sources of Indiana's First Constitution." *Indiana Magazine of History* XXXIX (1943): 55-94.

Cayton, Andrew R. L. *Frontier Indiana, History of the Trans-Appalachian Frontier.* Bloomington, Ind.: Indiana University Press, 1996.

Holman, William S. "The Constitutional Convention of Indiana of 1850-1851: The Reforms it Accomplished." Washington, IN.: Gibson Bros., 1886.

Madison, James H. *The Indiana Way: A State History.* Bloomington and Indianapolis: Indiana University Press; Indiana Historical Society, 1990.

Schlesinger, Arthur Meier. *The Age of Jackson.* Boston: Little Brown and Company, 1945.

Tarr, G. Alan. *Understanding State Constitutions*. Princeton, N.J.: Princeton University Press, 1998.

Thornbrough, Emma Lou. *Indiana in the Civil War Era, 1850-1880*. Volume II, *The History of Indiana*. Indianapolis: Indiana Historical Bureau, 1965.

Woollen, William Wesley, and Josiah Kirby Lilly. *Biographical and Historical Sketches of Early Indiana*. Indianapolis: Hammond, 1883.

INDEX

Selected Individuals

INDEX

Selected Subjects